AFRICA
and the BIBLE

AFRICA
and the BIBLE

Edwin M. Yamauchi

FOREWORD BY KENNETH A. KITCHEN

Baker Academic
Grand Rapids, Michigan

©2004 by Edwin M. Yamauchi

Published by Baker Academic
a division of Baker Publishing Group
P.O. Box 6287, Grand Rapids, MI 49516-6287
www.bakeracademic.com

Paperback edition published in 2006
ISBN 10: 0-8010-3119-2
ISBN 978-0-8010-3119-9

Printed in the United States of America

Library of Congress Cataloging-in-Publication Data has cataloged the hardcover edition as follows:

Yamauchi, Edwin M.
    Africa and the Bible / Edwin M. Yamauchi ; foreword by Kenneth A. Kitchen.
    p. cm.
    Includes bibliographical references and index.
    ISBN 10: 0-8010-2686-5 (cloth)
    ISBN 978-0-8010-2686-7 (cloth)
    1. Bible—Black interpretations. 2. Blacks in the Bible. 3. Afrocentrism—Religious aspects—Christianity. 4. Bible—Criticism, interpretation, etc. I. Title.
BS521.2.Y36 2004
220.6′089′96—dc22   2003057906

To
Win and Nancy Clark
Dick and Ruthie Pettit
for their faithful encouragement

Contents

ILLUSTRATIONS

FOREWORD

With its rich heritage of languages and cultures, the vast and varied continent of Africa has always exercised a fascination for those living in neighboring continents and, in modern times, for many people in far-distant continents also. So vast and diverse is Africa's cultural wealth, and so spread is it across millennia, that no proper study of it could ever be done by just one person in just one book—only an appropriately vast, multivolume encyclopedia could ever do justice to so grand a concept, covering the terrain that divides the Mediterranean from the Cape shores and the Atlantic from the Red and Arabian seas.

The scholar or student must perforce concentrate on Africa from much more modest perspectives. This present volume therefore focuses on the relationships between ancient Africa and the Bible, from far antiquity down into Roman times, and also on this topic in the context of Africa and its cultures as the heritage of many folk living both in Africa and worldwide. Dr. Yamauchi is well known for his versatility, immensely wide scholarship, thoughtful approach, and relaxed, readable style of presentation in other fields relating to the Bible (a central historical interest of his), and these qualities are well shown in this new book. This new work draws helpfully on the solid scholarly essays recently issued in an invaluable volume under Dr. Yamauchi's editorship: *Africa and Africans in Antiquity.*

In this new book, Dr. Yamauchi proceeds by themes from Noah's descendants to the present day. He opens by deftly exposing the gross abuse of the figure of Ham in medieval and recent times and then reviews the much-discussed question of the origins of Moses' "Cushite" wife: was she an African from Kush (closely linked with Egypt) or from Kush(an), an ancient term for Levantine Midian? Thereafter he deals with two later Old Testament periods, of Solomon and of Hezekiah. The epoch of Solomon leads into the varying ancient and later views that would (allegedly) link Solomon, the Queen of Sheba, and regions of East Africa. In Hezekiah's time, Egypt itself had passed into the control of the greatest early kings of Kush from the south; Shabako, Shebitku, and Taharqa boldly dared to engage in ancient Near Eastern wars and politics in the Levant against the formidable Assyrians. After this, Dr. Yamauchi indicates the true origin of the "Ethiopian eunuch" of the New Testament as hailing from the major kingdom of Meroe (successor to Kush), prefacing this with a chapter on Meroe and Rome and following it with one on Cyrene (in north Libya). Coming to our own epoch, Dr. Yamauchi reviews understandingly and sympathetically the questions and claims raised by Afrocentrism, while seeking judiciously to weed out misconceptions that too easily arise when enthusiasm outruns knowledge. In short, this book will provide a wide-ranging, readable, and helpful introduction to an absorbing subject of importance to a wide readership today.

Kenneth A. Kitchen
Personal and Brunner Professor Emeritus of Egyptology
University of Liverpool

PREFACE

As a graduate student, I had the privilege of studying the language and history of the ancient Egyptians under Cyrus H. Gordon and Dwight Young. Then, first at Rutgers University (1964–69) and since 1969 at Miami University, I have taught every third year a semester-long course on the history of ancient Egypt. My former students Robert Bianchi from Rutgers and Susan Doll from Miami pursued Ph.D.'s in Egyptology and worked respectively at the Brooklyn Museum and at the Boston Museum of Fine Arts.

In recent years I have also offered a graduate colloquium in ancient Africa. In 1991, I convened a conference at Miami University on the subject of ancient Africa. It featured leading authorities such as William Y. Adams (an anthropologist from the University of Kentucky), Reuben G. Bullard (a geologist from Cincinnati Bible Seminary), Stanley M. Burstein (a historian from California State University at Los Angeles), Carleton T. Hodge (a linguist from the University of Indiana), Edna R. Russmann (an art historian from the Brooklyn Museum), Frank M. Snowden Jr. (a classicist from Howard University), Maynard W. Swanson (a historian from Miami University), Donald White (an archaeologist from the University of Pennsylvania), and Frank J. Yurco (an Egyptologist from the Field Museum in Chicago). I edited their papers, together with contributions from Kathryn A. Bard (an archaeologist from Boston University) and Rodolfo Fattovich (an archaeologist from Naples, Italy), in a volume titled *Africa and Africans in Antiquity*, published in 2001 by Michigan State University Press. In all of these informative and erudite essays, there was but one reference to

Scripture: a note about Philip and the "Ethiopian eunuch" of Acts 8 in Snowden's chapter.

On the other hand, what I have found even in the bookstore of the Harvard Divinity School are popular works written either by preachers or by Afrocentric scholars, who are more or less oblivious to the wealth of archaeological discoveries and scholarly discussions bearing on the subject of Africa and the Bible. A desire to correct misconceptions and to supply relevant information has led me over the past fifteen years to research and to present papers on various topics involving ancient Africa and the Bible.

My interests have been threefold in exploring these topics: (1) to explore the historical and archaeological background of biblical texts that deal with Africa and the Bible, (2) to examine the exegesis of these texts, and (3) to trace the ramifications of later interpretations and misinterpretations of these texts.

Chapter 1, "The Curse of Ham," examines Genesis 9:25, an important verse that has Noah cursing Ham's son Canaan, but that was reinterpreted in subsequent centuries by various groups in both the Old and the New World to explain the blackness of Africans and to justify enslaving them or, in the case of the Mormons, excluding them from their priesthood.

Chapter 2, "Moses' Cushite Wife," discounts the view that this wife is to be identified with the Midianite Zipporah. Instead, the evidence is examined for the long-standing interrelationships between Egypt and Kush, the country to the south (modern Sudan), to demonstrate that Moses could very well have married a black woman from Nubia. Recent excavations at Kerma, near the Third Cataract of the Nile, shed new light on Kushite culture.

Chapter 3, "Solomon and Africa," explores the widespread international contacts of Solomon, which included Ophir, from which he obtained gold. The search for this site, which may have been in India, Arabia, or Africa, inspired Columbus's voyages of exploration. Though the Queen of Sheba came from southwest Arabia, later Ethiopian traditions claimed her and traced the royal dynasty to Menelik, her son by Solomon.

Chapter 4, "Tirhakah and Other Cushites," surveys the various Cushites mentioned in the Hebrew Bible, from the united monarchy to the Babylonian attack on Jerusalem. Tirhakah, though casually mentioned in 2 Kings 19:9 (cf. Isa. 37:9), turns out to be Taharqa, the most distinguished pharaoh of the Kushite 25th Dynasty, black kings from Nubia who ruled over Egypt for a half century.

Chapter 5, "Rome and Meroe," investigates the circumstances that led to the Roman invasion of Nubia under Augustus and the archaeological and historical background of the kingdom of Meroe, near the Sixth Cataract, which prospered for a millennium.

Chapter 6, "Why the Ethiopian Eunuch Was Not from Ethiopia," explains that in antiquity Ethiopia designated the area of the Sudan—not modern Ethiopia. The treasurer of Candace whom Philip converted (Acts 8:27) was from Meroe. The eventual Christianization of the kingdom of Aksum in Ethiopia occurred in the fourth century, while that of Nubia occurred only in the sixth century.

Chapter 7, "Cyrene in Libya," refutes the popular view that Simon of Cyrene who bore the cross of Christ was a black man. Cyrene was a famous Greek colony in Libya, and Simon was no doubt a member of the prominent Cyrenean Jews in Jerusalem who are mentioned in Acts. Excavations in Cyrene have shed much light on the Greek and Roman structures of the site, including signs of the devastation wrought by the Jewish revolt in A.D. 115.

Chapter 8, "Afrocentric Biblical Interpretation," surveys the views of scholars who, following the lead of Cheikh Anta Diop, assume that all Egyptians were black and that Greek civilization derived its essential concepts from Egypt. This has resulted in a school of interpretation that also holds that all biblical figures from Moses to Christ were black.

The appendix, "Martin Bernal's *Black Athena* Reviewed," addresses the challenge of a controversial scholar who has denounced the so-called Aryan model of ancient history, which denies that the Greeks owed anything to either the Egyptians or the Phoenicians. Bernal, like Afrocentric scholars, derives much of Greek civilization from Egypt.

The first four chapters are entirely new; the last four chapters have been previously published and are now revised. I am indebted to professor Sante Matteo and the publisher for permission to use "The Romans and Meroe in Nubia," originally published in *ItaliAfrica: Bridging Continents and Cultures*, ed. Sante Matteo (Stony Brook, N.Y.: Forum Italicum Publishing, 2001). I am grateful to Buist Fanning and Darrell Bock and Crossway for permission to use "Why the Ethiopian Eunuch Was Not from Ethiopia." I am also indebted to the editors of the respective journals for allowing me to reuse "Cyrene in Libya," published in *Archaeology in the Biblical World* 2 (1992); "Afrocentric Biblical Interpretation," published in the *Journal of the Evangelical Society Theological* 39 (1996); and "Martin Bernal's *Black Athena* Reviewed," published in the *Journal of Ancient Civilizations* 14 (1999).

I am especially indebted to professors Kenneth A. Kitchen, James K. Hoffmeier, and Frank J. Yurco for their suggestions and corrections, as well as to my colleagues Jack T. Kirby and Sherman Jackson. I am grateful to the following scholars for their generosity in sharing their publications with me: Charles Bonnet (University of Geneva), Stanley M. Burstein (California State University at Los Angeles), Scott T. Carroll (Cornerstone

University), David M. Goldenberg (University of Pennsylvania), W. W. Hallo (Yale University), J. K. Hoffmeier (Trinity Evangelical Divinity School), Timothy Kendall (Boston Museum of Fine Arts), Kenneth A. Kitchen (University of Liverpool), Peter Machinist (Harvard University), Alan Millard (University of Liverpool), Terence Mitchell (British Museum), William Spencer (Gordon-Conwell Theological Seminary), F. A. Pennacchietti (University of Turin), and Donald White (University of Pennsylvania).

For the maps, I am indebted to Carol Hill, Kenneth A. Kitchen, Michael Lucas, and Samuel Mutiti. For the photos, I am grateful to Art Resource, Bildarchiv Preussischer Kulturbesitz, Charles Bonnet, Michael Fuller, Cathy Geyer, Museo Civico Archeologico of Bologna, British Museum, Brooklyn Museum of Art, H. Budek, Alfred J. Hoerth, Joslyn Art Museum, Metropolitan Museum of Art, Museum of Fine Arts (Boston), Nelson-Atkins Museum of Art, Saint Louis Art Museum, Frank Sear, Steven E. Sidebotham, Thames & Hudson Publishers, Derek A. Welsby, and Frank J. Yurco.

For funds to acquire photos, I am indebted to grants from Miami University's College of Arts and Sciences and for matching funds from its History Department. Thanks to my department chair, Professor Charlotte Goldy, and to my secretary, Liz Smith, for their support and help. Staff at Miami University's audio-visual department and library, Hebrew Union College library, and University of Cincinnati Classics Library have been unfailingly helpful. I am grateful to Bob Evans and to Cameron Hines for their advice on computer issues. Thanks also to my wife, Kimi, for her help in countless ways. Finally, I wish to express my appreciation to Jim Kinney, Wells Turner, and Amy Sykes of Baker Academic.

A note on the spelling of Kush/Cush: Egyptologists conventionally spell the name of the area south of Egypt as *Kush,* whereas the loanword in the Hebrew Bible is consistently spelled *Cush* by English translators. Since both spellings are found in the literature, I also use both spellings, depending on whether the context is Egyptological or biblical.

1

THE CURSE
OF HAM

No other verse in the Bible has been so distorted and so disastrously used down through the centuries for the exploitation of Africans and African Americans as Genesis 9:25: "He [Noah] said, 'Cursed be Canaan! / The lowest of slaves / will he be to his brothers'" (NIV). It is quite clear that as the text stands, the curse was not upon Ham, one of Noah's three sons, but upon Canaan, the son of Ham.

Earlier interpreters assumed that the biblical flood was a global phenomenon, which killed all humankind,[1] and that all peoples were descended from Noah's three sons: Ham, Shem, and Japheth.[2] Since Ham was commonly reckoned as the progenitor of Africans, when African slavery became widespread, first among the Arabs and then among the Europeans and Americans, this verse was reinterpreted to justify enslaving the Africans.

1. For geological and archaeological problems with this view and attempts to harmonize Scripture and science, see Yamauchi, "Critical Comments on the Search for Noah's Ark." See also Young, *Creation and the Flood*; idem, *Christianity and the Age of the Earth*; idem, *Biblical Flood*.
2. See Yamauchi, "Meshech, Tubal, and Company."

That such a popular notion is still widespread is revealed in a comment by Fidel Castro: "I was taught that one of Noah's sons was punished by having black descendants. Somebody should check to see if this is being taught today and if it's really proper for religion to teach that being black is a punishment of God."[3]

Noah's Drunkenness

After the flood subsided, Noah became drunk and slept uncovered in his tent.[4] Most commentators believe that this was Noah's initial experience with the intoxicating effects of wine, leaving him unprepared for its effects. H. Hirsch Cohen, however, citing the incident of Lot's daughters with their father (Gen. 19:30–38) and the affair of David and Bathsheba (2 Sam. 11:12–13), fancifully suggests that Noah deliberately drank the wine as a preliminary to sexual intercourse: "First, he drank the wine to obtain the seminal potency necessary for the prodigious task of repopulating the earth."[5]

Ham's Deed

According to the biblical text, "Ham, the father of Canaan, saw his father's nakedness and told his two brothers outside" (Gen. 9:22 NIV). When Noah awoke, he somehow realized what Ham had done and uttered his fateful curse, not upon Ham himself, but upon his son, Canaan.[6]

Since the mere acts of looking and telling seem too trivial to warrant such a severe punishment, many read between the lines to detect some more monstrous deed. Some Christian writers (e.g., Theophilus of Antioch) and many Jewish rabbis speculated that either Ham or Canaan castrated Noah.[7] Citing parallels in Leviticus (e.g., 18:8), F. W. Bassett argues that Ham had incestuous relations with his mother: "It would also explain why Noah cursed only one of Ham's several sons, if it is further assumed that Canaan was the fruit of such a case of incest."[8]

3. From Betto, *Fidel and Religion*, 108, cited in Wittenberg, "Let Canaan Be His Slave," 46.
4. Elsewhere in Scripture (Lam. 4:21; Hab. 2:15) drunkenness and nakedness are associated.
5. Cohen, *Drunkenness of Noah*, 17.
6. Gen. 9:24 designates Ham as the youngest son, but in the typical recital of the three sons, Ham is named between Shem and Japheth. Though some regard this as a contradiction, other factors may be involved in the order of the three names. See Hoftijzer, "Some Remarks to the Tale of Noah's Drunkenness," 24; Merrill, "Peoples of the Old Testament," 12.
7. Cohen, *Drunkenness of Noah*, 13. See also Lewis, *Study of the Interpretation of Noah*, 153.
8. Bassett, "Noah's Nakedness and the Curse of Canaan," 235.

But the text itself simply indicates that Ham beheld his father's nudity and reported it to his brothers, Shem and Japheth. Marc Vervenne comments: "There is, however, more at stake than the acceptability of nudity. Contrary to the Hebrew terms עֲרֹום/עֲרֻמִּים which occur in the Eden story (Gen. 2.25; 3.7, 10, 11), the key-word here, עֶרְוָה (Gen. 9.22a, 23d, 23f), does have an erotic and sexual connotation and is, therefore, best rendered as 'genitals' *pudenda*)."[9] Quite unlikely is Cohen's surmise that Ham acquired his potency by looking on his nude father.[10]

As difficult as it is for many readers to comprehend, it appears that Ham's misdeed indeed consisted in gazing at the nakedness of his father. As Allen Ross notes: "Ham's frivolous looking, a moral flaw, represents the first step in the abandonment of a moral code. Moreover this violation of a boundary destroyed the honor of Noah."[11] Ham compounded his sin by tattle-taling what he had seen to his brothers. Anthony Tomasino suggests: "Furthermore, when Ham told his brothers about their father's nudity, he was undoubtedly tempting them with forbidden knowledge (the opportunity to see their father's nakedness)."[12]

Not to honor one's father even when he is drunk is a grave failing (cf. Isa. 51:17–18). Gordon Wenham cites an apposite parallel from the Ugaritic epic Aqhat 1.32–33, which states that a son takes his father "by the hand when he's drunk, carries him when he's sated with wine."[13] In an illuminating exposition, Leon Kass, after observing that Noah's drunkenness robbed Noah of his "dignity, paternal authority, and humanity," draws out some of the broader implications of Ham's deed for posterity:

> Besides, what Ham did is more than sufficiently odious, even though he did not lay a hand on Noah. . . . To put it sharply, Ham's viewing—and telling— is metaphorically, an act of patricide and incest, of overturning the father *as a father*. . . . Eliminated is the father as authority, as guide, as teacher of law, custom, and a way of life.[14]

The Curse on Canaan

Readers from the time of Philo have puzzled over why Noah cursed Canaan rather than Ham.[15] Most explain this as a reference to the con-

9. Vervenne, "What Shall We Do with the Drunken Sailor?" 49.
10. Cohen, *Drunkenness of Noah*, 16.
11. Ross, "Studies in the Book of Genesis," 230.
12. Tomasino, "History Repeats Itself," 128–30.
13. Wenham, *Genesis 1–15*, 200.
14. Kass, "Seeing the Nakedness of His Father," 41.
15. Lewis, *Study of the Interpretation of Noah*, 56–57. Some Septuagint manuscripts replace Canaan with Ham. A Dead Sea Scrolls fragment (4Q252) explains the enigma of the curse of

quest of the Canaanites by the Israelites, either as a prophecy[16] or as a prophecy after the event.[17] The Table of Nations in Genesis 10 lists the various ethnic groups descended from Ham, Shem, and Japheth.[18] Genesis 10:6 lists the sons of Ham as Cush, Mizraim, Put, and Canaan.

David Neiman offers his view that the curse was a contemporary "war cry" of Israelites, who in the Late Bronze Age were allied with the sons of Japheth, the Philistines, in their mutual antagonism against the Canaanites, the sons of Ham.[19] Cohen, following his novel view that Ham coveted Noah's sexual potency, avers: "To thwart Ham's scheme, Noah—if this hypothesis is correct—would have had to curse Ham's son, Canaan, who was not shielded by any such generative power."[20]

I agree with Kass's analysis, who argues for the appropriateness of Noah's response: "A little reflection shows the fitness of Noah's response. Measure for measure, Noah 'unfathers' Ham by driving a wedge between him and his (youngest) son Canaan. . . . Ham, who seeks to free himself from parental authority and law, will be held responsible *by his son*—as a parental authority—for the evils that befall that son."[21]

In any case, a simple reading of the text reveals that though the sin was Ham's, Ham was not the object of Noah's curse. As *The Original African Heritage Study Bible* points out, none of Ham's three other sons, Mizraim (Egypt), Put (Libya), or Cush (Nubia = Sudan), was cursed.[22]

The Curse of Ham among Jews

On the basis of some remarks made by Jewish rabbis in the Midrash (sermonic stories), Talmud, and later medieval texts, it has been alleged that the so-called curse of Ham, which holds that God cursed the descendants of Ham with a black skin and destined them to slavery, originated first in Jewish circles.[23] The Midrash on Genesis (fifth century), for example, contains the following stories:

Ham as follows: "And he said, 'Cursed be Canaan; he will be, for his br[others], the last of slaves!' [But he did not] curse Ham, but only his son, for God had blessed the sons of Noah" (translation from García Martínez, *Dead Sea Scrolls Translated*, 214).

16. Hamilton, *Book of Genesis*, 327.

17. Rice, "Curse That Never Was," 13, 15.

18. Borowski, "Table of Nations," 14–31, believes that the groups are arranged not according to ethnic but rather sociocultural categories.

19. Neiman, "Date and Circumstances," 113–34.

20. Cohen, *Drunkenness of Noah*, 29.

21. Kass, "Seeing the Nakedness," 45.

22. Felder, *Original African Heritage Study Bible*, 15.

23. McKenzie, "Ham/Canaan, Cursing of," 268: "This interpretation occurs first in the Talmud and has persisted in certain circles."

R[abbi] Huna said in R[abbi] Joseph's name (Noah declared), "you have prevented me from begetting a fourth son, therefore I curse your fourth son." R[abbi] Huna also said in R[abbi] Joseph's name: "You have prevented me from doing something in the dark (. . . cohabitation), therefore your seed will be ugly and dark-skinned." R[abbi] Hiyya said: "Ham and the dog copulated in the Ark, therefore Ham came forth black-skinned while the dog publicly exposes his copulation."[24]

The Babylonian Talmud (sixth century) contains this passage about Ham's sin and his punishment: "Our Rabbis taught: 'Three copulated in the ark, and they were all punished—the dog, the raven, and Ham. The dog was doomed to be tied, the raven expectorates [his seed into his mate's mouth], and Ham was smitten in his skin."[25]

From the *Tanhuma*, a medieval collection of legends and rabbinic exegesis, R. Patai and R. Graves offer this paraphrase:

> Moreover because you twisted your head around to see my nakedness, your grandchildren's hair shall be twisted into kinks, and their eyes red; again, because your lips jested at my misfortune, theirs shall swell; and because you neglected my nakedness, they shall go naked, and their male members shall be shamefully elongated. Men of this race are called Negroes. (*Tanhuma* 13.15)[26]

The famed Jewish traveler from Spain, Benjamin of Tudela (twelfth century), commented about some blacks he observed in the area around Aswan in southern Egypt:

> There is a people among them who, like animals, eat of the herbs that grow on the banks of the Nile and in the fields. They go about naked and have not the intelligence of ordinary men. They cohabit with their sisters and anyone they find. It is a very hot land. . . . When they come after the food, they are taken as slaves and sold in Egypt and the neighbouring countries. These sons of Ham are black slaves.[27]

On the basis of these texts, a number of scholars identify Jewish postbiblical interpretations as the source of the curse of Ham.[28] This allegation was expanded in an inflammatory way when the Nation of Islam[29] pub-

---

24. Freedman and Simon, *Midrash Rabbah: Genesis*, chap. 36.
25. Epstein, *Hebrew-English Edition of the Babylonian Talmud*, tractate *Sanhedrin* 108b.
26. Graves and Patai, *Hebrew Myths*, 121.
27. Hess, "Itinerary of Benjamin of Tudela," 17.
28. Sanders, "Hamitic Hypothesis," 521–32; Jordan, *White Man's Burden*.
29. On the ideology of the Nation of Islam, popularly known as "Black Muslims," see Tsoukalas, *Nation of Islam*.

lished a book, *The Secret Relationship between Blacks and Jews*, which charged Jews with major involvement in the African slave trade. When this book was used as a text in a course taught by Tony Martin, an African American professor at Wellesley College, Jewish students and their supporters demanded that the administration suspend or punish Professor Martin. Martin's Jewish colleague, Mary Lefkowitz, became so outraged at his Afrocentric views that she became the leading critic of Afrocentrism.

Martin defended himself by claiming that Lefkowitz, a distinguished professor of classics, did not know her sources, such as Herodotus. He held that the Hamitic myth was invented by Jewish talmudic scholars over a thousand years before the transatlantic slave trade began: "Now it is the turn of the Jews to retract, apologize and pay reparations for their invention of the Hamitic myth, which killed many millions more than all the anti-Jewish pogroms and holocausts in Europe."[30]

Closer examination of these texts and their overall contexts renders the theory of a Jewish origin of the curse of Noah implausible. Ephraim Isaac, a scholar from Ethiopia, concludes in a study published in 1980:

> Nevertheless, on the basis of the primary sources, one cannot apply or transfer the curse against Canaan and the prejudices against the Canaanites to Cush or his descendants. Both the Biblical story and the Rabbinic literary sources are unambiguous in the distinction they make between Canaan, the forefather of the Canaanites, and Cush, the forefather of black people.[31]

In a later study, Isaac concludes:

> In Rabbinic literature, we do not have or find an implication that the descendants of the accursed Canaan are black or African People. Indeed there was never a question in Rabbinic thought—it was Cush and not Canaan who inhabited Africa south of Egypt.[32]

Two Jewish scholars, David Aaron and David Goldenberg, independently reexamined these texts and pointed out that these are very isolated references and that questionable translations have sometimes been used by scholars who could not read the original texts. For example, Goldenberg points out that a more accurate rendering of the *Tanhuma* passage paraphrased by Graves and Patai (cited above) reads:

30. Martin, *Jewish Onslaught*, 35.
31. Isaac, "Genesis, Judaism" (1980), 17. See also idem, "Ham"; and idem, "Concept biblique et rabbinique de la malédiction de Noé."
32. Isaac, "Genesis, Judaism" (1985), 77.

Ham's eyes turned red, since he looked at his father's nakedness; his lips became crooked, since he spoke with his mouth; the hair of his head and beard
became singed, since he turned his face around; and since he did not cover
[his father's] nakedness, he went naked and his foreskin was extended.[33]

As more accurately rendered, this text may not refer to blacks at all; the
statement "men of this race are called Negroes," is not in the Hebrew text
but was an explanation inserted by Graves and Patai.

Rabbinic literature in general, following the Bible, holds that Canaan,
not Ham, was cursed. According to Isaac, for the rabbis, "Canaan's dark
complexion, which was not unlike that of the Israelites, was said to be
ugly; Cush's blackness, on the other hand, which was deep and distinguished, had no such stigma attached to it."[34] This was the view also of
the main medieval commentators, such as Rashi (d. 1105), Abraham ibn
Ezra (d. 1167), Ramban (d. 1274), and Sforno (d. 1550). The few texts from
the Midrash and the Talmud cited above, far from representing the talmudic view of the rabbis, are quite exceptional when judged against the
whole corpus. Aaron points out that the passage cited from the Babylonian Talmud stands alone in a collection of seventeen volumes with an
average volume containing 800 pages.[35] Goldenberg comments: "The
claim that two aggadic folktales, representing .0006 percent of the overall
talmudic corpus and transmitted by two of 1500 personalities, represents
'the talmudic view' sounds a little ridiculous."[36]

Furthermore, as talmudic literature was incomprehensible even to the
general Jewish population, its impact on non-Jews was probably nonex-
istent. No citation of rabbinic literature by non-Jews can be traced before
the twelfth century. Aaron concludes: "At the present time, no such documentation exists demonstrating a Christian or Islamic awareness of the
Jewish exegesis on the curse of Ham/Canaan."[37] The diary of Benjamin
Tudela was not published until four centuries after his travels.[38]

As to the charge that Jews played a major role in the African slave
trade, although Jews in England and in the Caribbean were involved, Eli
Faber concludes from a study of the primary sources that Jewish partici-
pation in the slave trade and in the ownership of slaves was quite small.[39]

33. Goldenberg, "Curse of Ham," 29. See also idem, "Scythian-Barbarian," 92–93; idem,
Curse of Ham.
34. Isaac, "Genesis, Judaism" (1980), 8.
35. Aaron, "Early Rabbinic Exegesis," 739.
36. Goldenberg, "Curse of Ham," 32; idem, "Image of the Black in Jewish Culture," 557–79.
37. Aaron, "Early Rabbinic Exegesis," 752. For a response to Aaron's criticism of McKenzie's "Ham/Canaan, Cursing of," see McKenzie, "Response: The Curse of Ham," 183–86.
38. Adler, Itinerary of Benjamin of Tudela.
39. Faber, Jews, Slaves, and the Slave Trade.

The Curse of Ham among Muslims

Though the Qur'an relates the story of Noah (11.36–48), there is no reference to Ham, unless he is the unnamed son (11.43) who went up to a mountain rather than enter the ark and perished as a result. After Muhammad's death (632), Muslim expansion brought the Arabs into contact with black Africans. Muslims became more and more involved in the slave trade, transporting black slaves eastward across the Red Sea and across the Sahara westward to northwest and west Africa.[40]

According to Bernard Lewis, some Muslims developed the concept of the curse of Ham to justify their enslavement of blacks: "The slaves of the Arabs were not Canaanites but blacks—so the curse was transferred to them, and blackness added to servitude as part of the hereditary burden."[41] Goldenberg notes that the following Muslim sources express versions of the curse of Ham:[42]

> According to Ibn ʿAṭāʾ (647–732): "Ham begat all those who are black and curly-haired. . . . Noah prayed that the hair of Ham's descendants would not grow beyond their ears, and that wherever his descendants met the children of Shem, the latter would enslave them."
>
> Ṭabari (9th cent.), quotes others as saying: "[Noah] prayed that Ham's color would be changed and that his descendants would be slaves to the children of Shem and Japheth."

According to David Davis, by the eighth and ninth centuries, Arab writers "increasingly invoked the biblical curse of Canaan to explain why the 'sons of Ham' had been blackened and degraded to the status of natural slaves as punishment for their ancestor's sin."[43] For most Arabs "slave" (ʿabdun) meant black; European slaves were called mamluks. The Banu Ham (Sons of Ham) were Sūdān (Blacks or Negroes).[44]

Evans observes that, by the tenth century, the curse of Ham had been modified to exempt Egyptians and Berbers:

> The reprieve was accomplished by one of two methods. Either the genealogy was revised so that North Africans, though still "sons of Ham," were descended through some son other than Canaan upon whom the curse had fallen; or the story itself was retold in such a way that these particular sons of Ham were forgiven the sin committed by their ancestor.[45]

40. See Willis, Slaves and Slavery in Muslim Africa, vol. 1.
41. Lewis, Race and Slavery in the Middle East, 55.
42. Goldenberg, "Curse of Ham," 33.
43. Davis, Slavery and Human Progress, 42.
44. Evans, "From the Land of Canaan," 29; Zoghby, "Blacks and Arabs," 12.
45. Evans, "From the Land of Canaan," 33. Blackburn, Making of New World Slavery, 72, observes: "However, neither the Papacy nor the Portuguese Crown chose to dwell on

After the Crusades Europeans learned about sugar cane from the Muslims. Since the cultivation of sugar cane was labor intensive, slaves were used to lower the cost of production. The cultivation of sugar spread westward from the Near East to Sicily, Spain, and then to the Madeira Islands (ca. 1432) and the Canaries (ca. 1480). Lewis suggests that as the cultivation of sugar and cotton and black slaves to harvest them spread from Spain and the Atlantic islands to the Americas, the myth of the curse of Ham was adopted by Christian defenders of slavery.[46]

The Curse of Ham among Europeans

In northwestern Europe slavery disappeared in the eleventh and twelfth centuries, though the system of serfdom continued long after.[47] In 1031 Conrad II forbade all traffic in slaves; in 1102 a synod held in London repeated the prohibition. But slavery continued in the Iberian Peninsula: in Spain the slaves were Moors from North Africa; in Portugal Negroes were imported from Africa after 1441.

A garbled version of the curse of Ham was reported by a mid-fifteenth-century Portuguese chronicler to Prince Henry, the patron of the navigators who explored the west coast of Africa: "'Here you must note,' the chronicler told the prince, 'that these blacks were Moors like the others, though their slaves, in accordance with the Deluge, Noah laid upon his son Cain [sic], cursing him in this way—that his race should be subject to all the other races of the world.'"[48]

Renaissance thinkers did not believe in the curse of Ham. According to Allen: "Early theologians had held that Ham was turned black because of his impiety, but Renaissance historians were quite aware that not all of Ham's descendants were black; moreover they were far more eager to discover the scientific explanation of the Negroid type than to accept miracles."[49]

In 1521 Johan Boemus, a German scholar of Hebrew, argued that all civilized peoples were descended from Shem and Japheth, while all barbarous peoples were descended from Ham.[50] According to Albert Perbal, a Lutheran writer named Hanneman from Kiel for the first time in Europe declared in 1677 that all peoples with black skins, including Africans, In-

Noah's curse since they aimed to win the friendship of African kingdoms, with the aim of fostering trade and making converts."
46. Lewis, *Race and Slavery*, 125.
47. The last serf was enfranchised in England in 1574, and in Scotland in 1799.
48. Evans, "From the Land of Canaan," 39.
49. Allen, *Legend of Noah*, 119.
50. Fredrickson, *White Supremacy*, 10.

dians, and Malays, were the children of Ham and were condemned to slavery for a thousand generations.[51]

The Curse of Ham among Americans

From 1562 British seamen took part in the slave trade that supplied the
Spanish colonies. African slaves were first offered for sale to the British
colony in Virginia in 1619. In 1644 Boston merchants organized an expedition to import slaves from Africa. The slave traffic into the British colonies
expanded rapidly in the latter half of the seventeenth century. Between
1680 and 1700 more than 300,000 African slaves were imported into the
British colonies.

The earliest use of the curse of Ham to justify slavery in America dates
to the 1670s. Some scholars argue that the curse of Ham played a relatively minor role until the late eighteenth and early nineteenth centuries,
the Antebellum era prior to the Civil War.[52] Thomas Peterson identifies
numerous southern writers from Louisiana, Mississippi, Alabama, Geor-
gia, South Carolina, North Carolina, Tennessee, Virginia, and Maryland
who reflected various versions of the Hamitic myth.[53] But the most influential purveyor of the myth was a New Yorker, Josiah Priest. Elizabeth
Fox-Genovese and Eugene Genovese comment: "But it took a northern
clergyman, Josiah Priest, to elaborate a fantastic rereading of the curse of
Ham that confused the color of Africans' skins with their purported sexual excesses, justifying slavery by a racism considered rabid even in the
slaveholding South."[54] In his *Bible Defense of Slavery* (1853) Priest avers:

> God, who made all things, and endowed all animated nature with the
> strange and unexplained power of propagation, superintended the forma-
> tion of two of the sons of Noah, in the womb of their mother, in an extraor-
> dinary and supernatural manner, giving to these two children such forms of
> bodies, constitution of natures, and complexion of skin, as suited his will.
> Japheth he caused to be born white, differing from the red color of his par-
> ents, while he caused Ham to be born black, a color still further removed
> from the red hue of his parents than was white.[55]

51. Perbal, "La race nègre et la malédiction de Cham," 159.
52. Davis, *Slavery and Human Progress*, 337 n. 144: "Before then, for Jews, Christians, and
Muslims alike, it was sufficient that blacks were Gentiles, pagans, or infidels, and the
Noachidian curse served as an occasional, if forceful, obiter dictum." For early American
slavery, see Greene, *Negro in Colonial New England*; Wood, *Origins of American Slavery*.
53. Peterson, *Ham and Japheth*, 104.
54. Fox-Genovese and Genovese, "Divine Sanction of Social Order," 224.
55. Cited by Bradley, "Curse of Canaan and the American Negro," 102.

Thornton Stringfellow's *Slavery: Its Origin, Nature and History* (1861) describes the Negroes as the "descendants of Ham, the beastly and degraded son of Noah."[56] Most southern intellectuals, however, rejected the use of the curse of Ham, but rather argued that slavery was justified since the Bible itself recognized slavery in both the Old and New Testaments.

But in opposition to the Genoveses' de-emphasis of the curse of Ham among southerners, Stephen Haynes identifies at least fifty primary documents from the Antebellum era that cite Noah's curse as the central justification for slavery. He asserts:

> By the 1830s—when the American antislavery movement became organized, vocal, and aggressive—the scriptural defense of slavery had evolved into the "most elaborate and systematic statement" of proslavery theory, Noah's curse had become a stock weapon in the arsenal of slavery's apologists, and references to Genesis 9 appeared prominently in their publications.[57]

The New Hamitic Hypothesis

With the recognition that Mizraim (Egypt) was descended from Ham, a counterhypothesis also arose early in the nineteenth century, which held that the Hamites were actually Caucasian or Europeans who were the inventors of the great civilizations in Africa. Such ideas were promulgated by clergyman such as M. Russell in his book *View of Ancient and Modern Egypt* (1831).

This viewpoint was held also by John Hanning Speke, who discovered the source of the White Nile in central Africa and named Lake Victoria after his queen. Even in the early twentieth century such a thesis was supported by anthropologist C. G. Seligman in such books as *Races of Africa* (1930). According to E. Sanders: "So it came to pass that the Egyptians emerged as Hamites, Caucasoid, uncursed and capable of high civilization."[58]

In 1871 some extraordinary stone structures, including walls and towers, called the "Great Zimbabwe Ruins," were discovered in southern Rhodesia by Karl Mauch, a German geologist, who ascribed them to Solomon. Still others attributed them to settlers from India. Under the influence of the Hamitic hypothesis, some scholars credited newcomers from the north rather than the indigenous Bantu peoples.[59] The Hamitic thesis even influenced the Belgians to favor the fairer and taller Tutsi over the

56. Cited by Buswell, *Slavery, Segregation, and Scripture*, 16.
57. Haynes, *Noah's Curse*, 8, 246 n. 13.
58. Sanders, "Hamitic Hypothesis," 527.
59. See Swanson, "Colonizing the Past."

darker Hutu, which contributes to the deadly enmity between these two
tribes even today.

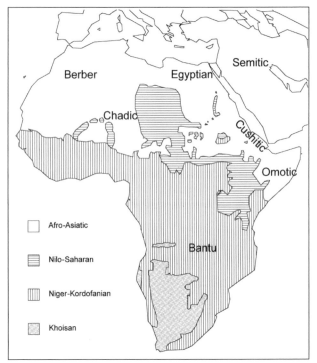

Figure 1.1. Distribution of African language stocks (Michael Lucas).

The Curse of Ham in South Africa

Between 1836 and 1846, ten thousand descendants of Dutch colonists
called Boers or Afrikaners escaped British jurisdiction in the Cape Colony
by trekking into the interior of South Africa. There they defeated the Zu-
lus in the battle of Blood River in 1838 and subjugated various tribes, such
as the Khoikhoi and the Hottentots. According to George Fredrickson, the
Trekboers invoked the curse of Ham to justify their expansion.[60] However,
there is only one documented case of such an expression in the early nineteenth century. According to André du Toit:

> The documentation usually adduced to support the alleged early Afrikaner
> tradition to invoke the curse on the sons of Ham as a justification for racial

60. Fredrickson, *White Supremacy*, 170: "Inevitably some of them invoked the curse on
Ham to justify their dominance over the Khoikhoi."

inequality has as its *locus classicus* a passage in the journal of Governor Janssens in 1803. One "brother of Thomas Ferreira," claiming some acquaintance with literature, "made the discovery" that the Hottentots were the descendants of Ham and subject to the curse.[61]

Although such a myth gained greater popularity late in the nineteenth century, it played no role in the development of the policy of apartheid developed by the Herenigde Party in 1945.[62] Instead, appeal was made to verses such as Deuteronomy 32:8: "When the Most High gave to the nations their inheritance, / when he divided all mankind, / he set up boundaries for the peoples / according to the number of the sons of Israel" (NIV); and Acts 17:26: "From one single stock he not only created the whole human race so that they could occupy the entire earth, but he decreed how long each nation should flourish and what the boundaries of its territory should be" (Jerusalem Bible). The supporters of apartheid cited the story of the Tower of Babel in Genesis 11 as a warning against humanity's sinful attempt to combine various groups of the human race.[63]

The Curse of Ham among Mormons

Joseph Smith (1805–44), who lived in upstate New York at Palmyra, claimed in 1827 that Moroni, an angel, led him to buried golden plates written in "reformed Egyptian." With the aid of stones that he called the Urim and Thummim, he translated these tablets as the Book of Mormon, which revealed that some Hebrews, led by a prophet Lehi, came to America about 600 B.C. Some of their descendants became the heathen Lamanites, who were the ancestors of the American Indians. Jesus revealed himself to another group, the Nephites, who were destroyed by the Lamanites about A.D. 400.

In 1835 when Joseph Smith was in Kirtland, Ohio, he purchased four ancient Egyptian mummies and papyri from Michael Chandler, who had inherited these objects from his uncle, Antonio Lebolo, who in turn had obtained them from Thebes in Upper Egypt in 1831. Smith translated some of these papyri and published them in 1842 as the Book of Abraham (later incorporated in the Pearl of Great Price). He also copied some of the vignettes found on the papyri. The Book of Abraham was canonized by the Utah church in 1880, but was not accepted by the Reorganized Church in Missouri.

61. Du Toit, "No Chosen People," 929.
62. Ibid., 930; de Klerk, *Puritans in Africa*, 220.
63. De Klerk, *Puritans in Africa*, 222; de Gruchy, *Church Struggle in South Africa*, 71.

In 1912 the Episcopal bishop of Utah enlisted eight prominent Egyptologists to challenge Smith's translation. But as the papyri were believed to have been lost in the great Chicago fire, the controversy faded away. Then a Coptic scholar, Aziz Atiya, who was a professor at the University of Utah, discovered that these papyri were in the possession of the Metropolitan Museum of New York City. The museum transferred them to the Mormon Church in 1967.[64]

When these documents were restudied by such noted Egyptologists as John Wilson, Richard Parker, and Klaus Baer, they turned out to be funerary texts from the Book of the Dead and the Book of the Breathings.[65] Comparisons between the original texts and Joseph Smith's notes and sketches were facilitated by the publication in 1966 of Joseph Smith's *Grammar and Alphabet of the Egyptian Language*. It appears that characters from less than four lines of one papyrus were rendered by Smith into forty-nine verses of the Book of Abraham. Since the papyri bear no resemblance to the translations produced by Joseph Smith, who was not aware of the decipherment of Egyptian by François Champollion in 1822, the episode created controversy among Mormon intellectuals and confirmed the suspicions of the critics of Mormonism.[66]

Of great significance is the fact that a passage in the Book of Abraham served as the basis for denying Mormon priesthood to blacks.[67] As Mormon historian Richard Howard observes: "But when one looks at the text of the *Book of Abraham* (Chapter 1:21–27), it appears that Joseph Smith in 1835–36 was making the so-called curse of Ham (through Canaanite blood) to extend from the mere condition of servitude to the denial of the right of priesthood to the nineteenth century Negro."[68] In 1841, Joseph Smith asserted "that the 'curse' on Ham, the alleged ancestor of black people, was promoted by Noah, not simply in a fit of drunken anger, but rather in a calm and deliberate fashion."[69] Four years later Apostle Orson Hyde explained that the subordinate status of blacks had been predetermined by their acts in their previous existence. Blacks such as Walker Lewis and Elijah Abel were ordained in the lifetime of Joseph Smith, but attitudes toward blacks later hardened.

In 1852 Brigham Young proclaimed that "the seed of Canaan will inevitably carry the curse which was placed upon them until the same author-

64. Atiya and Fischer, "Facsimile Found."
65. Wilson, "Joseph Smith Egyptian Papyri"; Parker, "Joseph Smith Papyri"; Baer, "Breathing Permit of Hôr." See Ritner, "Breathing Permit of Hôr."
66. Howard and Tanner, "Source of the Book of Abraham Identified"; Walters, "Joseph Smith among the Egyptians."
67. Bringhurst, *Saints, Slaves, and Blacks*, 45.
68. Howard, "Book of Abraham," 42.
69. Bringhurst, *Saints, Slaves, and Blacks*, 86.

THE CURSE OF HAM

ity which placed it there, shall see proper to have it removed."[70] After the 1880 canonization of the Pearl of Great Price, including the Book of Abraham, blacks could be received into the church but not granted priesthood. Neither could they receive temple endowments or temple marriages.

This denial was a source of embarrassment in the light of criticism by civil-rights advocates and was also a hindrance to the evangelism of areas like South America and Africa.[71] The Mormon Church, however, believes in the prospect of continuous revelation. It was a matter of great satisfaction to both Mormons and non-Mormons alike that the church's First Presidency received a revelation that led to the repeal of black priesthood denial on June 8, 1978: "The Lord . . . has heard our prayers, and by revelation has confirmed that the long-promised day has come when every faithful, worthy man in the Church may receive the priesthood, with power to exercise its divine authority, and enjoy with his loved ones every blessing that flows therefrom, including the blessings of the temple."[72]

Thus, we see that over the centuries an obscure text was so interpreted by medieval Jews to explain the blackness of Africans and was then used in turn by Arabs, Europeans, and North Americans to justify slavery and, until recently, by Mormons to exclude blacks from their priesthood.

70. Ibid., 68.
71. Mauss, "Mormonism and the Negro."
72. Bringhurst, *Saints, Slaves, and Blacks*, 178; cf. Embry, *Black Saints in a White Church*, 27.

2

MOSES' CUSHITE
WIFE

According to Numbers 12:1, Miriam and Aaron objected to Moses' marriage to a Cushite woman (*hāʾiššâ hakkušît*) and challenged his right to be God's sole spokesperson,[1] whereupon God punished Miriam—but not Aaron—with leprosy.[2] Since the Cushite woman was no doubt dark-skinned, some commentators infer that Miriam was turned white as an act of poetic justice.[3] Scholars with medical knowledge, however, point out that biblical leprosy is not the same as Hansen's disease and suggest that the point of the comparison was that her skin ailment produced flakes like snow.[4]

Elsewhere, in Exodus 2:21, we learn that Moses was married to Zipporah,

1. See Ashley, *Book of Numbers*, 224; Budd, *Numbers*, 136–39. Cf. also Burns, *Has the Lord Indeed Spoken?*; Coats, "Humility and Honor"; Diebner, "For He Had Married a Cushite Woman."

2. Bamberger, "Aaron: Changing Perceptions," 205.

3. Cross, *From Epic to Canaan*, 204; Felder, *Race, Racism, and the Biblical Narratives*, 135; Trible, "Bringing Miriam out of the Shadows," 22.

4. Browne, *Leprosy in the Bible*; Davies, "Levitical Leprosy"; Hulse, "Nature of 'Biblical Leprosy,'" 103; Robinson, "Jealousy of Miriam," 432 n. 8; Kiuchi, "Paradox of Skin Disease."

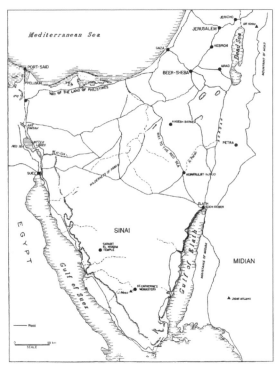

Figure 2.1. Sinai and Midian
(S. Mutiti).

the daughter of a Midianite priest.[5] Midian was an area in northwest Arabia across the Red Sea from the Sinai Peninsula.[6] Since Moses had not done so, Zipporah circumcised their son, according to Exodus 4:24–26.[7] She was sent away by Moses (18:2) and is not mentioned again until her father Jethro brings her back with their two sons, Gershom and Eliezer, to meet Moses (18:5).

A number of earlier writers (Augustine, Talmud, Targum Onkelos, Ezekiel the Tragedian, Ibn Ezra)[8] and some recent scholars suggest that the Cushite

5. See Hays, "Moses: The Private Man."

6. Montgomery, *Arabia and the Bible*; Mendenhall, "Midian"; Knauf, "Midianites and Ish-maelites." For a refutation of Cross's attempt (*From Epic to Canaan*, 60–68) to locate Mount Sinai in Midian, see Franz, "Is Mount Sinai in Saudi Arabia?"

7. Ackerman, "Why Is Miriam Also among the Prophets?" 75, concludes: "As Miriam could be imagined as holding the otherwise typically male position of prophet during the story of the liminal sojourn of the people of Israel in the wilderness, so too can Zipporah be depicted as if she occupies the otherwise exclusively male position of priest during the story of the wilderness sojourn of Israel's spiritual leader and microcosmic representative, Moses."

8. Schneider, "Semitic Influences and the Biblical Text," 94: "Ibn Ezra states: 'The Cushite woman was Tzipporah, the wife of Moses. She was a Midianite woman, and the Midianites, were black. T[zipporah] was black and was like a black person."

woman of Numbers 12 is to be identified with Zipporah on the basis of the parallelism between Cushan and Midian in Habakkuk 3:7: "I saw the tents of Cushan in distress, / the dwellings of Midian in anguish" (NIV).[9]

Most scholars, however, believe that the Cushite woman was a second wife who may have been part of the mixed multitude that left Egypt in the exodus (Exod. 12:38; Num. 11:4).[10] The Septuagint and the Vulgate translate the Hebrew word as "Ethiopian," which is derived from the Greek word *Aithiops* (lit., sunburned face), a general word used by the Greeks to describe dark-skinned people, chiefly from the area south of Egypt.

Later Jewish sources provide legendary embellishments of this union.[11] Artapanus (second century B.C.), an Egyptian Jew, was cited by Eusebius in *Preparation for the Gospel* 9.27. According to Artapanus, Moses was adopted by the barren wife of King Chenephres of Memphis, who became envious of Moses and sent him to fight the Ethiopians. Josephus (*Antiquities* 2.10.1–2 §§242–48) describes how Moses was led by ibises, who devoured serpents that were in the way.[12] He adds that Princess Tharbis of the Ethiopians was smitten with Moses and betrayed her city to him. The tradition that the Cushite woman was a queen of Ethiopia is also mentioned in Pseudo-Jonathan. This Jewish elaboration is reflected in later Christian sources such as letter 13 of Jacob of Edessa (d. 708), who declared: "'The 'Cushite woman' is not Sippora but the daughter of the king of the Cushites. For Moses was sent as general of the Egyptians by Pharaoh to fight with the Cushites, the Egyptians' neighbours and enemies."[13]

9. Cross, *From Epic to Canaan*, 204; Hidal, "Land of Cush in the Old Testament," 102.

10. Two contributors to *The Original African Heritage Study Bible* take opposing positions on the identification of the Cushite woman. On the one hand, Copher ("Black Presence in the Old Testament," 156) asserts: "This woman undoubtedly was Zipporah, daughter of Jethro, and not the Ethiopian princess referred to by Josephus." On the other hand, Bailey ("Beyond Identification: The Use of Africans in Old Testament Poetry and Narratives," 179) objects: "Most of the expositions of this passage revolve around either of two themes. The first is the attempt to de-Africanize this woman, to argue that she must come from some Cush other than the Cush in Africa."

11. Lévy, "Moïse en éthiope"; Ginzberg, *Legends of the Jews*, 5.407; Vermes, "La figure de Moïse"; Rajak, "Moses in Ethiopia"; Runnalls, "Moses' Ethiopian Campaign"; Feldman, *Josephus's Interpretation of the Bible*, 376, 402–3.

12. Silver, "Moses and the Hungry Birds."

13. Brock, "Some Syriac Legends concerning Moses," 242. Heliodorus of Emesa (third century A.D.) wrote a popular novel, *Aithiopica*, relating the romance between a Greek prince and an Ethiopian princess. This probably inspired Egyptologist Auguste Mariette (1821–81) to suggest a story to Camille du Locle, who wrote a libretto, which was then transformed into the opera *Aïda* by Giuseppe Verdi, first performed in Cairo in 1871, two years after the opening of the Suez Canal.

Cush and the Garden of Eden

Though scholars are unanimous that almost all of the biblical references to Cush are to the area south of Egypt, there continues to be sharp
disagreement about the enigmatic reference to Cush and one of the four
rivers associated with the garden of Eden.[14] Genesis 2:10–14 reads as
follows:

> A river watering the garden flowed from Eden; from there it was separated
> into four headwaters. The name of the first is the Pishon; it winds through
> the entire land of Havilah, where there is gold. (The gold of that land is
> good; aromatic resin and onyx are also there.) The name of the second river
> is the Gihon; it winds through the entire land of Cush. The name of the third
> river is the Tigris; it runs along the east side of Asshur. And the fourth river
> is the Euphrates. (NIV)

Whereas the names of the last two rivers, the Euphrates[15] on the west
and the Tigris[16] on the east, are well known from the land of Mesopotamia
(Greek: "Between the Rivers") in modern Iraq, the other two rivers are
problematic. Scholars are divided into two schools of thought: those who
regard Pishon and Gihon as actual rivers, and those who regard them as
mythological or symbolic. The former associate the Cush mentioned in
verse 13 with Mesopotamia; the latter take Cush in the usual sense of the
land south of Egypt.

The most promising attempt to identify real rivers is an essay by geologist Carol Hill, who uses evidence from satellite photographs to identify
the Pishon with a now-dry riverbed, Wadi al-Batin, coming from Arabia
into the area in lower Mesopotamia where the Tigris and Euphrates flow
into a single Shatt Al-Arab.[17] She suggests: "The Gihon is most likely the
Karun River, or less likely the Karkheh, both of which encircled the land
of the Kassites (Cush) in western Iran."[18]

14. Though most commentaries continue to derive the etymology of Hebrew *ʿēden* from a
Sumerian word meaning "steppe, plain," Millard, "Etymology of Eden," suggests a derivation from Semitic root *ʿdn* (to make abundant, to enrich), on the basis of the newly published
Akkadian-Aramaic bilingual from Tell Fekheriyeh; see Abou-Assaf, Bordreuil, and Millard,
La statue de Tell Fekherye, 62. The Septuagint translates Hebrew *gan-ʿēden* (garden of Eden)
with *paradeisos tēs tryphēs* (pleasure park of delicacies). On the Medo-Persian origin of the
word *paradise*, see Yamauchi, *Persia and the Bible*, 332–34.

15. Euphrates = Sumerian *buranun* = Akkadian *pūrattu*. Kramer, *Sumerians*, 40, notes that
the names of both the Euphrates and the Tigris are pre-Sumerian in origin.

16. Hebrew *ḥiddeqel* (Tigris) is derived from Akkadian *idiglat*. See Hallo, *Origins*, 326.

17. Hill, "Garden of Eden."

18. Ibid., 44. For the various rivers flowing out of southwestern Iran (Khuzestan), see
Yamauchi, *Persia and the Bible*, 280.

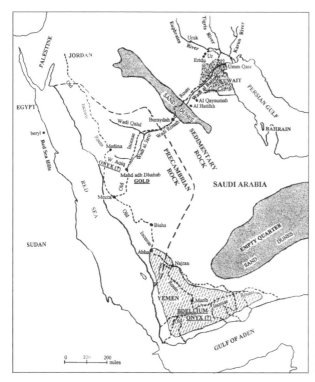

Figure 2.2. The four
rivers of the garden of
Eden (Carol A. Hill).

The identification of Cush in Genesis 2:13 with a Mesopotamian locale
rather than the usual African area was first suggested by Friedrich De-
litzsch in 1881. In the fourteenth-century B.C. Amarna letters, written in
Akkadian and found in Egypt, both areas are subsumed under the same
name: *Kaši*.[19]

The Kassites were a people from the Zagros Mountains east of Mesopotamia, who settled in Mesopotamia after the destruction of Babylon by
the Hittites in 1595 B.C. and established a four-century-long reign during
the Middle Babylonian era.[20] The Mesopotamian location is also favored
by the association in Genesis 10:8 of Nimrod as the son of Cush, who established well-known cities in Shinar (i.e., Mesopotamia).[21] This hypothesis is advocated by E. A. Speiser,[22] who maintains that in Genesis 2:10 "the
term 'heads' can have nothing to do with streams into which the river

19. Klengel, "Das Land Kusch in den Keilschrifttexten von Amarna." References to
Kushite soldiers are found in Amarna letters 49, 131, and 287.
20. See Yamauchi, "Kassites." Kassites are called *Kaššu* in Akkadian, *Kuššu* in the Nuzi
dialect, and *Kossaioi* or *Kissioi* in Greek.
21. Lipiński, "Nimrod et Aššur."
22. Speiser, "Rivers of Paradise."

breaks up after it leaves Eden, but designates instead four separate branches which have merged within Eden."[23]

The majority of scholars, however, disagree with Speiser's reading of this verse[24] and consider that it describes the branching out of four rivers from Eden, with the Gihon (associated with African Cush) identified as the Nile River[25] and the Pishon (associated with Havilah,[26] an area usually associated with Arabia) identified as the sea that surrounds Arabia.[27] T. Stordalen notes that "the motif of cosmic water running in four directions is well attested in ancient iconography."[28] In this interpretation the four rivers symbolize the watering of the lands in a centrifugal direction (cf. Ezek. 47:1–12).

The Names of Places and Peoples

The name of the continent Africa goes back to the Roman name of their province, which the Romans established in the area of Tunis after Carthage was destroyed in the Third Punic War (146 B.C.). According to S. Raven:

> Africa itself meant nothing to the Greeks, who regularly used the word Libya for all African territory west of Egypt; the Romans used "African" indiscriminately of the people, but confined the noun to Africa Proconsularis—roughly Tunisia. Only in the late third century did the "diocese" of Africa cover all the north-west African provinces except the area round Tingis (Tangiers). In Byzantine times, the north-west African provinces retrieved by Justinian became the exarchy of Africa. The original Afri were probably one tribal group in one small part of Tunisia. Later north-west Africa was called *Ifriqiya* by the Arabs.[29]

23. Speiser, *Genesis*, 20.

24. See, e.g., Wenham, *Genesis 1–15*, 66: "The greatest difficulty with this view is that, according to Genesis, the rivers as they flow from Eden split into four, whereas on Speiser's location they flow toward Eden to converge there." See also Westermann, *Genesis*, 1.292–98; Hidal, "Land of Cush in the Old Testament," 105. Cf. also Adamo, *Explorations in African Biblical Studies*, 73; Felder, *Original African Heritage Study Bible*, xi; *Holy Bible: African American Jubilee Edition*, 100–101.

25. Görg, "Zur Identität des Pischon," 11, suggests a derivation of Pishon either from Egyptian *pȝ šn* (the [great] waters) or *pȝ ḥnw* (the canal). See also idem, "Wo lag das Paradies?"

26. Simons, *Geographical and Topographical Texts*, 40; see also Yamauchi, "Havilah."

27. Neiman, "Eden: The Garden of God," 325–26: "Kush must be understood as the lands farthest to the south, and the Gihon as the sea circumfluent to them. Gihon, therefore, corresponds to the circumfluent Ocean Stream which most ancient geographers considered to be the rim of the disc of earth." Albright, "Location of the Garden of Eden," 22, suggests that the Pishon and the Gihon might be two rivers that joined to form the Nile, such as the Nile and the Atbara, or the Blue Nile and the White Nile.

28. Stordalen, *Echoes of Eden*, 275.

29. Raven, *Rome in Africa*, xxvi.

The word *Libyan*, which is derived from the *Libu* tribes who lived west of Egypt, was used by the Greeks of non-Punic peoples living west of Egypt. After the Punic Wars both Greeks and Romans used "Libyan" solely of Africans living in Carthaginian territory.

The most common name used by Greeks of black-skinned peoples living south of Egypt was *Aithiops* (lit., sunburned face). This name first appears in the Linear B tablets of the Mycenaean age (1400–1200 B.C.) as *ai-ti-jo-qo* (Aithioqᵘs) (Pylos 133 = EnO3).[30] For the Greeks and Romans this meant not only those with dark skins but also Africans with crinkly hair, thick lips, and a broad nose.[31] These "Negro" types of blacks were not encountered by the Egyptians until about 1600 B.C.[32]

The Septuagint and the Vulgate translate the Hebrew word *Cush* with *Aithiopia*. Cush occurs twenty-eight times, and Cushi (i.e., the Cushite) twenty-two times. Ezekiel 29:10 clearly places the boundary between Egypt and Cush at Aswan (Syene) at the First Cataract: "Therefore I am against you and against your streams, and I will make the land of Egypt a ruin and a desolate waste from Migdol to Aswan, as far as the border of Cush" (NIV). Isaiah 18:1–2 declares: "Woe to the land of whirring wings / along the rivers of Cush, / which sends envoys by sea / in papyrus boats over the water. / Go, swift messengers, / to a people tall and smooth-skinned, / to a people feared far and wide, / an aggressive nation of strange speech, / whose land is divided by rivers" (NIV). The proverbial statement in Jeremiah 13:23 ("Can the Ethiopian change his skin / or the leopard its spots?" [NIV]) alludes to the unusually black skin of the Cushite.[33]

The Hebrew word *Cush* is a loanword borrowed from the Egyptian term *Kush*, originally pronounced *Kash*.[34] This name first appears in a monumental inscription set up about 1950 B.C. by Senusret I of the 12th

30. Ventris and Chadwick, *Documents in Mycenaean Greek*, 99, 114.

31. Thompson, *Romans and Blacks*, 57–58. Cf. also Beardsley, *Negro in Greek and Roman Civilization*; Snowden, *Blacks in Antiquity*; idem, "Images and Attitudes"; idem, "Attitudes towards Blacks."

32. The word *Negro* is derived from Latin *niger* (black). Trigger, "Nubian, Negro, Black, Nilotic?" 33: "In the New Kingdom, when Egyptian rule extended above the Fourth Cataract, a more southerly African type was frequently portrayed. These southerners are shown with black skin, everted lips, and prognathous jaws." Cf. also Vercoutter, "Iconography of the Black in Ancient Egypt," 33; idem, "L'image du noir," 22. See also Strouhal, "Evidence of the Early Penetration of Negroes."

33. Yurco, "Were the Ancient Egyptians Black or White?" 24: "The ancient Egyptians, like their modern descendants, were of varying complexions of color, from the light Mediterranean type (like Nefertiti), to the light brown of Middle Egypt, to the darker brown of Upper Egypt, to the darkest shade around Aswan and the First Cataract region, where even today, the population shifts to Nubian." See also Trigger, "Nubian, Negro, Black, Nilotic?" 27; Adams, *Nubia*, 8.

34. See *kš̠, kš̠* in Zibelius, *Afrikanische Orts- und Völkernamen*, 165–69.

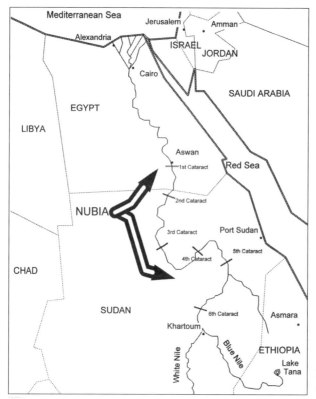

Figure 2.3. Location of Nubia (S. Mutiti).

Dynasty near Buhen.[35] On the basis of its appearance in certain execration texts,[36] Kush was originally restricted to a small territory just upriver from Semna.[37]

The Egyptians commonly added the epithet "wretched" or "miserable" whenever they mentioned Kush. Kush, however, developed into a powerful and wealthy state, especially between 1700 B.C. and 1500 B.C., at a time of Egyptian weakness, when its northern territories (Lower Egypt) were overrun by the Hyksos, Semitic invaders from Palestine.[38] Kush's capital was located at Kerma near the Third Cataract. At its height its forces occu-

35. Lüddeckens, "Nḥsj und kš in ägyptischen Personennamen"; Kendall, Kerma and the Kingdom of Kush, 27; cf. also Adams, "Coming of Nubian Speakers to the Nile Valley," 18.

36. Posener, Cinq figurines d'envoûtement.

37. Posener, "Pour une localisation."

38. Kemp, "Old Kingdom, Middle Kingdom," 721: "This is a geographical term with two levels of application: as a general geographical term for Upper Nubia, and one which remained as such throughout the New Kingdom, and as the name of a particular kingdom there, presumably the most powerful since the Egyptians used its name to characterize a much larger area, might also suggest a locally recognized political supremacy."

pied abandoned Egyptian forts at the Second Cataract, to the north. Its extent to the south is indicated by a settlement and a cemetery about 60 miles south of Kerma, near Bugdumbush. In 1992 a Kushite fort was discovered about 12 miles east of Kerma. To date, "we still do not know if the domain of the Kerma king extended to the west bank of the Nile; mysteriously, not a single Kerma site has yet been identified there."[39]

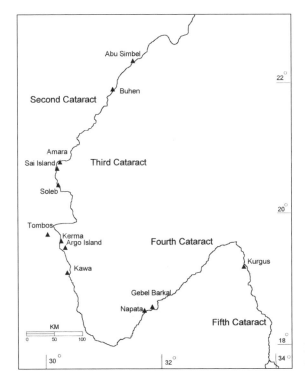

Figure 2.4. Upper Nubia (Kush) (Michael Lucas).

The name *Kush* was adopted for the area south of Egypt not only by the Hebrews but also by the Assyrians and the Persians. Taharqa (Tirhakah), the Kushite pharaoh who ruled over Egypt in the 25th Dynasty, is called the king of *Kûsu* by Esarhaddon and Ashurbanipal.[40] The area is called *Kūša* in the inscriptions of Darius.[41]

An older term (ca. 2600 B.C.) used by the Egyptians for those who lived to the south of them was *Nḥsjw*,[42] which is variously rendered Nehasyu

39. Kendall, *Kerma and the Kingdom of Kush*, 51.
40. *ANET* 292, 294.
41. Kent, *Old Persian*, 180.
42. Lüddeckens, "*Nḥsj* und *kš* in ägyptischen Personennamen," 284; Zibelius, *Afrikanische Orts- und Völkernamen*, 140–41; Faulkner, *Concise Dictionary of Middle Egyptian*, 137.

(by Kemp and O'Connor), Nehesy (by Kendall), and Nehesyou (by Posener). It is translated "Nubian" and seems to denote primarily those who lived in the Nile Valley as opposed to those who lived in the eastern desert, though it sometimes includes nomads and even those living as far away as Punt, on the Red Sea coast.[43]

In 1871 F. J. Lauth recognized that the Hebrew name *Pînĕḥās* (Phinehas) originally meant "the Nubian," as Egyptian *pʒ* before *Nḥsj* in *pi-nehase* is the definite article. As this was the name of Aaron's grandson (Exod. 6:25), it is an independent confirmation of intermarriage with Cushites in Moses' family.[44]

A more specific term for the nomads of the eastern desert is *mḏʒ* (Medjay), plural *mḏʒw* (Medjayu).[45] They appeared as early as the Old Kingdom and were recruited by the Egyptians to serve as soldiers, for example, in Kamose's army against the Hyksos. Their material remains are found in shallow pan graves. Their successors were the Blemmyes, who attacked the Coptic monasteries in Shenoute's time and who were the ancestors of modern Beja.[46]

The oldest term used for the area to the south of Egypt is *Tʒ Stj* or *Ta Sety* (The Land of the Bow). Pharaoh Aha of the Archaic Period claimed victory over this area.[47] Such southerners were famed for their skill and prowess as archers. A model of forty archers was found in the tomb of Mesehty at Asyut, who served the Egyptians. A well-preserved tomb of an archer was uncovered at the Kerma cemetery by C. Bonnet. Two bows were found, with the strings in his right hand and a supply of arrows nearby.[48] When Cambyses, the Persian king, had conquered Egypt in 525 B.C. and marched south, the Ethiopian king presented a bow to the Persian scouts, warning him not to invade unless the Persians could draw such a bow (Herodotus 3.21–22). B. G. Haycock comments: "Whether or not this incident is historical, as it may well be, it illustrates external attitudes and beliefs about Cush. The bow was indeed the weapon of the Nubians par excellence."[49]

The Persians included Kush as a tributary in their lists of the peoples of their vast empire. Panel 23 of the stairway relief from Darius's Apadana

43. O'Connor, *Ancient Nubia*, 3. Kitchen (personal communication to the author) observes: "Panehsi became a name among New Kingdom Egyptians that meant little more than 'darkie,' in the case of people born of wholly Egyptian parents."

44. Meek, "Moses and the Levites"; Albright, *From the Stone Age to Christianity*, 254; idem, *Yahweh and the Gods of Canaan*, 165.

45. Zibelius, *Afrikanische Orts- und Völkernamen*, 133–37; O'Connor, *Ancient Nubia*, 43.

46. Adams, "Kush and the Peoples of Northeast Africa," 9.

47. Posener, "Pour une localisation," 62.

48. Bonnet, *Kerma: Territoire et Métropole*, 43.

49. Haycock, *Sudan in Africa*, 38.

building at Persepolis depicts Kushites (Ethiopians), who are bringing an
exotic animal, perhaps a giraffe or an okapi.[50]

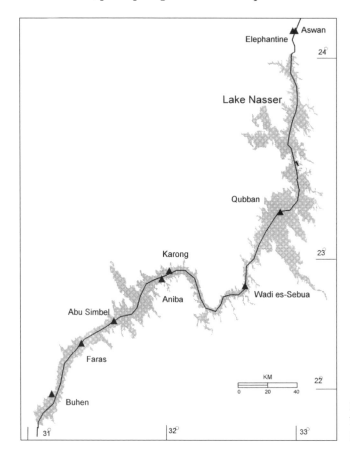

Figure 2.5. Lower
Nubia (Wawat)
(Michael Lucas).

The Egyptians themselves called the area between the First and Second
Cataracts *wꜣwꜣt* (Wawat). This term first appears in the inscription of Mer-
nere of the 6th Dynasty and his official Uni.[51] Scholars today often speak
of this area as Lower (i.e., northern) Nubia, and Kush as Upper (i.e.,
southern) Nubia. Today Lower Nubia is largely in southern Egypt, and
Upper Nubia is wholly in the Sudan.[52]

The term *Nubia* itself first occurs in Roman geographer Strabo, who wrote
at the time of Augustus, quoting the earlier Alexandrian scholar Eratosthenes:

50. Afshar, Dutz, and Taylor, "Giraffes at Persepolis."
51. Breasted, *Ancient Records of Egypt*, 1.146–50.
52. The name *Sudan* is derived from the Arabic phrase *Bilad as-Sudan* (land of the blacks).
See Wehr, *Dictionary of Modern Written Arabic*, 440.

"On the left of the course of the Nile live *Nubae* in Libya, a populous nation. They begin from Meroe and extend as far as the bends [of the river]." Some scholars[53] speculate that the name may be derived from the Egyptian word for gold (*nbw*),[54] as this area was famed for its gold mines. The modern-day tribe of the Nuba in Kordofan in the Sudan continues a three-millennium-long tradition of wrestling, which was depicted in Egyptian reliefs.[55]

A Land of Deserts and Cataracts

In his magisterial treatment of the area, W. Y. Adams calls Nubia the "corridor to Africa." He writes succinctly: "If I may sum up the definition of Nubia in a few words, it is the land of the Nile cataracts: that part of the Nile Valley, directly south of Egypt, which is occupied by peoples African in origin and speech but strongly influenced by Egyptian and Mediterranean culture."[56] He points out that for millennia Nubia was "the only dependable way across the great desert barrier of the Sahara, and the only contact between the civilized world and Africa."[57]

Herodotus, "the father of history," visited Egypt in the fifth century B.C. and famously described it as "the gift of the Nile."[58] The Nile, which floods regularly, provided not only water for irrigation but also rich silt. The cultivable land is a narrow band of green on either side of the river in the midst of barren desert lands, which include the Sahara to the west and the Arabian Desert to the east, as shown most dramatically in satellite photos. Over 99% of the population lives along the Nile.

The Nile provided easy transportation for the Egyptians: they could sail upstream, as the prevailing winds blew from north to south; and they could simply drift north with the current. The Nile is formed by the confluence of the Blue Nile from Ethiopia, which supplies most of the water, and the White Nile from Lake Victoria. From Lake Victoria the White Nile proceeds 2,185 miles before being joined by the Blue Nile near Khartoum, the capital of Sudan.[59] It then flows in a sinuous direction for 1,130 miles to Aswan in southern Egypt and then straight north for another 750 miles to the Mediterranean. The waters of the Nile in Nubia were less accessible

53. For example, Emery, *Lost Land Emerging*, 4.
54. Gardiner, *Egyptian Grammar*, 573.
55. Carroll, "Wrestling in Ancient Nubia"; cf. Luz and Luz, "Proud Primitives"; Riefenstahl, *Last of the Nuba*.
56. Adams, *Nubia*, 21.
57. Ibid., 19.
58. See Yamauchi, "Herodotus" (1992); idem, "Herodotus" (1999); idem, "Herodotus—Historian or Liar?"
59. See Moorehead, *White Nile*; idem, *Blue Nile*.

for irrigation than in Egypt. The *saqiya*, a waterwheel turned by animals, was introduced into Nubia only in the first century B.C.

Modern Sudan (as was the case, no doubt, with ancient Nubia) is subject to severe temperature extremes. It can rise to over 100 degrees Fahrenheit in the shade and then drop in the winter (January–February) to the 60s, with cold winds from the north. There is practically no rainfall except in the south, so that the humidity is at 10%.

Arable land was scarcer in the Nubian section of the Nile, and travel was also made much more difficult by the interruption of six major cataracts, granite outcroppings that create hazardous rapids. The first of these, numbered from north to south, is found at Aswan, forming the natural border between Egypt and Nubia.[60]

Figure 2.6. Aswan Cataract from Sehel Island (Frank Joseph Yurco).

Aswan yields a number of interesting sites. The Elephantine Island (called *Yeb* by the Egyptians) was where a Jewish mercenary force was garrisoned during the Persian period, and informative Aramaic letters have been recovered from the site.[61] The island of Philae, called "The Pearl of Egypt," was the setting of numerous temples and was the last stronghold of paganism during the early Christian era.

A series of dams were built at Aswan,[62] including the High Dam, which created the vast Lake Nasser that inundated most of the remains of Lower Nubia. The building of the High Dam was begun in 1959. Accord-

60. See Kees, *Ancient Egypt*; Baines and Málek, *Atlas of Ancient Egypt*.
61. See Porten, *Archives from Elephantine*.
62. The first dam on the Nile was built in 1902, the second in 1912 and raised further in 1934. These earlier efforts led to limited surveys, first in 1907–11.

ing to R. Keating: "To build it, some 30,000 men laboured round the clock
for five years in one of the fiercest summer climates on earth. It stands 360
feet high and the road on its crest is 2.25 miles long. Incidentally, someone
with a taste for irrelevancies has calculated that the volume of the dam is
17 times that of the Great Pyramid."[63]

Between the Second and First Cataracts the Nile flows placidly for
about 200 miles through a relatively flat area of sandstone and desert. On
the east bank rises Qasr Ibrim, now an island, the only important site that
was not flooded, because it stood on a high bluff. D. O'Connor comments
on the significance of this area of Wawat: "Lower Nubia was unlikely to
support a highly developed culture. It has access to some important resources (copper, gold and some valued types of stone) but only a small
amount of cultivable land, and throughout history it has acted as a buffer
zone between Egypt and the inhabitants of Upper Nubia."[64] Just 20 miles
north of the present Egyptian-Sudanese border stood the four colossal
statues of Ramesses II at Abu Simbel. These statues and adjacent temples
were saved from the waters of the dam by being cut apart and reassem-
bled on a higher level.[65]

The Second Cataract is located just south of the Egyptian-Sudanese border. During the Egyptian expansion southward in the Middle Kingdom,
various pharaohs built a dozen fortresses in this region. The 90-mile
stretch of the Nile between this cataract and the Dal Cataract is known in
Arabic as *Baṭn el-Hajar* (The Belly of Stones). As the name implies, there are
more than 350 islets, making navigation impossible. At Semna the Nile
narrows to a channel about 100 feet wide.[66] Beyond the Dal Cataract and
the Third Cataract is the Abri-Delgo Reach (the word *reach* denotes the
stretch between cataracts), which extends 120 miles, with some cultivable
land available. Adams notes that more Egyptian monuments were found
between Abri and Kerma than in any other comparable area of Nubia.[67]

The Dongola Reach of 200 miles between the slight Third Cataract and
the Fourth Cataract was the most fertile stretch of the Nile River in Nubia.
As the river is calm, navigation was easily accomplished. This favorable
situation no doubt was the reason for the establishment of the Kushite
capital at Kerma near the Third Cataract.

63. Keating, *Nubian Rescue*, 6–7.
64. O'Connor, "Ancient Egypt and Black Africa," 5.
65. In all, twenty-three temples and shrines were saved. See Säve-Söderbergh, *Temples and Tombs of Ancient Nubia*. One temple from Dendur, from the period of Augustus, is now housed in a special wing of the Metropolitan Museum in New York City. See Aldred, *Temple of Dendur.*
66. See Dunham and Janssen, *Second Cataract Forts*, 1.2.
67. Adams, *Nubia*, 28.

Near the Fourth Cataract is a sacred mountain called Gebel Barkal. Napata, the capital of the 25th Dynasty, which was briefly to rule Egypt, developed near this mountain. Nearby are royal cemeteries featuring small pyramids for the kings of this dynasty. The Abu Hamed Reach between the Fourth and Fifth Cataracts traces a great S curve, making sailing upstream on the western part of this curve impossible, as one has to sail against the prevailing winds from the north on this section of the Nile. This was one of the least populated areas of the Nile. Between the Fifth and Sixth Cataracts is the Shendi Stretch. Travel between the Shendi and the Dongola Reaches went overland through the Bayuda Desert.

A heated controversy has arisen over the location of a country called Yam,[68] which Harkhuf, a nomarch at Aswan, visited during the Old Kingdom.[69] Most scholars maintain that Yam should be identified with another place later called Irem[70] and should be located near Kerma.[71] They assume that Harkhuf began his seventy-day journey with donkey caravans from Memphis, the capital of the Old Kingdom, which is in Lower Egypt near the apex of the Nile Delta. On the other hand, O'Connor, who assumes that Harkhuf's starting point was at Elephantine, prefers to place Yam farther south in the Shendi Reach by the Sixth Cataract.[72]

Harkhuf (ca. 2300 B.C.) made four journeys south, the first with his father. His first journey took seven months, his second eight months. Whether Yam was near Kerma or farther south, the products that Harkhuf brought back were those that ultimately came from central Africa: "I came down with three hundred donkeys laden with incense, ebony, *ḥknw*-oil, *sꜣt*, panther skins, elephant's tusks, throw sticks, and all sorts of good products."[73] The young king, Pepi II, who was to reign for ninety-four years, wrote to Harkhuf, instructing him to carefully watch over a *dng*, a pygmy from central Africa: "When he lies down at night, get worthy men to lie around him in his tent. Inspect ten times at night! My majesty desires to see this pygmy more than the gifts of the mine-land and of Punt."[74]

68. For Yam, see under *iꜣm* in Zibelius, *Afrikanische Orts- und Völkernamen*, 78–81.
69. See, e.g., Dixon, "Land of Yam"; Goedicke, "Harkhuf's Travels." Cf. also Kadish, "Old Kingdom Egyptian Activity in Nubia." For the full text, see Breasted, *Ancient Records of Egypt*, 1.150–54.
70. For Irem, see under *jrm* in Zibelius, *Afrikanische Orts- und Völkernamen*, 84–85.
71. Edel, "Die ¨Ländernamen Unternubiens."
72. O'Connor, "Locations of Yam and Kush."
73. Lichtheim, *Ancient Egyptian Literature*, 1.26.
74. Ibid., 1.27. See also Yurco, "Egypt and Nubia," 40. The "mine-land" was a name for Sinai. Punt was an area on the east coast of Africa, located by some scholars on the Somali coast, but placed further north near Eritrea by Kitchen, "Land of Punt."

Figure 2.7. Autobiography of Harkhuf at Qubbet el-Hawa, Aswan
(sandstone, Dynasty 4) (Frank Joseph Yurco).

The Gold of Kush

Nubia was a source of important materials for the Egyptians. From the quarries of Aswan came pink granite, which was used for the great monoliths known as obelisks.[75] Diorite for royal statues was obtained from west of Toshka during the Old and Middle Kingdoms. Copper was worked at Buhen near the Second Cataract.

Excavations at Kerma uncovered furnaces for the working of bronze, an alloy of copper and tin.[76] The source of tin in the ancient world is still a problem.[77] The bronze foundry, which measured ten meters on a side, was placed near the main temple and was probably directed by the religious authorities.[78] The furnaces faced north to take advantage of the strong winds to stoke the fires needed to melt the metals. Radiocarbon dating yields a date of about 1910–1730 B.C.[79]

The greatest treasure that Nubia/Kush provided was gold, making Egypt the richest nation in antiquity. Though the hieroglyph for gold was already attested around 3200 B.C., it was only with the expansion of the Egyptians during the Middle Kingdom (ca. 1900 B.C.) that the Egyptians began to mention gold as one of the objects to be obtained from Wawat and Kush. After Egypt invaded and ruled parts of Upper Nubia (ca. 1500 B.C.), the pharaohs appointed a "viceroy of Kush" to collect taxes and extract gold from this area. The tribute for year 38 of Thutmose III (1479–1425) included 77 cattle, 16 slaves, and 2844 deben of gold (1 deben equals 20 pounds). During the reign of Tutankhamun (1340–1331) Kushites are depicted holding platters loaded with gold rings in the paintings in the tomb of Viceroy Huy. Setau, a viceroy of Kush under Ramesses II (1279–1213), declared: "I was appointed to be Viceroy of Nubia and [Superintendent of] the Gold [Lands]. I directed serfs in thousands and ten-thousands, Nubians by myriads, without limit. I brought in all the dues of this land of Kush in double measure."[80]

Three major areas had gold mines: (1) Coptos: a northern group of sites in the hilly region parallel to the Red Sea, by Wadi Hammamat and Wadi Abbad; (2) Wawat: various sites along Wadi Allaqi and Wadi Cabgaba; and (3) Kush: the southern area along the Nile Valley. According to J. Vercoutter: "For four years during the reign of Tuthmosis III, the Wawat mines produced more than 993 kg. of gold, with a yearly yield of more

75. Yamauchi, "Obelisks and Pyramids"; idem, "Obelisk."
76. See Yamauchi, "Metal Sources and Metallurgy."
77. DeFelice, "Tin and Trade."
78. Bonnet, "Les fouilles archéologiques de Kerma," 34.
79. Ibid., 39.
80. Kitchen, "Great Biographical Stela of Setau," 299.

than 248 kg."[81] In the reign of Amenhotep III (1427–1396), gold was obtained from Karoy near the Fourth Cataract. By the 19th Dynasty, however, gold production declined. Ramesses III (1185–1154) was able to ded-
icate only 26 kg. of gold to the temple of Amon.

The Egyptian gold workers were divided into various specialists: overseer of gold workers, priest of gold workers, reckoner of gold, overseer of
gold lands, and captain of the archers of gold.[82] Agatharchides of Cnidus
(ca. 140 B.C.) mentions specialists such as artificers who spot the vein, dig-
gers who cut the rock, pounders who pound the ore, grinders who work
the millstones, washers who separate the heavier gold, and cooks who
smelt the metal. He describes in great detail the harsh conditions under
which slaves and prisoners were forced to extract and work the gold ores:

> Tens of thousands of unfortunate men crush with iron sledges the rock that
> has been fragmented and can be broken up with little effort. A technician,
> who evaluates the rock, is in charge of the whole process and gives assign-
> ments to the workers. . . . It is impossible for an observer to not pity the
> wretches because of the extremity of their suffering. For they meet with no
> respite at all, not the sick, the injured, the aged, not a woman by reason of
> her weakness, but all are compelled by blows to strive at their tasks until,
> exhausted by the abuse they have suffered, they die in their miseries.[83]

It is probable that many condemned persons were sent to work in these
efforts. One oath reads: "If I lie, may my nose and ears be cut off—or let
me be sent to Kush."[84] A text of Ramesses II reports that

> if a few of the caravaneers of the gold washing went thither, it was only half
> of them that arrived there, for they died of thirst on the road, together with
> the asses which they drove before them. There was not found for them their
> necessary supply of drink, in ascending and descending, from the water of
> the skins. Hence no gold was brought from this country, for lack of water.[85]

Vercoutter found two structures that were sloping tables used to
spread the slurry of water and crushed gold ore.[86] Diodorus 3.14.1–3 (cit-

81. Vercoutter, "Gold of Kush," 135. According to Keating, *Nubian Rescue*, 162, during the
reign of Thutmose III, "translated into modern terms, 31,000 ounces of gold were extracted
from Wawat alone over a span of eight years."
82. Vercoutter, "Gold of Kush," 144–47.
83. Burstein, *Agatharchides of Cnidus*, 61, 63. See also Lucas and Harris, *Ancient Egyptian
Materials and Industries*, 228–29.
84. Trigger, *Nubia under the Pharaohs*, 113.
85. Cited by Emery, *Egypt in Nubia*, 193.
86. Vercoutter, "Gold of Kush."

ing Agatharchides) describes the process that earlier goldworkers must have also used:

> (They spread the crushed gold ore) upon a broad table a little inclined, and pouring water upon it rub the pulverised stone until all the earthy matter is separated, which flowing away with the water leaves the heavier particles behind on the board. This operation is often repeated, the stone being rubbed lightly with the hand: they then draw up the useless and earthy substance with fine sponges—gently applied until the gold comes out quite pure.

Reliefs from the Mastaba of Mereruka at Saqqara include scenes showing workers weighing the gold and working the gold into jewelry.

Figure 2.8. Dwarfs at work as jewelers. From the tomb of Mereruka at Saqqara (limestone, Dynasty 6) (Frank Joseph Yurco).

Gold was used in international diplomacy, as vividly illustrated in the Amarna letters. In letter 19 sent by King Tushratta of Mitanni to Amenhotep III we read this plea: "May my brother send me in very great quantities gold that has not been worked, and may my brother send me much more gold than he did to my father. In my brother's country, gold is as plentiful as dirt."[87] There is no more spectacular example of Egypt's gold than the solid gold coffin of Tutankhamun, which weighs over 200 pounds.[88]

Between 1901 and 1903 British geologists identified eighty-five ancient gold-mining sites in what was then the Anglo-Egyptian Sudan. Between

87. Moran, *Amarna Letters*, 44.
88. Saleh and Sourouzian, *Official Catalogue of the Egyptian Museum*, no. 175.

1989 and 1994 German investigators identified more than a hundred additional sites. Neither the earlier British efforts nor the more recent Sudanese attempts were able to recover much gold from these areas.[89]

Egypt and Nubia

From the very beginning there were contacts between Egypt and Nubia. In fact, on the basis of finds, including a stone incense burner with pharaonic symbols, at Qustul north of Buhen near the Second Cataract, B. Williams argues for the priority of the development of a royal state in Nubia.[90] He is supported by F. J. Yurco,[91] but his conclusions are questioned by a number of scholars.[92]

During the Archaic Period (1st–2d Dynasties; ca. 3200–2700), Pharaoh Djer (Zer) of the 1st Dynasty left an inscription at Jebel Sheikh Suleiman near Wadi Halfa.[93] Kha-Sekhem is shown triumphing over a Nubian. During this period an agricultural population known as the A-Group occupied Lower Nubia.

As noted above, Egyptians sent peaceful expeditions south to obtain valuable trade; these groups were led by officials such as Harkhuf during the Old Kingdom (3d–6th Dynasties; ca. 2700–2200). But earlier under Sneferu of the 4th Dynasty, according to the Palermo Stone, armed expeditions brought back 7,000 prisoners and as much as 110,000 cattle in a single expedition. These incursions wreaked havoc on the A-Group settlements. During the 5th Dynasty (ca. 2400) a new population called the C-Group began to settle in Lower Nubia. They had a highly developed pottery and raised long-horned cattle.[94] This C-Group culture, which is called the "most uniquely Nubian of all cultures," lasted for a thousand years.[95] Only two settlements of the C-Group, Areika and Wadi es-Sebua, have ever been excavated.

89. Vercoutter, "Das Gold Nubiens," 12, 18.

90. Williams, "Lost Pharaohs of Nubia"; idem, "Forbears of Menes in Nubia: Myth or Reality?"

91. Yurco, "Egypt and Nubia," 28–34.

92. Adams, "Doubts about 'the Lost Pharaohs'"; Leclant, "Introduction to the Civilization of Nubia," 15–18. According to O'Connor, *Ancient Nubia*, 21: "Williams' theory is exciting but the evidence for it is not convincing. At the time his theory was published, the Qustul 'royal' tombs antedated the earliest royal tombs of Egypt, of Nakada phase IIIB. But recently an Abydos royal tomb of IIIA has been found, so Qustul loses chronological primacy." See also O'Connor, "Chief or Kings?"

93. Emery, *Archaic Egypt*, 59–60.

94. Hintze and Hintze, *Civilizations of the Old Sudan*, 12.

95. Adams, *Nubia*, 142. Though an intermediate B-Group was originally identified, this has proved to be an illusory culture.

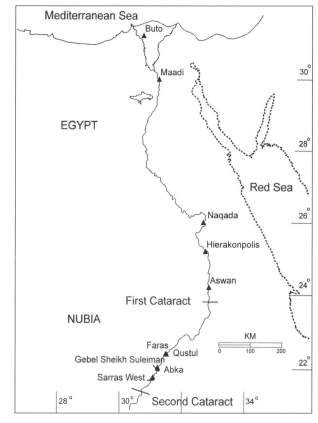

Figure 2.9. Predynastic Egypt and Nubia (Michael Lucas).

The First Intermediate Period (7th–10th Dynasties; ca. 2200–2040) was a brief era of instability, with four ephemeral dynasties succeeding each other. Nubians are depicted as mercenaries in the Egyptian army from this period on.[96] The famous model of Nubian archers from Asyut comes from this period. Adams comments: "There is almost no literary record of Egyptian-Nubian relations during the 1st Intermediate period (Dynasties VII–X)."[97]

During the Theban reconsolidation of the Middle Kingdom (11th–12th Dynasties; 2134–1786), the Egyptians also resorted to execration texts written on clay to defeat their enemies by magic.[98] Aggressive pharaohs not only invaded Nubia but also established over a dozen forts between Wadi Halfa and Semna near the Second Cataract.

96. Hays, "From the Land of the Bow."
97. Adams, *Nubia*, 67.
98. Sethe, *Die Ächtung feindlicher Fürsten*; Posener, *Princes et pays d'Asie*; idem, *Cinq figurines d'envoûtement*.

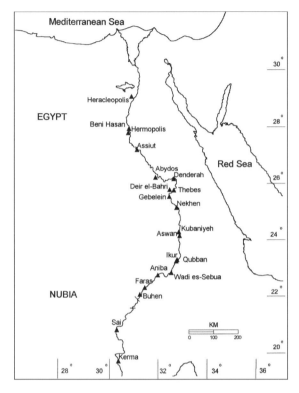

Figure 2.10. Middle
Kingdom Egypt and Nubia
(Michael Lucas).

Senusret I (1965–1920) was the first to campaign in Upper Nubia, and his sandstone stela at Buhen is the first mention of Kush. Senusret III (1874–1855) cut a channel through the First Cataract and established nine forts along the Second Cataract. An inscription from his eighth year indicates that the forts were built to "prevent any Nubian [*Nehsy*] from going north, whether by boat or on foot, and also any Nubian animals, except for Nubians coming to the market at Iken (the great fort of Mirgissa) or Nubian messengers."[99]

In his sixteenth year Senusret III set up duplicate boundary stelae at Uronarti and Semna. They read in part:

> I have made my boundary further south than my fathers.
> . . . .
> Since the Nubian listens to the word of mouth,
> To answer him is to make him retreat.
> Attack him, he will turn his back,
> Retreat, he will start attacking.

99. Trigger, *Nubia under the Pharaohs*, 67.

Figure 2.11. Senusret I
(Frank Joseph Yurco).

Figure 2.12.
Senusret III
(courtesy, The
Metropolitan
Museum of Art,
gift of Edward S.
Harkness, 1916–
17 [17.9.2]).

Figure 2.13. Senusret
III's stela from
Elephantine
(©British Museum).

They are not people one respects,
They are wretches, craven-hearted.
My majesty has seen it, it is not an untruth.
I have captured their women,
I have carried off their dependents,
Gone to their wells, killed their cattle,
Cut down their grain, set fire to it.[100]

Ironically, in later generations Senusret III was worshiped as a protective
deity at Buhen, Toshka, Uronarti, Semna, and Kumma.

All the forts except Kumma were situated on islands or on the west
bank. Each fort had massive walls of mud brick, with loopholes for archers. It is estimated that each had a complement of about three hundred
soldiers and their families. These were among the most impressive monu-

100. Lichtheim, *Ancient Egyptian Literature*, 1.119.

Figure 2.14. Uronarti Fort, southeast wing, south wall looking southeast
(December 25, 1928) (©2002 Museum of Fine Arts, Boston).

ments from the Middle Kingdom. George Reisner investigated some of
the forts between 1924 and 1932.[101] Others were investigated by archaeologists before they were all inundated by Lake Nasser.

An ancient list of fortresses gives some of their original names, such as
Waf-Khastiu (Subduing the Foreign Lands) for Shelfak.[102] The major forts
from south to north (upstream to downstream) are the following:

1. Semna	7. Dabenarti
2. Semna South	8. Mirgissa
3. Kumma	9. Abu Sir
4. Uronarti	10. Dorginarti
5. Shelfak	11. Mayanarti
6. Askut	12. Buhen

The first four fortresses guarded the most constricted passage along the
Nile, the Semna Cataract. At Uronarti, Reisner found about five thousand

101. Dunham and Janssen, *Second Cataract Forts.*
102. Gardiner, "Ancient List of the Fortresses of Nubia."

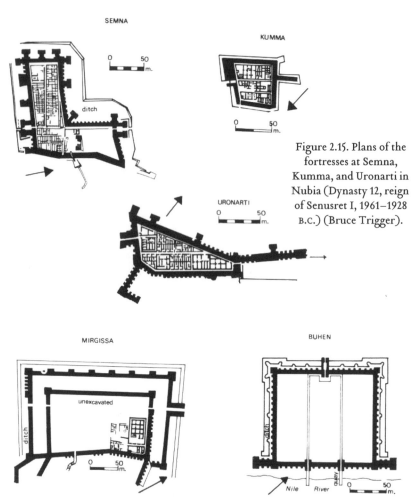

Figure 2.15. Plans of the fortresses at Semna, Kumma, and Uronarti in Nubia (Dynasty 12, reign of Senusret I, 1961–1928 B.C.) (Bruce Trigger).

Figure 2.16. Plans of the fortresses at Mirgissa and Buhen in Nubia (Dynasty 12, reign of Senusret I, 1961–1928 B.C.) (Bruce Trigger).

clay sealings. The five hundred different seals indicate a high level of literacy there.

Shelfak was built on a rocky eminence, which rises steeply 60 meters above the river level. The fortress occupied 1,800 square meters. Askut was located on an island about 25 miles upstream from Buhen. It was cleared by A. M. Badawy in 1968. He found evidence of the garrison's barbershop, including a copper razor and lumps of curly black hair.[103]

103. Smith, "Askut and the Role of the 2nd Cataract Forts"; idem, *Askut in Nubia*.

Mirgissa guarded the upper end of the Second Cataract. Work at this site, which was not completed, revealed two forts, an inner and an outer fort.[104] Excavations uncovered the armory, in which weapons such as hide shields were made. More than seventy-five spears and javelins were stored there. At Mirgissa could be seen mud lines of slipways, a mile long, over which boats were dragged to avoid the dangerous rapids.

Only Buhen was completely excavated by W. B. Emery.[105] It was surrounded by walls 16 feet thick and 36 feet high. Outside the walls a ditch 30 feet wide and 23 feet deep was carved out. Buhen's walls were almost a mile in circumference. It enclosed a rectangle 560 feet by 525 feet. The walls were penetrated by ingenious triple loopholes, which enabled an archer to fire in three directions. The fort could have supported a garrison of two thousand troops. Adams comments: "Buhen staggers the imagination not only by its size but by the complexity of its defences. Bastions, loopholes, fosse, drawbridge, glacis—virtually all of the classic elements of medieval fortification are present in this structure which was built 3,000 years earlier in the Nubian desert."[106]

The fortunes of Egypt and Kush have shown an inverse relationship: when Egypt was strong, Kush was weak; when Egypt was weak, Kush became bold. During the 13th Dynasty the Egyptians abandoned these forts, which were then occupied by Kushites from the area of Kerma.[107]

During the Second Intermediate Period (13th–17th Dynasties; 1786–1540), Lower Egypt was overrun by the Hyksos, Semites (so-called Asiatics) from Palestine, who may have introduced the chariot into Egypt. Manfred Bietak discovered and excavated their capital of Avaris at Tell el-Debᵓa, a site just south of Khataaneh-Qantir that is also identified as the biblical city of Rameses (Exod. 1:11).[108] Even before the invasion, Semites like Joseph had been sold as slaves into Egypt, as highlighted by the Brooklyn Museum Wilbour Papyrus, dated to the reign of Sobkhotep III (1743–1740), which listed 79 servants, 45 of them Semites. The Hyksos formed an alliance with the Kushites, as demonstrated by a large number of Hyksos sealings discovered at Kerma.

Seqenenre Taᵓa of the 17th Dynasty from Thebes was the first to drive the Hyksos back to the area of Asyut. His mummy reveals that he died of a head wound. His son Kamose complained in the Carnar-

104. Vercoutter, *Mirgissa*.
105. Emery, Smith, and Millard, *Fortress at Buhen*; Smith, *Fortress of Buhen*.
106. Adams, *Nubia*, 181.
107. Bourriau, "Relations between Egypt and Kerma," 132.
108. Bietak, "Avaris and Piramesse"; Hoffmeier, *Israel in Egypt*, 62–68.

von Tablet, which is a copy of his inscription at Karnak: "Let me understand what this strength of mine is for! (One) prince is in Avaris, another is in Ethiopia, and (here) I sit associated with an Asiatic and a Negro! Each man has his slice of this Egypt, dividing up the land with me."[109] Kamose's inscription reveals that the Thebans had luckily captured a Hyksos messenger asking the Kushites to cooperate against the Thebans:

> I captured a messenger of his high up over the Oasis travelling southward to Cush for the sake of a written dispatch, and I found upon it this message in writing from the chieftain of Avaris. . . . Have you (not) beheld what Egypt has done against me, the chieftain who is in it, Kamose the Mighty, ousting me from my soil and I have not reached him—after the manner of all that he has done against you, he choosing the two lands to devastate them, my land and yours, and he has destroyed them. Come, fare north at once, do not be timid. . . . Then we will divide the towns of this Egypt between us.[110]

The Theban 18th Dynasty succeeded in expelling the Hyksos from Egypt, establishing the New Kingdom (18th–20th Dynasties; 1550–1069), the most glorious period of a far-flung empire. Under the aggressive King Thutmose III (1479–1425), Egypt established its hegemony over Palestine and Syria.

Thutmose I (1504–1492) led an army beyond Kerma to the Fourth Cataract. A naval officer, Ahmose, boasted: "His majesty sailed down-river, with all countries in his grasp, that wretched Nubian Troglodyte being hanged head downward at the [prow] of the ba[rge] of his majesty, and landed at Karnak."[111]

Thutmose III captured and destroyed Kerma, a destruction that radiocarbon dating indicates took place between 1460 and 1450 B.C.[112] He also established the first permanent garrison south of Kerma, at Gebel Barkal near the Fourth Cataract, as a stela from his forty-seventh year indicates. He also erected rock inscriptions at Kurgus, between the Fourth and Fifth Cataracts.[113]

During the Egyptian occupation of Nubia numerous temples were built, for example, by Amenhotep III (1386–1349) in the Abri-Delgo

109. *ANET* 232.
110. Cited by Gardiner, *Egypt of the Pharaohs*, 167–68.
111. Breasted, *Ancient Records of Egypt*, 2.34.
112. Kendall, *Kerma and the Kingdom of Kush*, 73. Recent excavations at Kerma by Bonnet uncovered the fortifications, including ditches, bastions, and a large gate of Kerma. See Bonnet, "Kerma: Rapport préliminaire sur les campagnes de 1999–2000 et 2000–2001," 201–3.
113. Morkot, "Nubia in the New Kingdom," 294.

Figure 2.17.
Thutmose III
(1479–1425 B.C.)
(Frank Joseph
Yurco).

Reach and by Amenhotep IV = Akhenaten (1356–1340) at Sesebi and Kawa. Excavations near Kerma uncovered a Meroitic temple resting on the foundations of an earlier Napatan temple, which in turn lies over a temple established in the Amarna period, as indicated by inscriptions.[114] The jubilee temple of Amenhotep III at Soleb near the Third Cataract is described as a masterpiece. One of the bases of the pillars depicts a tribe that is interpreted as the "Shasu of Yahve."[115]

Figure 2.18. Nubian tributes to Tutankhamun, from the Tomb of Huy (courtesy, The Metropolitan Museum of Art [30.4.21]).

We have a wealth of information from the tomb of Huy, the viceroy of Kush under Tutankhamun (1340–1331). A temple to Amon was erected by this king at Sesebi. A scene depicts three chiefs of Wawat bringing as tribute platters full of gold rings. Huy boasts that he was given authority over areas as far south as Gebel Barkal and Karoy near the Fourth Cataract. Haremhab (1347–1295) built a temple at Silsileh to commemorate his visit to Nubia.

During the 19th Dynasty Ramesses I (1295–1294) during his short reign managed to build a temple to Amon-Min at Buhen. Seti I (1294–1279) led at least one campaign south, setting up stelae at West Amarna and Sai. In his eighth year he sent troops from the Third Cataract to suppress aggression from the natives of Irem. Kitchen describes the action and its significance:

> First, the desert-dwellers of Irem may well have coveted the relatively richer lands of the Dongola Reach along the Nile Valley. Seizure of this stretch would, however, have disrupted local peace and Egyptian control and communications southward to Napata and the bounds of the empire—and perhaps also have posed a threat to Egyptian interests in the "gold of Kush," named from the second to third Cataract area perhaps on both sides of the Nile.[116]

114. See Bonnet, "Kerma: Rapport préliminaire sur les campagnes de 1999–2000 et 2000–2001," 205–9; cf. Valbelle, "Kerma: Les inscriptions."
115. The Shasu were Semitic bedouin whom scholars compare with the Israelites. See Giveon, *Les bédouins shosou des documents égyptiens*; idem, *Impact of Egypt on Canaan.*
116. Kitchen, "Historical Observations on Ramesside Nubia," 218.

Figure 2.19.
Nubians
bringing tribute
(©British
Museum).

About twenty years later Ramesses II (1279–1213) sent his forces to Irem and returned with 7,000 prisoners.[117] This great king built seven temples in six locations,[118] most spectacularly at Abu Simbel. There his four colossal statues towered 67 feet high. The chambers of his temple were carved 200 feet into the cliffside. After his reign it was almost five hundred years before another temple was built in Nubia.[119]

Merenptah (1213–1204) set up at Buhen a triumphal stela showing him slaughtering captives.[120] In year 5 and probably in coordination, as Kitchen suggests, the Libyans attacked Egypt, and the region of Wawat rebelled. The pharaoh declared:

117. Kitchen, *Pharaoh Triumphant*, 72.
118. Säve-Söderbergh, *Temples and Tombs of Ancient Nubia*, 38.
119. Adams, *Nubia*, 225.
120. Smith, *Fortress of Buhen*, 213.

Figure 2.20. Wadi es-Sebua temple, Nubia
(reign of Ramesses II, year 44, 1235 B.C.) (Frank Joseph Yurco).

The hot blast of his (King's) mouth (went) against the land of Wawat. They were destroyed at one (blow), they have no inheritance, having been brought to Egypt altogether. . . . (As for) the rest, the hands of some were cut off because of their crimes (i.e., revolt); (as for) others, ears and eyes were removed, and they were taken (back) to Kush. They were made into heaps in their settlements. . . . Never again will Kush repeat rebellion.[121]

Though Ramesses III (1185–1154) was able to defeat the invasion of the Sea Peoples, including the Philistines, his reign was beset by a harem conspiracy, which was abetted by the chief of the archers of Kush. During the reign of Ramesses XI an uprising at Asyut was suppressed by Pa-Nehesy, the viceroy of Kush, and his Nubian troops. After the Ramesside kings of the 20th Dynasty, Egypt went into a period of decline known as the Third Intermediate Period.[122] Darkness also fell upon Nubia for two centuries between 1070 and 850 B.C.[123]

121. Cited in Kitchen, "Historical Observations on Ramesside Nubia," 223.
122. Kitchen, *Third Intermediate Period in Egypt*.
123. Adams, *Nubia*, 67; Trigger, *Nubia under the Pharaohs*, 139.

The Archaeology of Kerma

Whereas Egypt's antiquities became well known in Europe because of Napoleon's invasion in 1798, especially through the efforts of V. Denon's monumental collection of sketches, Nubia remained largely unknown except for a few hardy travelers like Lewis Burckhardt who journeyed by camel between Aswan and the Dongola Reach.[124] Former circus strongman Giovanni Belzoni cleared the sand to the entrance of the Abu Simbel temple in 1817. Prussian Karl Richard Lepsius traveled throughout Egypt and Nubia in 1842–44 and published twelve volumes of Nubian and Egyptian antiquities. And in 1907, E. A. W. Budge wrote the first modern history of Nubia. Early in the twentieth century, limited surveys were conducted in connection with the building of dams at Aswan.

In 1959, with the beginning of the construction of the High Dam at Aswan, an unprecedented international survey and rescue effort, which would last twenty years, was undertaken, resulting in a comprehensive and exhaustive collection of data from Lower Nubia. More than forty separate expeditions were undertaken.

In contrast, Upper Nubia has had relatively little attention paid to it. The exceptions are an unsatisfactory excavation at Meroe by John Garstang and the foundational work of George Reisner of Harvard University on behalf of the Boston Museum of Fine Arts at many different sites. Reisner, a genius, correctly ascertained the presence of the so-called A-Group and C-Group cultures and established the basic chronology for Nubian archaeology. At the same time he overestimated Egyptian influence and underestimated the indigenous culture.[125]

Reisner conducted extensive investigations both at the town site and the cemetery of Kerma,[126] the capital of Kush, but because of the discovery of the statues of an Egyptian official and his wife, he misinterpreted Kerma as an Egyptian outpost and the structure known as the Western Deffufa as a fortress. According to Adams:

> Although Reisner initially regarded the Kerma people as Nubians, his subsequent identification of the great Tumulus K.III as the burial place of an Egyptian Prince became an idée fixe which colored and distorted his overall interpretation of Kerma and its place in history. He came to regard the site as a

124. Lewis, "John Lewis (Johann Ludwig) Burckhardt."
125. See Burstein, "Kingdom of Meroe," 135–38; Adams, "Coming of Nubian Speakers to the Nile Valley," 12.
126. Reisner's work at the cemetery in 1913–16 was published in the three-volume *Excavations at Kerma*. After Reisner's death in 1942, Dows Dunham published a supplementary volume: *Excavations at Kerma*. Reisner also worked at Gebel Barkal (1912–16), Meroe (1921–24), Napata (1916–20), and the Second Cataract forts (1924–32).

whole as an Egyptian colony, and the southernmost in the great chain of Egyptian fortresses which were built in Nubia during the Middle Kingdom.[127]

After nearly a century of neglect, the key site of Kerma has yielded much new information over the last quarter century, thanks to the excavations conducted by Charles Bonnet on behalf of the University of Geneva.[128] We do not know the ancient name of the city,[129] which is by the modern village of Kerma, but there is no doubt that it was the capital of the kingdom of Kush during its acme of power (ca. 1700–1500). It is situated on the east bank of the Nile River at the northern end of the Dongola Reach, near the Third Cataract.

Figure 2.21. View of the excavations at Kerma, with the Western Deffufa in the background (C. Bonnet).

In 1820 the first Europeans saw the striking monument known as the Western Deffufa. In 1844 Lepsius gave a detailed description of the structure. As now revealed by excavations, the city was defended by a mudbrick wall and a ditch 3 to 6 meters deep. It covered an area of about 60 acres and is estimated to have held as many as two thousand persons within the walls. According to O'Connor, "Kerma was also Nubia's earliest city, indeed the earliest city in Africa outside of Egypt."[130]

127. Adams, "Reflections on the Archaeology of Kerma," 41.
128. Bonnet, "Kerma: An African Kingdom"; idem, *Kerma: Territoire et métropole*; idem, *Kerma: Royaume de Nubie*; idem, "Excavations at the Nubian Royal Town of Kerma"; idem, *Édifices et rites funéraires à Kerma*. For preliminary reports on the continuing excavations, see *Genava* 26 (1978): 107–27, and following issues.
129. Kendall (*Kerma and the Kingdom of Kush*, 2) suggests that the city's name, like that of the kingdom, may also have been Kush.
130. O'Connor, *Ancient Nubia*, 50.

Thanks to the work of B. Gratien on the basis of levels of Kerma culture found at Sai island,[131] a relative chronology of Kerma culture can be established:

Pre-Kerma	3500–2500
Early Kerma	2500–2050
Middle Kerma	2050–1750
Classic Kerma	1750–1580
Final Kerma	1580–1500

We can highlight only a few discoveries, concentrating on the Western Deffufa, the Grand Hut, and the great tumuli of the cemetery.

The Western Deffufa

The Western Deffufa[132] is a solid mass of mud brick more than 150 feet long and 75 feet wide. It has been preserved up to 60 feet of its original height. As to the shape of this structure and a similar one (the Eastern Deffufa, which is preserved up to about 30 feet of its height) by the cemetery, Williams suggests: "It is likely that the *deffufa* structures at Kerma were representations in brick of the butte-like *gebels* (i.e., mountains) that dot the landscape of Upper Nubia at wide intervals, providing distinctive landmarks in an otherwise repetitive landscape and a kind of natural religious focus."[133] The function of this striking brick structure has been much debated. Reisner thought that it was a fortress; Adams suggested that it might have been a watchtower.[134] It is clear from Bonnet's excavations that it was in fact a temple, surrounded by other religious structures. The solid structure contains a narrow corridor, with a stairway leading to the top of the monument. In the corridor is a stone base, which Bonnet suggests may have functioned as an altar.[135] Like other chapels in the cemetery, the soil has been colored with red ochre. We do not know the names of the gods the Kushites worshiped. Elsewhere they accepted Egyptian gods.

The Grand Hut

Bonnet discovered the postholes of a Grand Hut, which has no parallel in Egyptian architecture, but which is quite reminiscent of audience huts

131. See Gratien, *Les cultures Kerma*; cf. O'Connor's review.
132. The word *deffufa* is a local name for a brick structure.
133. Williams's review of Kendall's *Kerma and the Kingdom of Kush*, 197.
134. Adams, "Reflections on the Archaeology of Kerma," 44; idem, *Nubia*, 201–2.
135. Bonnet, "Les fouilles archéologiques de Kerma," 47–48.

Figure 2.22. Grand Hut (2000–1500 B.C.) (C. Bonnet).

of African monarchs. The large hut must have been at least 33 feet high. It was used for several centuries from the Early Kerma period and was not abandoned until the Classic Kerma phase.

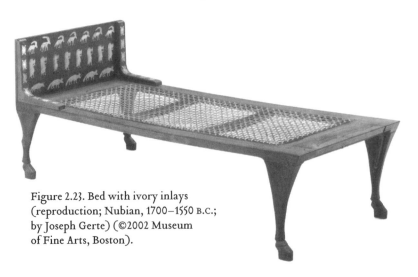

Figure 2.23. Bed with ivory inlays
(reproduction; Nubian, 1700–1550 B.C.;
by Joseph Gerte) (©2002 Museum
of Fine Arts, Boston).

Figure 2.24. Model of Kerma (C. Bonnet).

The Tumuli

Reisner was mistaken in thinking that the cemetery, 4 kilometers east of the city, developed from south to north. This vast necropolis, nearly a mile long and half as wide, is estimated to contain between 15,000 and 25,000 burials.

An ordinary person was placed on a bed, with the head always to the east. Animals were sacrificed. Hundreds of terra-cotta cattle figurines were also offered. Bucrania (ox skulls) lined the south of the tomb, probably the remains of a funerary feast. In one case Reisner found up to 500 bucrania. More recently Bonnet excavated a royal tomb covered by a mound 40 feet in diameter and discovered 4,500 "cattle frontal bones arranged in a crescent of several rows."[136]

There are four massive tumuli, which must have been royal tombs,

136. Bonnet, "Kerma: Rapport préliminaire sur les campagnes de 1999–2000 et 2000–2001," 205.

Figure 2.25. Funerary chapel K XI (C. Bonnet).

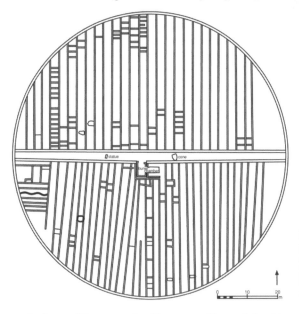

Figure 2.26. Tumulus K III, royal tomb of Kushite king, Kerma (Second Intermediate Period) (Bruce Trigger).

each about 90 meters in diameter. One of the kings may have been Ned-jeb, a Kushite king named at Buhen.[137] What is most striking are the numerous retainers who were sacrificed to accompany their lord to the

137. Kendall, *Kerma and the Kingdom of Kush*, 65.

next world. They evidently went voluntarily and then were buried
alive. Adams comments: "To complete the picture of barbarian magnifi-
cence it may be added that the number of human sacrifices in Tumulus
X at Kerma—322 by actual count, and perhaps as many as 400 before
plundering—is larger than in any other known tomb of any civilization."[138] This practice was retained in Nubia and is attested in Meroitic
times, in the medieval period,[139] and in relatively modern times, as recently as 1926.[140]

Figure 2.27. Nubian prisoner (New Kingdom, 1550–1307 B.C.)
(courtesy, Saint Louis Art Museum [purchase]).

Egyptianized Nubians

Some scholars interpret the Cushite wife of Moses as Zipporah, perhaps because they were not aware of the extensive contacts between
Egypt and Kush and the presence of many Nubians in Egypt, from slaves
to members of the royal household in the New Kingdom. Those who hold

138. Adams, *Nubia*, 203. A Mesopotamian parallel is the sixty-eight women and six men
buried with the Sumerian king discovered by Woolley at Ur (Woolley, *Ur of the Chaldees*, 58–
61). On the subject of human sacrifices in antiquity, see Green, *Role of Human Sacrifice*; Day,
Molech: God of Human Sacrifice; idem, "Molech: A God of Human Sacrifice"; Derchain, "Les
plus ancient témoignages"; Jesi, "Rapport sur les recherches"; Margalit, "Why King Mesha
of Moab Sacrificed His Oldest Son"; Stager and Wolff, "Child Sacrifice at Carthage."
139. Keating (*Nubian Rescue*, 148) cites the account of Abd-el Aziz el Bakri (eleventh century), who describes the burial of a king of the Sudan: "Placed near him are his jewelry, his
arms and his eating and drinking vessels. Into the cupola are put food and drink together
with some of his servants after which the door is closed and earth heaped upon the structure
until it becomes a huge hill. After this a moat is dug around the hill and animals are slaugh-
tered to the dead therein."
140. Fairservis, *Ancient Kingdoms of the Nile*, 113–14.

Figure 2.28. Nubian-Kushite prisoners from the Memphite tomb of Haremhab (limestone relief, Dynasty 18, reign of Tutankhamun, 1334–1325 B.C.) (courtesy, Museo Civico Archeologico, Bologna [KS 1869 = 1887]).

the early date of Moses place him in the reign of Thutmose III, in the fifteenth century; those who favor the late date place him in the thirteenth century. At either time many Kushites were resident in Egypt.

As a number of scholars observe, there was no such thing as color prejudice in the ancient world. Though Egyptians might speak of their Asiatic and Kushite enemies with bravado and contempt, this did not prevent those who were assimilated into Egyptian culture from rising to positions of prominence, even to the rank of the vizier, which was second only to the pharaoh in responsibility and power. An example is the discovery of the tomb of Aper-El, a Semite who was a vizier.[141]

Even the Old Kingdom gives evidence of intermarriage between Egyptians and Kushite women. Yurco observes:

> The deported Nubians (under Sneferu), it has been suggested, or their descendants, appear as titled servants of Old Kingdom nobles in the Fifth Dynasty. Other Nubians in Egypt may have descended from these captives. One, possibly, is the woman, with non-Egyptian, distinctly Kushite features, buried in Giza mastaba no. 4440, in the reign of Khufu, with her Egyptian husband and prince.[142]

With the rise of Theban pharaohs, because of the relative proximity to Nubia, contacts and intermingling increased. It became impossible to distinguish acculturated Nubians from Egyptians. Mentuhotep II of the 11th

141. Stannish, "Evidence for the 'Amarna Period."
142. Yurco, "Egypt and Nubia," 36. See O'Neill, *Egyptian Art*, 238. Another example of a Kushite from the Old Kingdom is Pepi-ankh (the Black), who is depicted in wooden statues both as a youth and as an adult (ibid., 67).

Dynasty was known for his Nubian wives.[143] The prophecy of Amenemhet, the founder of the 12th Dynasty, was said to have a mother from Ta-Seti.[144] A vivid illustration of intermarriage at the lower level is a grave stela from Gebelein in Upper Egypt, showing a man called Nehesy, holding a typical Nubian bow, with an Egyptian wife.[145]

Figure 2.29. Stela of the Nubian soldier Nenu
(painted limestone, Egyptian, Dynasty 9 to early Dynasty 11, 2100–2040 B.C.)
(©2002 Museum of Fine Arts, Boston).

In light of the ample Egyptian evidence of the presence of many Nubians in Egypt from as early as the Old Kingdom and of intermarriage between Egyptians and Nubians, we should not doubt the possibility of Moses' marriage to a Kushite or Nubian woman.

143. Kendall, *Kerma and the Kingdom of Kush*, 15.
144. Lichtheim, *Ancient Egyptian Literature*, 1.143.
145. Kendall, *Kerma and the Kingdom of Kush*, 13. This grave stela from Gebelein in Upper Egypt is now in the Boston Museum of Fine Arts (03.1848).

3

SOLOMON
AND AFRICA

Solomon, the son of David and Bathsheba, was the third and last of three kings who ruled over the united monarchy of the twelve tribes of Israel. Solomon ruled for forty years (1 Kings 11:42), from 971 to 931 B.C.[1] He began construction on the temple in his fourth year (6:1),[2] a project that lasted seven years (6:38). He then spent thirteen years building his palace (7:1).

Solomon made a drastic reorganization of his kingdom into twelve administrative districts, which were with some exceptions not based upon the old tribal areas (1 Kings 4:1–19).[3] Each of the districts was to provide food for the court for one month (4:7). Some scholars believe that Solomon's administration owed much to Egyptian prototypes, as

1. Kitchen, "How We Know."
2. This event is dated 480 years after the exodus, which gives us the basis for the early date of the exodus (ca. 1448 B.C.), a date favored by Kaiser, *History of Israel*, 108; and Merrill, *Kingdom of Priests*, 58. The late date of the exodus (ca. 1265 B.C.) is favored by Kitchen, *Pharaoh Triumphant*, 71; and Hoffmeier, *Israel in Egypt*, 125–26. For a discussion of the arguments for these alternative dates, see Yamauchi, *Stones and the Scriptures*, 48–50.
3. Aharoni, "Solomonic Districts."

the titles of his various officers seem to be the Hebrew equivalents of Egyptian titles.[4]

Solomon introduced a fundamental change in Israel's military organization—a reliance upon chariotry. His father David had disabled the horses that he captured from the king of Zobah in Syria (2 Sam. 8:4). We are told that Solomon had 4,000 stalls for horses and 12,000 horses (2 Chron. 9:25). If for each chariot one assumes teams of three horses, including a reserve horse, the number of stalls accords with the 1,400 chariots that Solomon is said to have had (1 Kings 10:26).

The biblical description of Solomon's empire is often dismissed as legendary, for example, by J. Maxwell Miller.[5] But K. A. Kitchen, using extrabiblical materials, demonstrates that it is exactly the twelfth to tenth centuries, after the collapse of the Hittite Empire and the decline of the Egyptian Empire and before the rise of the Assyrian Empire, which provided the opportunity for the rise of "mini-empires" such as Solomon's (as well as Tabal and Carchemish) to flourish.[6] To those who object that we have no inscriptional evidence for Solomon, A. R. Millard notes: "When a rapid calculation reveals that only 16 out of 113 kings ruling in the Levant between 1000 and 600 B.C., including the kings of Israel and Judah, are known from their own inscriptions, the absence of Solomon becomes less remarkable."[7]

Building Activities

Solomon was the greatest builder in Israel's history before Herod the Great. Some earlier scholars dismiss the biblical accounts of Solomon's building activities as late inventions. A considerable number of archaeological discoveries now lend substance to these accounts. The so-called Solomon's Stables at the key site of Megiddo were demonstrated by Yigael Yadin in 1960 to belong to the later city of Ahab (ninth century).[8] The excavators estimate that originally there were about 450 stalls. J. B. Pritchard and Y. Aharoni challenge the interpretation of these structures as stables, since somewhat similar buildings at Beersheba were used as storerooms.[9] But Yadin vigorously defended their identification as sta-

4. Mettinger, *Solomonic State Officials*; Redford, "Studies in Relations between Palestine and Egypt."
5. Miller, "Solomon: International Potentate or Local King?"; idem, "Separating the Solomon of History from the Solomon of Legend." For a survey of skepticism about Solomon and his age, see Knoppers, "Vanishing Solomon."
6. Kitchen, "Controlling Role of External Evidence."
7. Millard, "King Solomon in His Ancient Context," 46.
8. Yadin, "New Light on Solomon's Megiddo."
9. Pritchard, "Megiddo Stables"; Aharoni, "Beersheba."

bles.[10] Since these have been left in place, it is possible that Solomonic stables may lie underneath those that are visible.

Yadin identified as Solomonic a magnificent triple-chambered gate at Hazor. He also pointed out nearly identical gates, excavated by the University of Chicago at Megiddo and by Macalister at Gezer,[11] though the latter did not realize it.[12] Israel Finkelstein argues for a ninth-century date for these gates, but his views are idiosyncratic and are rejected by other archaeologists.[13]

David Ussishkin identifies two splendid palatial buildings at Megiddo as Solomonic: building 6000 in the north and building 1723 in the south. Both are built of fine ashlar blocks similar to those used in the Solomonic gate. The northern palace is compared to Assyrian buildings called *bit hilani*, which were used as ceremonial palaces. The southern building is compared to the ninth-century palace of Kilamuwa at Zincirli and may have served as the residence of the governor.[14]

Though almost nothing has been recovered from tenth-century Jerusalem,[15] from detailed textual descriptions we can visualize how Solomon's temple must have looked.[16] The biblical text (1 Kings 5:6–18; 7:13–14) furthermore states explicitly that Solomon employed workers provided by his ally, King Hiram of Tyre. Tell Tayinat and Hama provide a number of close parallels from Syria from about the same date as Solomon.[17] Recently a most striking parallel to the Solomonic temple was uncovered in northern Syria at ʿAin Dara.[18]

Various features of the temple appurtenances may be illustrated by archaeological finds. The winged cherubim that served as decorative devices may have been similar to winged figures found on ivories from

10. Yadin, "In Defense of the Megiddo Stables"; idem, "Megiddo Stables."
11. The Hebrew Union College reexcavation at Gezer confirms Yadin's intuition. See Dever et al., "Further Excavations at Gezer."
12. Yadin, "Solomon's City Wall and Gate at Gezer"; idem, *Art of Warfare in Biblical Lands*, 371–74; idem, "Megiddo of the Kings of Israel."
13. Zevit, "Three Debates about Biblical Archaeology," 22, observes: "The archaeological community as a whole rejects Finkelstein's ceramic chronology on well argued archaeological grounds." See also Rainey, "Stones for Bread"; Shanks, "'Centrist' at the Center."
14. Ussishkin, "King Solomon's Palace." Cf. idem, "King Solomon's Palaces."
15. Kenyon, *Jerusalem*, 56, identifies a small wall north of Ophel as coming from the tenth century. The title of her article "New Evidence on Solomon's Temple" is misleading. For her evidence, see Kenyon, *Royal Cities of the Old Testament*, 39–40.
16. Oulette, "Basic Structure of Solomon's Temple."
17. Aharoni, "Solomonic Temple," 8; Ussishkin, "Building IV in Hamath"; Davey, "Temples of the Levant"; Schmid, "Der Tempelbau Salomos." Dever, "Palaces and Temples," 608–9, writes: "The biblical texts, at least the vivid descriptions in 1 Kings would appear to be based on early, authentic accounts."
18. Abou-Assaf, *Der Tempel von ʿAin Dara*; Monson, "New ʿAin Dara Temple."

Megiddo and Nimrud. The bronze laver resting on oxen (1 Kings 7:23–26) may be compared to a large stone basin from Cyprus that rests upon bulls' heads. Basins on wheels (eleventh century B.C.) from Cyprus must have been similar to the wheeled stands (New English Bible: "trolleys"; 7:27) used in the temple.

Solomon's International Marriages

Solomon's great international prestige is demonstrated by his marriage to a pharaoh's daughter. References are made to this Egyptian wife in no less than five passages (1 Kings 3:1; 7:8; 9:16, 24; 11:1; 2 Chron. 8:11). Since the Bible does not give us the name of the pharaoh in question, scholars speculate upon the identity of Solomon's Egyptian father-in-law. They favor one of the last two kings of the 21st Dynasty: Siamun (978–959) or Psusennes II (959–945).[19] Evidence in favor of Siamun includes a monument found at Tanis showing the king smiting an enemy who holds a double axe,[20] an Aegean weapon perhaps of the Philistines, and a scarab with the pharaoh's name found at Tell el-Far'ah (Sharuhen). The pharaoh captured Gezer and gave the city to Solomon as a dowry (1 Kings 9:16). Hebrew Union College excavations at Gezer yielded dramatic evidence of a destruction in the mid-tenth century that left up to four feet of debris and ash.

According to 1 Kings 11:3, Solomon had seven hundred wives and three hundred concubines, among whom were Moabite, Ammonite, Edomite, Sidonian, and Hittite women (11:1). The mother of Rehoboam, Solomon's successor, was Naamah, an Ammonite princess (14:21, 31). Hellenistic sources suggest that Solomon also married the daughter of Hiram of Tyre.

Trading Activities in the Mediterranean

Phoenicia, which is in the area of modern Lebanon, was blessed with both excellent harbors (Tyre, Sidon, Byblos, Beirut) and great stands of coniferous wood (the so-called cedars of Lebanon) for the construction of ships. As a consequence Phoenicians became the most daring seafarers in the ancient world.[21] King Hiram of Tyre, who had also been David's ally (1 Kings 5:1–12), actively aided Solomon by supplying him with timber and artisans and by

19. Kitchen, "How We Know," 36; idem, *Third Intermediate Period in Egypt*, 281–83, 531–32, 574.
20. Lance, "Solomon, Siamun, and the Double Ax"; Malamat, "Kingdom of David and Solomon"; Horn, "Who Was Solomon's Egyptian Father-in-Law?"; Green, "Solomon and Siamun." For an updated discussion of the broader background of Solomon's international relations, see Kitchen, "Egypt and East Africa"; idem, "Sheba and Arabia."
21. See Ward, "Phoenicians"; Harden, *The Phoenicians*; Markoe, *Phoenicians*.

cooperating with Solomon in his maritime ventures.[22] In exchange for these favors Solomon ceded to Hiram a district in the area of Akko.

The Tarshish ships (1 Kings 10:22) employed by Solomon in coopera-tion with Hiram were originally vessels that may have gone to Tarshish, a word that W. F. Albright analyzes as "smeltery" but that Cyrus Gordon associates with a wine color, as in Homer's "wine-dark" sea.[23] Some scholars think that Tarshish may refer to the distant Phoenician colony of Tartessus in southern Spain. In any case, the phrase *Tarshish ship* seems to refer to a long-distance craft.[24]

There was once a question of how early the Phoenicians penetrated into the western Mediterranean. Some classical scholars maintained that Phoe-nicians did not expand there before the Greeks, who established colonies in western Italy and Sicily in the late eighth century. On the other hand, Albright held that the Phoenician expansion westward should be dated to the era of Solomon and Hiram.[25] A ninth-century Phoenician inscription from Nora in Sardinia contains the word *Tarshish*. F. M. Cross dates the Nora fragment still earlier, to the eleventh century.[26] Other scholars, how-ever, date this fragment to the beginning of the ninth century.[27]

Though Solomon was content to leave the Mediterranean maritime trade in the hands of Hiram, he controlled the overland trade and in par-ticular the important traffic in horses. The King James Version of 1 Kings 10:28 obscures this by translating a Hebrew phrase as "linen yarn"— when it actually means "from Que," that is, from Cilicia, the region in southeastern Turkey where some of the best horses were to be obtained. Solomon also obtained horses and chariots from Egypt, which he sold elsewhere at a profit.[28] Solomon thus served as the middleman between Egypt and the Neo-Hittite and Aramean states (10:29).

Solomon's Copper Mines?

Nelson Glueck attributed the considerable evidence of copper min-ing in the Arabah, the valley between the Dead Sea and Elath, to Sol-

22. See Briquel-Chattonet, *Les relations entre les cités.*
23. Gordon, "Wine-Dark Sea."
24. Much information about earlier Late Bronze ships has been recovered by marine ar-chaeologists from shipwrecks off the southern coast of Turkey. For a comprehensive ac-count, see Wachsmann, *Seagoing Ships and Seamanship*. In 1997 two shipwrecked Phoenician ships of the eighth century B.C. were discovered in deep water off the coast of Ashkelon. See Ballard et al., "Iron Age Shipwrecks."
25. Albright, "Role of the Canaanites," 347.
26. Cross, "Early Alphabetic Scripts," 103–4.
27. Sass, *Genesis of the Alphabet*, 91–93.
28. Ikeda, "Solomon's Trade in Horses and Chariots."

omon.[29] Additional sites were discovered in the 1950s and 1960s by
Benno Rothenberg, who demonstrated that the copper-bearing ores
were smelted in open pits on charcoal fires fanned by bellows.[30] In 1969
Rothenberg discovered at the base of the so-called Solomon's Pillars, a
favorite tourist site at Timnah north of Elath, an Egyptian temple with
inscriptions of the 19th–20th Dynasties from Seti I (1294–1279) down to
Ramesses V (1153–1147). He therefore concludes that these Egyptian
kings, rather than the Judean kings of the tenth–sixth centuries, were
responsible for all the copper mines in the Arabah.[31] J. Muhly and P. J.
Parr criticize John Bimson's arguments (based on radiocarbon dates)
that some of the slag from these mining operations might have come
from Solomon.[32]

Solomon's Red Sea Port

Solomon established a port at Ezion-geber near Elath (1 Kings 9:26) to
give him access to trade in the Red Sea and beyond. In 1938–40 Glueck excavated Tell el-Kheleifeh, a small tell a short distance from the shore now
located in Jordanian territory, which he identified as Ezion-geber.[33] A
building enclosed in an area protected by a casemate wall was originally
interpreted by Glueck as a smeltery because of holes in the wall, which he
thought were flue holes, but this building was later reinterpreted as a
storehouse and/or granary. Reexamination of the site and its finds by
Gary Pratico proves that Tell el-Kheleifeh could not be Ezion-geber.[34]
Rothenberg suggests that the port of Ezion-geber may be located at Jeziret
Fara'un (now called the Coral Island by the Israelis), eight miles southwest of Elath.[35]

Because the fleet that carried gold from Ophir to Solomon is described
as the fleet of Hiram (1 Kings 10:11–12), Yutaka Ikeda suggests that the
Phoenicians built the Tarshish ships, disassembled them on the Palestinian coast, and then transported them overland to Ezion-geber, just as the
Egyptians did when they wanted to sail the Red Sea, transporting the disassembled ships from the Nile through Wadi Hammamat in the Eastern
Desert.[36] B. S. J. Isserlin makes the interesting observation that the Cru-

29. Muhly, "Solomon, the Copper King."
30. See Yamauchi, "Metal Sources and Metallurgy."
31. Rothenberg, "Ancient Copper Industries"; idem, *Timna*.
32. Bimson, "King Solomon's Mines"; Muhly, "Timna and King Solomon"; and Parr,
"Pottery of the Late Second Millennium B.C."
33. Glueck, *Rivers in the Desert*.
34. Pratico, "Where Is Ezion-geber?"
35. Flinder, "Is This Solomon's Seaport?"
36. Ikeda, "King Solomon and His Red Sea Trade," 114–16.

saders in 1182–83 also carried disassembled ships from the Palestinian coast to the Red Sea.[37]

Solomon's Gold

The staggering amounts of gold that Solomon received and accumulated raise questions for most scholars, who dismiss such descriptions as fantasy or propaganda.[38] The Queen of Sheba brought a gift of 120 talents (1 Kings 10:10), as did the King of Tyre (9:14), and 420 talents came from Ophir (9:28; 10:11), so that the annual sum was 666 talents (10:14). A talent weighs about 33 kilograms or 73 pounds, so the first two sums would be about 4.4 U.S. tons, the third 15.3 U.S. tons, and the total about 24.3 U.S. tons. Citing parallel amounts from nonbiblical sources, Millard argues that we should not so lightly dismiss such amounts.[39]

The joint Red Sea fleet of Solomon and Hiram made voyages every three years (1 Kings 10:22) to distant lands, from which they brought back a variety of objects, including fine gold (Isa. 13:12; Job 28:15–16). That Ophir was not an imaginary land is proved by the discovery of an eighth-century ostracon at Tell Qasile with the text "Ophir gold to Beth-horon 30 shekels."[40] Because scholars identify Ophir as the destination of Solomon's Red Sea fleet, it has been placed in India, Africa, Arabia, and even North America![41]

Ophir in India?

The King James Version reports (1 Kings 10:22) that Solomon "had at sea a navy of Tharshish with the navy of Hiram: once in three years came the navy of Tharshish, bringing gold, and silver, ivory, and apes, and peacocks" (see also 2 Chron. 9:21). If indeed the fleet brought back peacocks, then this would favor a location in India.[42]

Arguments for the possible identification of Ophir with (S)upara, a port 60 miles north of Bombay mentioned by Ptolemy, is the translitera-

37. Isserlin, *Israelites*, 189.

38. Montgomery and Gehman, *Book of Kings*, 211: "Only the exaggerated figure for the gold is to be corrected"; Cogan, *1 Kings*, 313: "Rather than being a fixed sum deemed the correct amount to be delivered to a great sovereign, the number is typological, standing for completeness."

39. Millard, "Solomon in All His Glory"; idem, "King Solomon's Gold"; idem, "Does the Bible Exaggerate King Solomon's Golden Wealth?"; idem, "King Solomon's Shields."

40. Maisler, "Two Hebrew Ostraca from Tell Qasile."

41. See Christidès, "L'enigme d'Ophir"; Görg, "Ophir, Tarschisch und Atlantis"; idem, "Ofir und Punt"; Baker, "Ophir." The best article on the subject is North, "Ophir/Parvaim."

42. Cansdale, *All the Animals of the Bible Land*, 168.

tion of its name in the Septuagint as *Soupheir* and the interpretation of Josephus (*Antiquities* 8.6.4 §164): "Hiram sent pilots to the land then called Sopheria but now Golden, 'This being in India,' to bring him gold." Jerome's Vulgate renders Ophir in Job 28:16 as India. R. D. Barnett suggests that the Hebrew words for sandalwood (*ʾalmug/ʾalgum*),[43] peacock (*tukkî*), and ape (*qôph*) are related to the Indian words *agil, tokei,* and *kapi*.[44] But Albright renders the last word as another kind of monkey.[45] Apes, monkeys, and baboons were greatly prized as pets by both Egyptian and Assyrian monarchs.[46] Scholars are still not agreed as to the translation of *tukkî*; according to Oded Borowski it has been translated as "monkeys," "poultry or baboons," and "peacocks."[47] North concludes: "From all these scraps of evidence and of controversy, it would seem that India is not precluded as the site of Ophir, but neither is it established."[48]

Ophir = Punt in Africa?

Ikeda, along with other scholars, associates Ophir with the area that the Egyptians called Punt: "The location of Ophir has been much disputed, but it was probably on the East African coast in the vicinity of the land of Punt."[49] As Punt was, above all, the source of incense for the Egyptians,[50] earlier scholars identified it with Somalia, on the eastern horn of Africa, an area noted for its myrrh and frankincense trees. Recent studies by R. Herzog[51] and K. A. Kitchen[52] indicate that Punt was farther

43. On the identification of *ʾalmug/ʾalgum*, see Montgomery and Gehman, *Book of Kings,* 218; Gray, *I and II Kings,* 261. The word *ʾlmg* occurs in Ugaritic (UT 120.8). See Greenfield and Mayerhofer, "ʾalgummīm/ʾalmuggīm-Problem Reexamined"; Greenfield, "Small Caves of Qumran," 138. Greenfield therefore believes that *ʾlmg/ʾllgm* was not sandalwood. It may have been tree aloe, which grows on both coasts of the Red Sea.
44. Barnett, *Illustrations of Old Testament History,* 40. See also Montgomery, *Arabia and the Bible,* 177–78; Schreiden, "Les entreprises navales du roi Salomon," 587; Groom, *Frankincense and Myrrh,* 48.
45. Albright, "Ivory and Apes of Ophir," 145.
46. Ikeda, "King Solomon and the Red Sea Trade," 120–22.
47. Borowski, *Every Living Thing,* 206.
48. North, "Ophir/Parvaim," 200. Groom (*Frankincense and Myrrh,* 49) writes: "The case for placing Ophir in Malaysia has been propounded by Innes Miller and rests on the unconvincing suggestion that a figure on one of three carved stone megaliths on the coast of the Malacca Strait resembles in appearance and dress a Phoenician as portrayed in Phoenician reliefs; it is therefore argued that these megaliths may have been set up by Hiram's men."
49. Ikeda, "King Solomon and the Red Sea Trade," 117. See Albright, "Location of the Garden of Eden," 20.
50. Dixon, "Transplantation of Punt Incense Trees"; Posener, "L'or de Pount."
51. Herzog, *Punt.* See the review by Kadish and the review essay by Kitchen, "Punt and How to Get There"; see also Bradbury, "*Kpn*-boats, Punt Trade."
52. Kitchen, "Land of Punt"; idem, "Further Thoughts on Punt."

north, in eastern Sudan and northern Ethiopia, extending to the Red Sea near Port Sudan and Eritrea, where such incense trees also grew.[53]

Figure 3.1. Hatshepsut (courtesy, The Metropolitan Museum of Art, Rogers Fund and Edward S. Harkness gift, 1929 [29.3.2]).

The Egyptians from at least the 5th Dynasty (ca. 2500 B.C.) sent expeditions to Punt to obtain products such as gold, incense, ebony, ivory, slaves, monkeys, and baboons. The most extensive visual evidence comes from the reliefs carved on the walls of Hatshepsut's (1479–1457) mortuary temple at Deir el-Bahri. This famous queen sent an expedition to Punt that brought back myrrh trees to be replanted at this temple. After Ramesses III early in the twelfth century, Punt virtually disappears from Egyptian records.[54]

If the three years that it took the Tarshish ships to return home (1 Kings 10:22; 2 Chron. 9:21) is the amount of time needed for a round trip,[55] then

53. See also Fattovich, "Problem of Punt"; Cozzolino, "Land of Pwnt"; and Fattovich, "Punt."
54. Kitchen, "Land of Punt," 606.
55. Albright argues that this could mean part of a year, a year, and part of another year; others hold that the phrase means only that the fleets were sent out at three-year intervals.

we might look farther afield. Intrigued by the coincidence with the three years that Phoenician sailors under Necho II (ca. 600 B.C.) took to circumnavigate Africa from east to west, Robert Stieglitz makes the daring suggestion that Solomon's fleet anticipated this remarkable Phoenician feat of navigation by four centuries:[56]

> So the Phoenicians set out from the Red Sea and sailed the southern sea; whenever autumn came they would put in and sow the land, to whatever part of Libya [i.e., Africa] they might come, and there await the harvest; then, having gathered in the crop, they sailed on, so that after two years had passed, it was in the third that they rounded the Pillars of Heracles [i.e., the Straits of Gibraltar] and came to Egypt. There they said (what some may believe, though I do not) that in sailing round Libya they had the sun on their right hand. (Herodotus 4.42)

A. B. Lloyd questions this account,[57] but its truth is accepted by M. Cary and E. H. Warmington, especially as the observation of the Phoenicians that they sighted the sun on the right (i.e., north) as they sailed from east to west indicates that they were in the southern hemisphere.[58]

Since many of the objects (e.g., ivory, apes, and baboons) are associated with Africa, some scholars sought to locate Ophir even farther south on the continent. John Milton in his *Paradise Lost* 11.400 (1660) wrote of "Sofala thought Ophir." Sofala was a province of Mozambique. In 1867, A. Petermann expressed his belief that gold fields found by German geologist Karl Mauch "are identical with the Ophir of the Bible and with the places from which Salomo obtained his wealth in gold."[59] In September 1871, Mauch became the first European since earlier Portuguese in the sixteenth century to stumble upon the stupendous ruins now known as the Great Zimbabwe, located 250 miles west of the Indian Ocean between the Zambezi and Limpopo Rivers in the country now known as Zimbabwe (formerly Southern Rhodesia). The name comes from the Shona phrase *dzimba dza mabwe* (houses of stone).

Covering almost 1,800 acres, the site consists of a hill complex and a lower monumental enclosure, 800 feet in circumference, with walls up to 30 feet high, 14 feet at their base. There is also a tower 30 feet high and 56 feet in circumference at the base, as well as other structures all built of carved granite stones, over one million in number. Mauch believed that the Queen of Sheba returned here and built these structures in imitation of Solomonic structures. According to M. W. Swanson: "His

56. Stieglitz, "Long-Distance Seafaring," 141.
57. Lloyd, "Necho and the Red Sea."
58. Cary and Warmington, *Ancient Explorers*, chap. 5.
59. Carroll, "Solomonic Legend," 237.

Figure 3.2. The courtyard of the Great Enclosure, Zimbabwe (Robert Harbison/1993 ©*The Christian Science Monitor*).

imagination was fixed upon the Biblical account of Solomon, Sheba and Ophir, and he concluded that here, or nearby, were the legendary mines of Solomon."[60] This belief inspired Rider Haggard, an Englishman who served in South Africa, to pen his famous novel *King Solomon's Mines* in 1885.[61] According to W. Minter: "Building on speculation linking the abandoned stone city of Zimbabwe and King Solomon's gold mines in the biblical land of Ophir, he concocted a tale of three English gentlemen . . . following a yellowed Portuguese map, fighting through danger and winning at last a treasure in diamonds."[62] This adventure was produced as a movie in 1950, featuring Stewart Granger as Allan Quatermain, who finds the mine.[63]

60. Swanson, "Colonizing the Past," 294. Other writers ascribe the ruins to Phoenicians, Indians, or Nilotic Hamitic peoples, but most recent studies ascribe the work to indigenous Shona people, built between A.D. 1100 and A.D. 1600. See Huffman, *Symbols in Stone*; Ndoro, "Great Zimbabwe."

61. The publisher, Cassell, proclaimed *King Solomon's Mines* "the most amazing book ever written." It sold 31,000 copies in Britain and went through thirteen editions in the United States in the first year alone. Before his death in 1925, Haggard wrote fifty novels, including *She*, about a mysterious Amazon-like queen who was three thousand years old, and *Queen Sheba's Ring*.

62. Minter, *King Solomon's Mines Revisited*, 3.

63. This was the sixth film based on the novel. In the original story three men searched for the mine; Hollywood's version introduced a beautiful Englishwoman searching for her husband. In 1987 Richard Chamberlain appeared as the hero of the film *Allan Quatermain and the Lost World of Gold*.

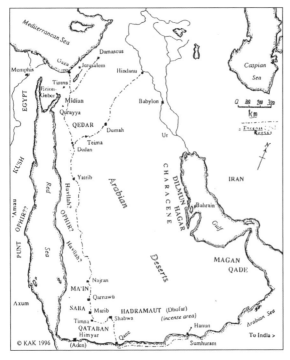

Figure 3.3. Ancient Arabia
and environs (Kenneth A.
Kitchen).

Ophir in Arabia?

According to Genesis 10:25–29, Ophir and Havilah were sons of Joktan,[64]
who was the son of Eber. The association of Ophir with Havilah,[65] a name
derived from "sand," inclines a number of scholars to place Ophir in Arabia.[66] R. North concludes that "Havilah is envisioned as a single locality

64. Mormons associate Joktan with Yucatan in Central America, inspiring them to con-
duct excavations there with the aim of confirming the Book of Mormon's account of the mi-
gration of some Israelites to the New World. In 1842 Joseph Smith read John L. Stephens, *Incidents of Travel in Central America, Chiapas, and Yucatan* and was convinced that the ancient
cities he describes in the Book of Mormon were to be found in that region. According to
Goodkind, "Lord Kingsborough Lost His Fortune," 58: "Some of the finest archaeological
work in southeastern Mexico has been conducted by a Mormon organization, the New
World Archaeological Foundation (NWAF)."
    65. See Yamauchi, "Havilah."
    66. Chastel, "La légende de la Reine de Saba," 211: "Selon toute vraisemblance, c'est en
Arabie du Sud qu'il faut placer Ophir"; Montgomery and Gehman, *Book of Kings*, 212: "No
exact location for Ophir has been discovered; it doubtless lay in Arabia, despite extravagant
theories"; Simons, *Geographical and Topographical Texts*, 70: "The exact localization of O[phir]
remains an unsolved problem, although generally speaking a district in South Arabia is
most likely (not in India or Africa)"; Wakely, "Ophir," 322: "But South Arabia seems to be
the most probable location."

spreading rather widely south of Sinai. In or near it, Ophir is on a horizon extending from Sheba in the mid-Arabian peninsula toward East Africa in a westerly direction, and perhaps not excluding a similar extent from Sheba toward the distant east." Kitchen also makes this connection: "In recent years, H. von Wissmann presented a persuasive case for locating Ophir in Western Arabia north of Wadi Baysh, between a southern and northern pair of lands each called Hawila (the Havilah of our English Bible)."[67] He further observes: "An Ophir in Western Arabia would have been close to the camel-caravan route that mattered so much to Sheba; so Tyrian/Hebrew intervention there might well have stimulated the kind of Sabaean response that is exemplified by the episode of the queen of Sheba."[68]

N. Groom notes: "Gold could have been obtained from the coast of 'Asir, being found in the area of Wâdi Dhahabân (a word meaning 'gold'); it was noted there by the classical authors and some mining is carried on there today."[69] Though there is evidence of a rich source of gold at adh-Dhahab between Medina and Mecca,[70] some of the other products would have been imported from elsewhere.[71] This was the case, for example, with products associated with Dilmun in ancient Mesopotamian texts, a site now identified with the island of Bahrain, which served as an entrepôt for the goods associated with it.[72]

Ophir in America?

A major goal of Christopher Columbus's expedition into the western Atlantic was to find Solomon's Ophir.[73] This is most clearly articulated in a compilation of notes written in Latin in 1501–2, which Columbus

67. Kitchen, "Ancient Arabia and the Bible," 29.
68. Kitchen, "Egypt and East Africa," 122.
69. Groom, *Frankincense and Myrrh*, 51.
70. Twitchell, *Saudi Arabia*, 247–50; Berkowitz, "U.S. Geological Survey." See especially Roberts, *Passion for Gold*, chap. 11: "Ophir: Mahd adh-Dhab 'Cradle of Gold.'"
71. Gray, *I and II Kings*, 256: "In view of the biblical tradition that Ophir was in Arabia, known to the Phoenicians as auriferous (Ezek. 27.22; cf. Job 28.16), it is safest to regard Ophir as South Arabia, and as an important *entrepôt* for merchandise from the further East and also from East Africa." Cf. Kitchen, "Egypt and East Africa," 123: "The other remaining possibility is that the further destination reached by ships of Hiram and Solomon (beyond Ophir) was African, or included African ports-of-call *en route*, going or returning. . . . Thence came gold, silver, ivory, apes and baboons. Except for the silver, all of these could well have come from East Africa; the silver may bespeak a more remote final port-of-call. Further, in the present state of knowledge, we cannot profitably go."
72. See my review of Al-Khalifa and Rice's *Bahrain through the Ages*.
73. Henning, *Terrae incognitae*, 31: "Columbus hat sie sich später zu eigen gemacht und wurde zu seiner weltgeschichtlichen Tat nicht zumindest durch die Hoffnung angeregt, auf einer Westfahrt über den Ozean nach Ophir-Hinterindien zu gelangen."

originally called *Notebook of authorities, statements, opinions and prophecies on the subject of the recovery of God's holy city and mountain of Zion, and on the discovery and evangelization of the islands of the Indies and of all other peoples and nations.* Today this book is simply called *Libro de las profecías* (Book of Prophecies).[74] Columbus's mission was to obtain gold that would enable King Ferdinand to rebuild the temple in Jerusalem for a gathering of Christians.[75] Since Josephus identified Ophir with India, Columbus sought a more direct route to India by sailing west.[76] Later writers such as Alvaro Mandana (1568) and Joãn dos Santos (1609) identified Ophir with Peru, comparing it with biblical Parvaim, which was also a source of the gold Solomon used in decorating his temple (2 Chron. 3:6). North contends that Parvaim is a synonym and variant of Ophir.[77]

Gene Savoy (b. 1927), who presents himself as "Author, Explorer, Scholar and Cleric,"[78] believes that he has found Ophir in Gran Vilaya, Peru. To demonstrate that such a long-distance voyage was possible in antiquity, he constructed a ship, the Feathered Serpent III–Ophir, a 73-foot double-hulled catamaran, to attempt to sail around the world.

The Location of Sheba

The numerous biblical references (e.g., Isa. 45:14; 60:6; Jer. 6:20; Ezek. 27:22) to Sheba and its merchants and incense convince most scholars that these are references to the kingdom of Saba in South Arabia (in southwest Yemen), as this was the area noted in classical sources for the growing and export of myrrh and frankincense.[79] On the basis of references in Job and in Assyrian texts, some scholars argue for a northern Sabean kingdom,[80] a no-

74. West and Kling, *Libro de las profecías of Christopher Columbus*, 2.

75. Ibid., 61. Metzger, *Introduction to the Apocrypha*, 232–34, notes that 2 Esdr. 6:42 gave rise to the notion that only one-seventh of the earth was covered with water, thus inspiring Columbus to believe that he had only a short distance to traverse and encouraging Ferdinand and Isabella to sponsor his voyage.

76. West and Kling, *Libro de las profecías of Christopher Columbus*, 70.

77. North, "Ophir/Parvaim," 201.

78. See his website: www.genesavoy.org.

79. Van Beek ("Land of Sheba," 45) notes that frankincense is derived from the resin of the Boswellia carterii and Boswellia frereana trees, which grow primarily in Dhofar in South Arabia and in Somalia, and that myrrh is derived from the Balsamodendron myrrha tree, which grows primarily in the southern coast of Arabia to the west of Dhofar and in the hills of Somalia. See idem, "Frankincense and Myrrh." On the Magi, who brought such gifts together with gold to the Christ child, see Yamauchi, "Episode of the Magi"; idem, *Persia and the Bible*, chap. 13.

80. Groom, *Frankincense and Myrrh*, 44. Others who advocate a northern Sheba include Gray, *I and II Kings*, 260; Wissmann, *Das Grossreich der Sabäer*, 45.

tion dismissed by Kitchen.[81] Since the 1990s the route of the famed incense
trade has been explored by Juris Zarins.[82]

The Queen of Sheba

Solomon's far-flung renown resulted in the visit of the Queen of Sheba.
According to 1 Kings 10:1–3, the queen came to test Solomon's famed wisdom.[83] That she "came from the ends of the earth to listen to the wisdom
of Solomon" is used by Jesus as a condemnation of his generation, for
they refused to listen to one who was greater than Solomon (Matt. 12:42//
Luke 11:31, New Revised Standard Version). As this episode is placed between the account of Solomon's naval voyages in the Red Sea (1 Kings
9:26–28) and the account of his revenues from various sources (10:14–22),
it is quite probable that she made the arduous journey of 1,500 miles
through rugged terrain with commercial interests also in mind. According to Ikeda: "The real purpose of the visit is apparent: to establish an official commercial (exchange and barter) relationship with Israel, in the new
situation that Solomon's maritime activity in the Red Sea would endanger
the land route monopoly of the South Arabians."[84]

The Kingdom of Sheba

Earlier critics reject this account as folkloristic, arguing that the Sabeans were still nomadic at this period.[85] As R. G. Hoyland remarks: "It

81. Kitchen, "Sheba and Arabia," 128: "Hence, the distant realm of Sheba in the Hebrew
record is to be understood as the Saba of Yemen. That there was ever another Saba up in NW
Arabia is excluded: (i) positively by the existence of a totally-different series of kingdoms
there, leaving no room for a theoretical northern Saba, and (ii) negatively by the *total absence*
of any clearly Sabean inscriptions, in stark contrast with (*e.g.*) Minean texts and local Qedar-
ite, Dedanite, Taymanite, Lihyanite and other inscriptions. So, our understanding of the nature and workings of ancient Sheba is tied to that of Saba in Yemen."
82. Zarins, "Persia and Dhofar"; cf. Roberts, "On the Frankincense Trail."
83. Scott, "Solomon and the Beginnings of Wisdom," 262–79, dismisses much of the biblical text as a later legendary embellishment., though he concedes (265): "Certainly it must be
acknowledged that the assertions of 1 Reg. v 9ff. and x 1ff. that Solomon (or his court) was
famous for developing Wisdom on the Egyptian model are not, on general historical
grounds, improbable."
84. Ikeda, "King Solomon and His Red Sea Trade," 127. So also Malamat, "Political Look
at the Kingdom of David," 204: "She came not only to conclude commercial ties and thus secure her hold over trade with South Arabia, which Solomon has long been circumventing,
for both she and Solomon, we can assume, foresaw the restoration of Egyptian trade in the
Red Sea under the forceful Shishak and would have sought to counter this threat." See also
Van Beek, "Land of Sheba," 48; Ricks, "Sheba, Queen of."
85. Groom (*Frankincense and Myrrh*, 53) writes: "In the first place, nothing has yet been
discovered in the archaeological investigation of south Arabia, admittedly so far very lim-

used to be thought that states were not yet in existence in south Arabia at such an early date, and so this account was rejected as a fabrication or a retrojection of a later situation."[86] As of 1920, no South Arabian site had been excavated, making South Arabia one of the least-known areas of the ancient world.[87] Work by Wendell Phillips and W. F. Albright in 1950–53 established that the Sabeans preceded the Mineans in the early first millennium B.C. and that they had a sedentary and even literate civilization.

For a time scholars were divided between Albright, Van Beek, and Jamme, who proposed a high date (1300–1100 B.C.) for the beginning of Sabean culture, and those who followed J. Ryckmans and J. Pirenne in preferring a low date (550–500 B.C.).[88] Pirenne argued that the monumental South Arabic script was adopted from the Greek script at the beginning of the fifth century B.C. and that South Arabian architecture and sculpture was influenced by Greco-Persian culture. She was, however, proved wrong by excavations and radiocarbon dates, which vindicate the advocates of a high dating.[89] J. A. Sauer and J. A. Blakely, who have worked at Wadi al-Jubah in North Yemen since 1982, assert, "Although some scholars have disputed this tradition (e.g., Pirenne . . .) our project in Yemen so far supports the presence of South Arabian cultures as early as ca. 1300 B.C."[90] Investigation by German scholars demonstrates that already by the middle of the third millennium B.C. efforts were made to maximize the use of precious water and that dams were already being built early in the first millennium B.C.[91] Kitchen compiled a list of rulers of Saba going back to Karibil A, who may be dated to 820 B.C. or, on a non-

ited, or in the much more considerable epigraphical study of south Arabia's history, to indicate that any developed and organised kingdom existed there as early as the time of Solomon." He then adds: "The earliest south Arabian rulers so far known from epigraphical testimony do not seem, on the latest reasoning, to have lived much before 500 B.C." Cf. also Delcor, "La reine de Saba et Salomon," 309: "Enfin le problème de l'historicité du récit est complique par le fait que nous ne savons pratiquement rien de Saba, ce royaume du sud de l'Arabie avant le VIIIème siècle av. J.C." See also Cogan, 1 Kings, 315.

86. Hoyland, Arabia and the Arabs, 38.

87. For an account of exploration and archaeology in southwest Arabia, see Breton, Arabia Felix, 7.

88. Ryckmans, L'institution monarchique; Pirenne, La Grèce et Saba; idem, Le royaume sud-arabe.

89. Blakely and Sauer, "Road to Wadi al-Jubah," 6, citing a radiocarbon date of 1440–1220 B.C., suggest: "This dating evidence clearly supports the 'early' chronology that was noted above, and it probably even pushes it back somewhat further in time to the 13th century B.C." Blakely and Sauer also add (9): "The dates also support the biblical tradition of the Queen of Sheba (ca. 950 B.C., contemporary with Solomon), as well as the later Assyrian and Babylonian references to the Sabaeans and other Arabs."

90. Sauer and Blakely, "Archaeology along the Spice Route of Yemen," 91.

91. Brunner, Die Erforschung der antiken Oase, 123.

overlapping scheme of rulers, to 900 B.C.[92] Some of these rulers were called *Mukarribs* (Uniters), that is, paramount rulers.

Queens of Arabia are mentioned in Assyrian records.[93] Although a queen of Sheba is not mentioned in any inscription that goes back to the tenth century, that these queens are mentioned only in the period 740–690 B.C. and not later is significant. Kitchen concludes: "On this ground alone, the role of the biblical Queen of Sheba places her squarely in the period *before* c. 700 B.C.—she cannot be some imaginary 'deuteronomic' or other late invention of the sixth to fourth centuries B.C."[94]

The capital of the kingdom of Sheba was the city of Marib, located 140 miles inland at an altitude of 3,900 feet above sea level on the left bank of the Dhana Valley. Though inscriptions at Marib date only to the eighth century B.C., German scholars date the origins of the city back to around 2200 B.C. Nearby is a famed dam, 720 meters long and about 15 meters high. The dam, built in the sixth century B.C., collapsed in A.D. 572.[95]

About three miles away from Marib is the sanctuary of Mahram Bilqis (the Arabic name for the Queen of Sheba). Excavation of the site by Wendell Phillips and F. P. Albright in 1951–52 was cut short by dangerous political developments.[96] Renewed excavations were begun in 1998 by William Glanzman under the sponsorship of the American Foundation for the Study of Man.[97] Glanzman notes that this is "the largest, and perhaps historically the most important pre-Islamic sanctuary in all of South Arabia."[98] The origins of the sanctuary go back to at least the fifteenth century B.C. The temple area is circumscribed by an oval wall, 112 meters along the longer axis and 75 meters along the shorter axis. The entrance is an elaborate peristyle building. There are eight tall limestone pillars before the temple. The sanctuary was dedicated to the moon god Almaqah (or Ilumquh). Other key Arabian gods were the sun god Shams and the goddess Athtar (cf. Astarte).

92. Kitchen, *Documentation for Ancient Arabia*, 1.110–11.
93. Abbot, "Pre-Islamic Arab Queens." Ullendorff, "Queen of Sheba," 488, comments: "Again, queens have been attested among the ancient Arabs, and we have therefore no reason to suspect the genuineness of the Biblical tradition. Cuneiform records enumerate many North Arabian queens [e.g., *ANET* 283], but to assert that there were none in the south would merely be an *argumentum e silentio.*"
94. Kitchen, "Ancient Arabia and the Bible," 29.
95. Van Beek, "Rise and Fall of Arabia Felix," 38–39.
96. Albright, "Excavation of the Temple of the Moon." For an account of the dangerous situation that caused the excavators to hastily evacuate the scene, see Clapp, *Sheba*, 198–201.
97. The German Archaeological Institute excavated dozens of mausoleums to the southwest.
98. Glanzman, "Digging Deeper," 101.

Figure 3.4. South Arabian
stela with a camel and
rider (©British Museum).

The Role of Camels

The Queen of Sheba came to Solomon with a caravan of camels
(1 Kings 10:2). The development of the long-distance overland trade de-
pended on the domestication of the camel. References to camels in the pa-
triarchal narratives are regarded by scholars as anachronistic,[99] but in
view of the new accumulation of evidence, Borowski concludes that such

---

99. See Yamauchi, *Stones and the Scriptures*, 42–43. Albright (*Archaeology and the Religion of
Israel*, 132) argues that camels were domesticated not long before the eleventh century B.C. A
similar date is maintained by Phillips, *Qataban and Sheba*, 106.

references can now be defended.[100] Though textual references come from a later period, evidence from bones and artistic depictions indicate that camels were domesticated earlier.

R. W. Bulliet traces the domestication of the camels in stages over centuries: The first stage occurred in southeastern Arabia in the fourth or third millennium B.C. and then spread to southwestern Arabia.[101] The second stage, some time after 2000 B.C., involved the use of camels to transport incense from southwestern Arabia north.[102] Wissmann notes that camel trips between Midian and Dedan are first recorded in the thirteenth century;[103] Blakely and Sauer suggest that the development of camel caravans occurred at the same time as the development of the South Arabian states.[104]

Evidence of Early Contacts with South Arabia

Indirect evidence for early contact between Palestine and South Arabia is an inscription in an alphabetic Ugaritic script in which the consonants are in the South Arabian order. P. Bordreuil comments: "We have therefore an abecedary, of alphabetic sequence, that refers to another language besides Ugaritic, thus testifying to the existence of more ancient relations between the Arabian peninsula and the northern coast of Syria than we had previously thought."[105] Kitchen observes: "How this came to be, we cannot know. But clearly, it reflects contact between Canaan and Saba in the field of writing at about 1200 B.C."[106] Kitchen furthermore concludes that this evidence is also important for the date of the emergence of the South Arabic script.[107] In 1957 J. Kelso discovered at Bethel an inscribed

100. Borowski, *Every Living Thing*, 114.

101. Ripinsky, "Camel in Ancient Arabia," 297, argues for an extremely early date: "Contrary to the prevailing views, the domestication of the camel in the Old World must have occurred not later than the fourth millennium B.C."

102. Bulliet, *Camel and the Wheel*. According to Roberts ("On the Frankincense Trail," 121): "Around 2000 B.C., thanks to the domestication of the camel, a complex trade network evolved to transport the priceless resins from the remote valleys where the trees grow to the markets where kings and emperors vied for the finest grades."

103. Wissmann, *Das Grossreich der Sabäer*, 44.

104. Blakely and Sauer, "Road to Wadi al-Jubah," 8. This is also the view expressed in Daum, *Die Königin von Saba'*, 12: "Regelmässigen Fernhandel im grossen Stil—eben das, was wir unter der Weihrauchstrasse verstehen—kann es jedoch erst ab der etwa im 13.–12. Jh. v. Chr. erfolgen Domestikation des Kamels gegeben haben."

105. Bordreuil, "South-Arabian Abecedary," 197.

106. Kitchen, "Ancient Arabia and the Bible," 28.

107. Kitchen, "Sheba and Arabia," 133: "The date of origin of the ancient South-Arabian script has been considered anew in recent years. Some 30 to 40 years ago, Cross suggested its emergence in the fourteenth/thirteenth centuries B.C., while very recently, Sass has argued for the eleventh/tenth centuries B.C. For more than one reason, a 'middle date' may be wiser, *i.e.* about the thirteenth/twelfth centuries B.C. In the first place, we have the remark-

South Arabian clay seal dated to the ninth century.[108] Despite doubts raised by Yadin,[109] G. W. Van Beek and A. Jamme, authorities on South Arabia, stoutly affirm the seal's authenticity.[110] A South Arabian altar dated to around 800 B.C. was found in Moab.[111]

Until recently the earliest textual evidence of contacts between South Arabia and Mesopotamia dated to no earlier than 715 B.C. Kitchen calls attention to an important study by M. Liverani establishing that the camel caravan trade from Sheba by way of Teima reached the Middle Euphrates kingdom of Hindanu by the early ninth century B.C. under Tukulti-Ninurta II (891–884 B.C.).[112] There is evidence to believe that Hindanu's trade with camel caravans in South Arabia was already established in the tenth century, that is, in the age of Solomon. According to Liverani:

> A starting phase of the South-Arabian trade in the second half of the 10th century would perfectly agree both with the Old Testament traditions and with the Assyrian royal inscriptions—and would also fit in the technological development of the Arabian mastery of the "desert" environment and its caravan network, as it is presently reconstructed. Needless to say, a beginning of the South-Arabian trade in the (late-)10th century, implies the existence of the Yemeni caravan cities (at least in an embryonic form) at the same time and probably even before. This is also in accordance with the results of the most recent archaeological and epigraphical research in Yemen.[113]

Nicholas Clapp helpfully sets out in tabular form the remarkable changes in evidence from excavations and studies of the last decade:[114]

Horizon	Theory in the Early 1990s	Current Theory
Neolithic settlement and local trade	suspected but not substantiated	5000–3000 B.C.

---

able case of the tablet from Beth-Shemesh inscribed with letters in Ugaritic script, but in the order of the Old South Arabian alphabet! Clearly, for this even to happen, *somebody* had already invented that very characteristic letter-order by *ca.* 1200 B.C. and as that order has no place whatsoever in the Mediterranean Semitic world, it is far more likely to have been someone from Arabia." The South Arabian alphabet has twenty-nine consonants, more than any other Semitic alphabet. More than ten thousand South Arabian inscriptions have been copied.

108. Van Beek and Jamme, "Inscribed South Arabian Clay Stamp."

109. Yadin, "Inscribed South-Arabian Clay Stamp from Bethel?"

110. Van Beek, Jamme, and Kelso, "Authenticity of the Bethel Stamp Seal."

111. Hoyland, *Arabia and the Arabs*, 38.

112. Kitchen, "Ancient Arabia and the Bible," 29; idem, *Documentation for Ancient Arabia*, 2.737–47.

113. Liverani, "Early Caravan Trade," 114.

114. Clapp, *Sheba*, 217.

development of artificial irrigation	1000–800 B.C.	ca. 2400 B.C.
distinctive Early South Arabian alphabet and rise of civilization	600–500 B.C.	1500–1200 B.C.
beginning of long-range trade	ca. 800 B.C.	ca. 1000 B.C.
journey of biblical Queen of Sheba (Saba)	unlikely; there was no writing and thus no civilization	ca. 950 B.C.

The Queen of Sheba in Jewish Traditions

Josephus, a Jewish historian writing at the end of the first century A.D., greatly embellished Old Testament stories in his *Antiquities*.[115] He calls the queen Nikaulē or Nikaulis and identifies her as the "queen of Egypt and Ethiopia" (*Antiquities* 8.10.2 §158; 8.10.5–6 §§165–75). This reference to her is the earliest outside the Gospels. Josephus describes the training and wisdom of the queen and relates that she brought Solomon 20 talents (instead of 120 talents) of gold. Josephus claims that the balsam trees of his country were derived from the plants she brought.

According to 1 Kings 4:32–33, God gave Solomon wisdom and "he spoke three thousand proverbs and his songs numbered a thousand and five. He described plant life, from the cedar of Lebanon to the hyssop that grows out of walls. He also taught about animals and birds, reptiles and fish" (NIV). In the second-century B.C. Wisdom of Solomon 7:18–20, the king also knows astrology, "virtues of roots," and "powers of spirits." According to Josephus (*Antiquities* 8.2.5 §45), "God granted him knowledge of the art used against demons for the benefit and healing of men. He also composed incantations by which illnesses are relieved, and left behind forms of exorcisms with which those possessed by demons drive them out, never to return." In the *Testament of Solomon* 19.3, dated between the first and third centuries A.D., Solomon, after receiving further magical powers over angels and demons, is visited by "Sheeba, Queen of the South," a witch, who tours his temple and gives him gifts.[116]

F. A. Pennacchietti remarks: "The fact remains that there is no mention of his relationship with the Queen of Sheba in the Jerusalem Talmud, nor in the Babylonian Talmud, nor in the oldest *Midrashim*, nor in any other kind of rabbinical literature."[117] As a matter of fact, the Babylonian Talmud contains one reference to the Queen of Sheba, albeit an

115. See Yamauchi, "Josephus and the Scriptures"; Feldman, *Josephus's Interpretation of the Bible.*
116. Duling, "Testament of Solomon," 982. See also idem, "Solomon, Exorcism, and the Son of David."
117. Pennacchietti, "Queen of Sheba," 225.

SOLOMON AND AFRICA

incidental one (tractate *Baba Bathra* 15b) in a dispute over the date of Job. Rabbi Nathan declared on the basis of Job 1:15 that Job lived in the days of Sheba. Rabbi Jonathan asserted that Sheba was not a woman but a kingdom.[118]

There is a remarkable version of the Queen of Sheba story in the second Targum (Targum Sheni) or Aramaic paraphrase of the Book of Esther. Its date is much disputed. L. H. Silberman dates it as early as the third or fourth century A.D.;[119] L. Munk dates it to the eleventh century; and B. Grossfeld believes that it was composed around 800.[120] According to the targum, Solomon sends a bird (translated variously as "hoopoe"[121] or "wild rooster") to the queen, demanding her presence. The queen, who is a worshiper of the sun, receives the message at her capital city of Qitor. She at first sends him 6,000 boys and girls, all of whom were born at the same time. When she herself finally arrives, she finds Solomon sitting in a bathhouse. Thinking that he was sitting in water, she raises her skirt to cross over. Whereupon Solomon observes that she has hairy legs! He remarks rather unchivalrously, "Your beauty is the beauty of women, but your hair is the hair of men. Now hair (i.e., on the legs) is beautiful for a man but shameful for a woman."[122] She then challenges the king with three riddles about a cosmetic box, naphta, and flax, which he successfully solves. This leads her to praise the eternal God of Israel.

Though Targum Sheni has no reference to a union between Solomon and the Queen of Sheba, a later Jewish text called the *Alphabet of Ben Sira* (dated to the ninth/tenth century) relates that after the unsightly hair on her legs was removed by a depilatory, Solomon slept with her. Their offspring turned out to be none other than Nebuchadnezzar![123]

Pennacchietti offers an intriguing theory on how the Queen of Sheba acquired hair on her legs. He notes that later Jewish and Islamic traditions held that the queen was buried at Palmyra. She then became associated with Queen Zenobia, whose revolt against Rome was crushed by the emperor Aurelian in A.D. 273.[124] Zenobia's name in Palmyrene was Bat Zabbay (daughter of Zabbay), but this became misunderstood in Arabic as *az-Zabba'*, which means "the hairy woman."[125]

118. Ullendorff, "Queen of Sheba," 492.
119. Silberman, "Queen of Sheba in Judaic Tradition," 65.
120. Grossfeld, *Two Targums of Esther*, 20.
121. This was the lapwing, a bird with an erect crest on its head and barred black-and-white patterns on its wings.
122. Grossfeld, *Two Targums of Esther*, 116.
123. Lassner, *Demonizing the Queen of Sheba*, 19; see also idem, "Ritual Purity and Political Exile."
124. Stoneman, *Palmyra and Its Empire*.
125. Pennacchietti, "Queen of Sheba," 228–30.

Furthermore, since hairy creatures were associated in various cultures with the demonic, later Jewish midrashic and mystical literature associated the Queen of Sheba with Lilith, the first wife of Adam.[126] The word *lilith* ultimately goes back to a demon in Sumerian/Babylonian mythology, a succubus who had intercourse with men at night and then attacked human babies.[127] Mesopotamian magic bowls written in Aramaic, Syriac, and Mandaic (dated ca. A.D. 600) contain many spells against her.[128]

Pennacchietti also speculates that Josephus's name for the queen, Nikaulis, may be connected with the Greek epithet *onokelis* (donkey-legged), given to the famous demon Empusa in, for example, the *Testament of Solomon* 4.2. Pennacchietti further suggests that this name was ultimately transformed to give rise to the Arabic name for the queen: Bilqis.[129] He concludes: "In the light of this hypothesis the Jewish and Islamic versions of the legend of the Queen of Sheba emerge afresh as an etiological tale, designed to confirm or invalidate the assimilation of the queen into a female demon with the hooves of a donkey."[130]

An even more curious transformation seems to have arisen from a scribal miscopying of a Latin phrase describing the queen's legs. Instead of *asininos* (ass), a scribe seems to have written *anserinos* (goose). Thus, by the twelfth century the queen was said to be noted for her *pedes anserios et oculos lucentes ut stellae* (feet of a goose and eyes that shone like stars). Paintings from fifteenth-century and sixteenth-century Europe depict the queen with webbed feet as she crosses a stream when moving toward Solomon. In France, statues of the queen as *reine pédauque*—that is, a queen with the feet of a goose—were erected in the eighteenth century.[131]

126. For example, in the Zohar, the queen is identified as Lilith. See Fontaine, "More Queenly Proverb Performance," 210.

127. Lassner (*Demonizing the Queen of Sheba*, 4) has an interesting comment on the current revaluation by feminists, converting a negative image into a positive one: "Reflecting a different sensibility, current feminists have made political icons of both the Queen of Sheba and the demonic Lilith, with whom the queen is explicitly linked in Jewish sources. As regards the queen, it is her intelligence; her desire for political independence; her sagacity in dealing with men at their own game; and above all her ability to make and enforce decisions about her own life that make her a kindred soul to the modern woman. The demonic Lilith provides in turn a model of sexual independence; a rejection of biological imperatives that relegate women to roles of procreation and nurturing; and, more generally, a defiance of male authority."

128. See Yamauchi, "Aramaic Magic Bowls"; idem, *Mandaic Incantation Texts*; idem, "Cyrus H. Gordon and the Ubiquity of Magic."

129. Pennacchietti, "Queen of Sheba," 230–31.

130. Ibid., 252. Others suggest that the name Bilqis is derived from Hebrew *pylgš*, which in turn was derived from the Greek *pallakis* (concubine). See Canova, "La leggenda della Regina di Saba." For an exhaustive discussion of various suggestions for the etymology of Bilqis's name, see Stiegner, "Die Königin von Saba'."

131. Pennacchietti, "Queen of Sheba," 232.

The Queen of Sheba in Islamic Traditions

Solomon (Arabic *Sulaimun*) is depicted in the Qur'an (6.84; 4.163) and in Islamic traditions as one of the prophets of Allah, like Jesus and Muhammad himself. He is a wealthy king with power over the birds, beasts, and the jinn, or spirits (21.78–82). The Qur'an recounts a somewhat disjointed story (27.15–44) about Solomon and the Queen of Sheba, which seems to assume the tradition narrated in the later Targum Sheni of Esther.[132] Solomon, who understands the languages of the birds, is disturbed by the absence of the hoopoe (Arabic *hudhud*). When it arrives, it reports that it observed a female ruler of Sheba who worshiped the sun instead of Allah. Solomon then commands it to deliver a letter to her, demanding her presence. He also commanded a jinn to bring her throne to him. When she arrived, she was told to enter the hall: "And when she saw it she deemed it a pool and bared her legs. [Solomon] said: Lo! it is a hall, made smooth, of glass. She said: My Lord! Lo! I have wronged myself, and I surrender with Solomon unto Allah, the Lord of the Worlds" (27.44).[133]

This Qur'anic story is elaborated in two books, both called the *Stories of the Prophets*, written in the eleventh century by al-Kisaʾi and athThaʿlabi.[134] According to these accounts, when Solomon was at Mecca, the hoopoe reported that the Queen of Sheba had built a castle at Sanʿaʾ (the capital of Yemen) and had instituted the worship of the sun there. The hoopoe brought Solomon's letter to the queen at Marib, where she had a council of 12,000 lords, each of whom had 100,000 warriors.[135] There were rumors that she had legs like a donkey's, because though her father was a king of Yemen, her mother was a jinn.[136] But when stepping over a glass floor, which she mistook for water, she uncovered her feet, and Solomon saw that they were human but hairy. She was given depilatories and then converted to Islam. Some versions report that she married Solomon, but according to Ibn Abbas, she was married to a king of Hamadan.[137]

The Queen of Sheba in Ethiopian Traditions

The modern country of Ethiopia, formerly known as Abyssinia, on the eastern coast of Africa, is an unusual African country because of its prox-

132. Schedl offers a learned but highly speculative suggestion that the Qur'anic version is a transformed Persian myth. See "Sulaiman und die Königin von Saba."
133. Pickthall, *Meaning of the Glorious Koran*, 274.
134. Canova, *Talʾabî Storia di Bilqîs*.
135. Watt, "Queen of Sheba in Islamic Tradition," 97.
136. This rumor is reported by commentator Zamakhshari. For another commentary, see Johns, "Solomon and the Queen of Sheba."
137. See Lassner, *Demonizing the Queen of Sheba*, 47–64.

imity across the narrow Red Sea to Arabia.[138] Its ancient language, Geᶜez[139] (like its modern language Amharic), belongs to the South Semitic language family (like Arabic) rather than to the Afroasiatic languages.[140] Ethiopia was the home of the Falashas or black Jews, some 40,000 of whom were resettled in the 1970s and 1980s in Israel.[141] Ethiopian Christianity also has a very high degree of Jewish elements in its practices and traditions, such as the observation of the Sabbath, circumcision, fasts, and food taboos.[142]

Edward Ullendorff notes: "Nowhere else in the world are the story of the Queen of Sheba and the Solomon-Sheba notion of kingship as important, as vital, and as pregnant with practical significance as in Ethiopia."[143] Though the origins of the national epic *Kebra Negast* (Glory of the Kings) may go back some centuries earlier,[144] the canonical version was translated into Geᶜez between 1314 and 1344 by Yeshaq of Aksum.[145] Its purpose was to lend support to the new "Solomonic" dynasty that had gained power in 1270, replacing the Zagwe dynasty. The first complete translation was published by C. Bezold in 1905–9, then in English by E. A. W. Budge in 1922. Of its 117 chapters, chapters 21–63, 84–94, and 113–17 are concerned with the Solomon-Sheba cycle. The most thorough analysis of its sources is a dissertation by David Hubbard under the direction of Ullendorff.[146] Hubbard concludes that the original might have been written by an Arabic-speaking Egyptian priest living in Ethiopia and not, as claimed, translated from Coptic.

According to the *Kebra Negast*, a merchant brought news of Solomon's kingdom to Makeda, the Queen of Sheba. Solomon is reported to have understood the language of birds and animals and also to have power over demons (*Kebra Negast* 18). Makeda goes to Jerusalem with a retinue and is so impressed by Solomon and his city that she rejects the worship of the sun to worship the God of Israel. The queen extracts a promise from Solomon that he will not take her by force; he agrees to her request on condition that she not steal anything. But then Solomon gave her spicy

138. See Buxton, *Abyssinians*; Pankhurst, *Ethiopians*; Ullendorff, *Ethiopians*.

139. Lambdin, *Introduction to Classical Ethiopic*. Many important texts such as Enoch are preserved in full only in Geᶜez. See Fisher, "Some Contributions of Ethiopic Studies."

140. See Hodge, "Afroasiatic," 15–27.

141. Quinn, *Evolution of the Ethiopian Jews*; Onolemhemhen and Gessesse, *Black Jews of Ethiopia*.

142. Isaac, *Ethiopian Church*; see also Master, "Origin of Jewish Elements."

143. Ullendorff, "Queen of Sheba in Ethiopian Tradition," 104.

144. Scholars reject the claim that *Kebra Negast* was copied from a third-century manuscript in the library of Saint Sophia in Constantinople.

145. Budge, *Queen of Sheba*, viii.

146. Hubbard, "Literary Sources of the Kebra Nagast."

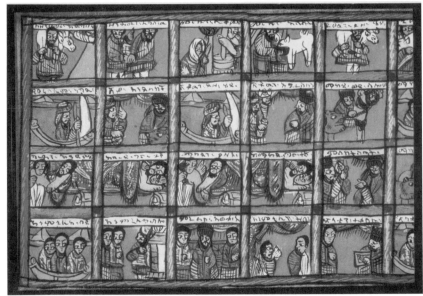

Figure 3.5. Left side of panel illustrating the *Kebra Negast* (C. Geyer).

food that he knew would make her thirsty.[147] So during the night when she arose for a drink, he seized her and slept with her. She bore a son, Menelik, who when grown came to visit his father. After a warm welcome, Menelik stole the ark (*Tabot*) and took it back to Ethiopia, where it supposedly resides today in the Church of Mary Zion in Aksum.[148] This story is traditionally illustrated in a painted panel of four rows of eleven scenes each.[149] Ethiopian Christians have also conflated the Queen of Sheba with Queen Candace, who sent her treasurer, the eunuch, who was converted by Philip (Acts 8:27).[150]

Tafari Makonnen, born in 1892, who became known as Ras (Prince) Tafari, became the emperor of Ethiopia in 1930 and took the name Haile Selassie (Might of the Trinity), supposedly the 111th emperor descended from Solomon. The Ethiopian constitution of 1931 declared him the "Son of King Solomon of Jerusalem and the Queen of Ethiopia." The 1955 constitution declared him the son of the Queen of Ethiopia, the Queen of

147. A different version of the seduction episode is found in a Tigre legend. A girl named Etiye-Azeb (Queen of the South) goes to Solomon to have her deformed foot, which was shaped like an ass's heel, healed. See Littmann, *Legend of the Queen of Sheba*.

148. Hancock, *Sign and the Seal*, suggests that the ark came to Ethiopia in the fifth century B.C. by way of the Jewish garrison at Elephantine.

149. Isaac, "Legend of Solomon and Sheba."

150. Ullendorff, "Candace (Acts 8.27)."

Figure 3.6. Right side of panel illustrating the *Kebra Negast* (C. Geyer).

Figure 3.7. Detail of panel illustrating the *Kebra Negast*: Solomon accuses the Queen of Sheba of stealing his water (C. Geyer).

Figure 3.8. Detail of panel illustrating the *Kebra Negast*: Solomon seduces the Queen of Sheba (C. Geyer).

Sheba, and King Solomon of Jerusalem. During a visit to England in 1954, when he was asked about the tradition of the *Kebra Negast*, he replied forcefully: "This is not a legend. It is based on the most universal book in the world—the holy Bible."[151]

In Jamaica black leaders in 1930 hailed the emperor as either God come to earth or Jesus Christ as black in a new dispensation, thus giving rise to the important Rastafarian religion, a popular movement associated with the smoking of *ganja* (hemp), dreadlocks, and reggae music popularized by Bob Marley.[152] Jamaican Leonard Howell sold five thousand pictures of Haile Selassie, declaring that "the glory that was Solomon greater still reigns in Ethiopia. We can see all the Kings of earth surrendering their crowns to His Majesty Ras Tafari the King of Kings and Lord of Lords."[153]

151. Hubbard, "Literary Sources of the Kebra Nagast," 5.
152. Malloch, "Rastafarianism."
153. Spencer, *Dread Jesus*, 11. Selassie himself resisted Marcus Garvey's appeal to him as a "Negro" head of state and the Rastas's belief that he was divine. Marcus Garvey (1887–1940) was an impassioned and visionary Jamaican who strove for the freedom of all Negroes. It is

An abridged edition of Budge's translation of the *Kebra Negast* was published as scripture for the Rastafarians.[154]

Some Afrocentric scholars try to use the Ethiopian *Kebra Negast* traditions, Josephus's description of the Queen of Sheba as the "Queen of Egypt and Ethiopia," and citations from the church fathers to support the view that the queen came from Africa and not from Arabia.[155] But these are late and unreliable sources that cannot be used to overturn the biblical and archaeological evidence that Sheba was in southwest Arabia.[156]

---

an irony that though he disdained the Rastas, they exalt him to a position second only to Selassie in their rituals. See Chevannes, *Rastafari*, 109, 180.

154. Hausman, *Kebra Nagast*.

155. Felder, *Troubling Biblical Waters*, 33; Copher, "Black Presence in the Old Testament," 158. Other arguments such as a comparison with African wisdom traditions and with matriarchy are enlisted by other writers for this identification; see Bailey, "Beyond Identification," 181–82; C. A. Morris, "Queen of Sheba," 77.

156. Ash, *David, Solomon, and Egypt*, 123–25. Kitchen (personal communication to the author) notes: "It is, of course, impossible to put Sheba in Africa, given the thousands of Sabean texts in southwest Arabia that prove otherwise. Saba did have a satellite kingdom, Daamat or Diamat, in Eritrea/northwest Ethiopia, ca. 700–500 B.C."

4

TIRHAKAH AND OTHER CUSHITES

During the period of the united monarchy (Saul, David, Solomon) and the divided kingdoms that followed, a few Cushites appear in the biblical narratives.[1] In these centuries (tenth–sixth centuries B.C.) Egypt experienced fragmentation and decline in what is called the Third Intermediate Period,[2] while first the Assyrians expanded (eighth–seventh centuries B.C.), only to be overturned by the Neo-Babylonians (sixth century B.C.). This led first to the overthrow of the northern kingdom of Israel in 722 B.C. by the Assyrians and then to the conquest of the southern kingdom of Judah in 605 B.C. by the Babylonians. During the period of Assyrian hegemony, for a half century a Kushite dynasty, the 25th, ruled Egypt and attempted to intervene in Palestine. The most important ruler of this dynasty was Taharqa (biblical Tirhakah).

W. Y. Adams comments: "Taharqa, the next-to-last 'Ethiopian' pharaoh, is the only Nubian to be mentioned by name in the Bible."[3] Tirhakah is mentioned in passing in parallel passages (2 Kings 19:9; Isa. 37:9). As

---

1. See Hidal, "Land of Cush in the Old Testament"; Hays, "Cushites."

2. The definitive work on this era is Kitchen's *Third Intermediate Period in Egypt.*

3. Adams, *Nubia*, 248. In the Septuagint Taharqa is called *Tharaka*; in cuneiform texts he is *Tarqû*. See Janssen, "Que sait-on actuellement du Pharaon Taharqa?" 23.

other Cushites are actually named in Scriptures, Adams's statement must be qualified to be understood that Taharqa is the only Cushite named in the Bible who is attested in extrabiblical sources.

The pharaohs of the 25th Dynasty, who hailed from Napata near the Fourth Cataract, can be rightly called "black pharaohs," as R. G. Morkot titles his book about them: *Black Pharaohs: Egypt's Nubian Rulers.* E. R. Russmann comments: "The newcomers did not look like Egyptians. Their skin was darker, their physiognomy that of the Sudan. In fact, they looked like the Nubians whom the Egyptians had pictured since time immemorial, but always as vile conquered enemies, as servile tributaries or as mercenaries."[4] The Kushite rulers are depicted with a darker "chocolate brown" color than the reddish-brown Egyptians in the wall paintings of the temple of Taharqa at Qasr Ibrim and also on a papyrus fragment (Brooklyn 47.218.3).

Joab's Cushite Messenger

When against David's orders Joab killed Absalom, David's rebellious son, Joab chose a Cushite to bear the unwelcome news to the king (2 Sam. 18:19–33). Most commentators regard him as a slave.[5] R. R. Hutton proposes that the later superscription added to Psalm 7, "which he sang to the LORD concerning Cush, a Benjamite" (NIV), refers to this Cushite messenger, which means that this psalm is "a declaration of innocence as David distanced himself from the treachery of Joab."[6]

Zerah the Cushite

Second Chronicles 14:9–15 relates that Zerah the Cushite led an enormous army against the forces of Asa in the latter's fourteenth year (897 B.C.). When Asa cried to the Lord for help, he was able to defeat the enemy's superior forces at Mareshah in southern Judah. E. A. Knauf dismisses the episode as unhistorical.[7] But other scholars such as John Bright and Jacob Myers accept this account.[8]

M. J. Selman comments that "Zerah's army (v. 9) is best understood as comprising 1,000 units, which would be more likely along with *three hundred chariots* than 'a million' soldiers (GNB etc.)."[9] Following the conjecture

4. Russmann, *Representation of the King*, 9.
5. But see Adamo, "Images of Cush," 69.
6. Hutton, "Cush the Benjaminite," 135.
7. Knauf, "Zerah."
8. Bright, *History of Israel*, 234–35; Myers, *II Chronicles*, 85; see also Hays, "From the Land of the Bow," 31–32.
9. Selman, *2 Chronicles*, 388–89; cf. also Dillard, *2 Chronicles*, 120. On the general problem, see Wenham, "Large Numbers in the Old Testament"; Fouts, "Defense of the Hyperbolic In-

of W. F. Albright,[10] some hold that Zerah's army was derived from the Hamites mentioned in 1 Chronicles 4:40, who may have been a colony of mercenaries established by Pharaoh Shoshenq I (Shishak I) after he invaded Judah in the fifth year of Rehoboam (2 Chron. 12:3).[11] K. A. Kitchen maintains that Zerah was probably a commander on behalf of the Libyan pharaoh Osorkon I (924–889 B.C.), the son of Shoshenq I.[12] That Libyan contingents are mentioned in his army is significant.[13] Dynasties 21–24 consisted of pharaohs who arose from Libyans who had settled in Lower Egypt. D. O'Connor comments:

> In 925 B.C. Shoshenq I, then pharaoh of Egypt, invaded Judah and Israel, and had Nubians ("Kushites") in his army. Later, his son Osorkon I sent against Judah another army, headed by a general called Zerah the Kushite. In both cases, Nubians who had been settled in Egypt for generations might have been involved, but it is equally possible that the Nubians in question were recruited in Upper Nubia . . . or even dispatched from thence by some Nubian "ally" of the Egyptians.[14]

The Appeal from Hoshea to "So" of Egypt

As the Assyrian juggernaut expanded westward through the efforts of Tiglath-pileser III,[15] who destroyed the Aramean state of Damascus in 732 B.C., and of his son Shalmaneser V, who besieged Samaria, the last king of Israel, Hoshea, sent out a desperate plea for help to So (Hebrew *Sôʾ*) of Egypt (2 Kings 17:4), prefiguring a pattern of vain appeals that would continue for the next century and a half. The call for help was made about 725 B.C.[16] Scholarly debate continues as to the identification of this enigmatic figure, inasmuch as Egypt was not united at this time, with several dynasties ruling concurrently in the Delta.

Kitchen concludes that the only possible candidate for So is Osorkon IV (728–716), a ruler in the Delta city of Bubastis during the 22d

---

terpretation." An appropriate rendering might be "myriads of soldiers." The English word is derived from Greek *myrias*, which literally meant "10,000," but often conveys the more general sense of "large numbers."

10. Albright, "Egypt and the Early History of the Negeb."
11. See Yamauchi, "Shishak."
12. Kitchen, "Zerah" (1980).
13. Hofmann, "Kuschiten in Palästina."
14. O'Connor, *Ancient Nubia*, 67.
15. See Yamauchi, "Tiglath-pileser."
16. There is a current debate as to whether Samaria fell in 722 in the reign of Shalmaneser V as the Bible (2 Kings 17:6) claims or in 720 in the reign of Sargon II, who claimed credit for the capture. See Yamauchi, *Stones and the Scriptures*, 75; Na'aman, "Historical Background"; Becking, *Fall of Samaria*; Younger, "Fall of Samaria"; Tetley, "Date of Samaria's Fall."

Dynasty.[17] He notes that relations had been established with this dynasty, dating back to Osorkon II. Less likely identifications are put forward by other scholars. D. L. Christensen and J. Day favor an identification with the Delta city of Sais, whose ruler was Tefnakht I of Dynasty 24.[18] They concur with the interpretation of D. B. Redford in this regard.[19] W. H. Shea and A. R. W. Green favor Piankhy, the Kushite ruler who conquered Egypt.[20] Green cites the Lucianic Septuagint gloss on 2 Kings 17:4: "Adrammelech the Ethiopian, living in Egypt," and avers: "In 726, the year after Piankhy's victorious campaign, it was clear where the real power lay. It was not in Tanis, Bubastis, or Sais but rather at Napata in Nubia, and it was held by Piankhy."[21]

The Kushite Dark Age

After the Egyptian conquest of Kerma (see chap. 2) a "dark age" seems to have descended on developments in Kush until the meteoric rise of the 25th Dynasty. The great warrior Pharaoh Thutmose III established Egyptian control in Kush as far as the Fourth Cataract by his thirty-first year (1460 B.C.). He erected monumental buildings at Gebel Barkal (The Pure Mountain), located nine miles from this cataract, which arises in spectacular fashion more than 300 feet above the plain. T. Kendall demonstrated that the Kushites believed that they had received authority over Egypt from the god Amon, who resided in this sacred mountain.[22] The capital of this new state was Napata, which was near the mountain but has not been found by excavators. According to D. A. Welsby: "The main settlement at Napata may have lain at Sanam, the term Napata relating to the region around Barkal rather than to the Barkal religious complex itself."[23]

Inasmuch as the last Egyptian building in the area was a temple of Ramesses II (1279–1213 B.C.) and the last artifact a statue of Ramesses IX (ca. 1100 B.C.), a considerable gap of about 250 years in the historical record precedes the rise of the 25th Dynasty.[24] The traditional chronology was established by George Reisner on the basis of his investigations of the

17. Kitchen, *Third Intermediate Period in Egypt*, 182, 372–76, 551–52.
18. Christensen, "Identity of 'King So'"; Day, "Problem of 'So, King of Egypt.'"
19. Redford, "Sais and the Kushite Invasions," 15; idem, *Egypt, Canaan, and Israel*, 346.
20. Shea, "'So,' Ruler of Egypt"; Green, "Identity of King So of Egypt."
21. Green, "Identity of King So of Egypt," 101, 106.
22. Kendall, "Origin of the Napatan State," 69.
23. Welsby, *Kingdom of Kush*, 148. Adams (*Nubia*, 254) considers that Napata referred to the district downstream from the Fourth Cataract and questions if there "was ever a specific town named Napata."
24. See Myśliwiec, *Twilight of Ancient Egypt*, 71.

Figure 4.1.
Temple of
Amon, built by
Thutmose III
at the base of
Gebel Barkal
(Derek A.
Welsby).

royal cemeteries at el-Kurru on the right bank of the Nile in the vicinity of
Gebel Barkal.

Reisner, who mistakenly believed that the new Napatan rulers had a
Libyan background, reckoned from the el-Kurru burials that there had
been five ancestral generations before Piankhy, thus dating the earliest
burial there to about 860–840 B.C. Kendall, who examined the unpub-
lished records of Reisner, defends his "short" chronology, noting that

the temple at Gebel Barkal "was almost certainly *not* operational and was perhaps even abandoned" during the interim.[25] He comments concerning the area of el-Kurru: "Further exploration here would be certain to yield more information about the earliest Napatan period, and would likely begin to fill in the still enigmatic archaeological 'gap' between the end of the New Kingdom and the construction of [el-Kurru] Tum[ulus] 1."[26]

L. Török, who favors a "long" chronology, postulates twelve ancestral generations, which dates the first tumulus at el-Kurru to 1020 B.C.[27] He and Welsby point out that the "short" chronology has to discount certain Egyptian objects as heirlooms.[28] Another scholar who argues for the long chronology is R. G. Morkot,[29] one of a group of scholars who have attempted to shorten or eliminate dark ages throughout the Mediterranean and the Near East by radically revisionist chronologies.[30] In a scathing review, Kitchen dismisses such revisionism[31] and even compares efforts by these scholars to the imaginative reconstructions of Immanuel Velikovsky.[32]

Alara

Alara (ca. 780–760 B.C.)[33] is the first member of the new Kushite dynasty to be attested.[34] His name is known only from later monuments. As his name in a cartouche is preceded by partial (or pseudo-)Egyptian titles, Russmann suggests that "Alara did not himself pretend to be king of Egypt."[35] His name is recorded in a dedication of his sister Pebatma's installation as a sistrum player for the god Amon-Re. Török concludes:

25. Kendall, "Origin of the Napatan State," 55.
26. Ibid., 49.
27. Török, "Emergence of the Kingdom of Kush," 208. Cf. idem, "Origin of the Napatan State."
28. Welsby, *Kingdom of Kush*, 14.
29. Morkot, *Black Pharaohs*, 131–33.
30. See Morkot, "Empty Years of Nubian History."
31. Kitchen, "Egyptian Chronology: Problem or Solution?" For other critical reviews, see Kemp, "Explaining Ancient Crises"; also see W. Ward's and Kohl's reviews of *Centuries of Darkness*.
32. See Yamauchi, "Immanuel Velikovsky's Catastrophic History."
33. Some argue that the standard dates given, for example, by Kitchen in *Third Intermediate Period in Egypt* for the pharaohs before Taharqa may all have to be revised a few years earlier because of the important Assyrian inscription of Sargon II, which names Shebitku rather than Shabako as the ruler who extradited the rebel Yamani to the Assyrians. See Kahn, "Inscription of Sargon II." But Kitchen disagrees with this interpretation; see Kitchen, "Regnal and Genealogical Data," 50–51.
34. Eide et al., *Fontes Historiae Nubiorum*, 41.
35. Russmann, "Egypt and the Kushites," 116.

"The installation of Alara's sister as priestess of Amon marked the creation of a system of royal succession and the ideology of royal power in which traditional Kushite concepts and practice were united with contemporary Egyptian concepts of kingship."[36]

Kashta

Kashta, whose name means "the Kushite," was the brother of Alara.[37] Kashta probably married his sister Pebatma (like Egyptian pharaohs, Kushite kings often married their sisters) and took the title *Sȝ-Re Nb-Tȝwy Kȝ-š-t* (Son of Re, Lord of Two Lands, Kashta). He reigned about thirteen years (760–747 B.C.). A stela in the temple of Khnum by the First Cataract suggests that he already controlled Lower Nubia.

In contrast to Morkot's view that Kashta forcibly seized Thebes,[38] Török suggests that the Thebans welcomed the Kushites as an ally against other rulers who had divided Lower Egypt among themselves. As evidence, he cites the double dating of the Divine Adoratrice, Shepenwepet I (the daughter of Osorkon III) and Amenirdis I (the daughter of Kashta), who was adopted as the wife of Amon, at Thebes.[39] Both Adams and Welsby believe that Kashta may have forced the high priestess of Amon to adopt his daughter.[40] Kashta was buried in tomb 8 in el-Kurru.

Piankhy (Piye)

The name of Kashta's son, Piankhy, means "the Living One." His standard dates are 747–716 B.C. Russmann explains the spelling of the name *Piye*:[41]

K. H. Priese has convincingly demonstrated that native speakers of this Kushite name did not vocalize the ankh sign with which it is written. On these grounds, the name is better transcribed as Piye; this form has become almost standard in the subsequent literature. However, inasmuch as this account deals primarily with Egyptian history and monuments, I prefer to retain an Egyptian transliteration of the name.[42]

36. Török, *Kingdom of Kush*, 144.
37. Eide et al., *Fontes Historiae Nubiorum*, 43.
38. Morkot, *Black Pharaohs*, 161.
39. Török, *Kingdom of Kush*, 149–50.
40. Adams, *Nubia*, 260; Welsby, *Kingdom of Kush*, 63.
41. Earlier scholars thought that Piankhy and Piye referred to different individuals. See Morkot, *Black Pharaohs*, 20.
42. Russmann, "Egypt and the Kushites," 127 n. 17.

Piankhy was the real founder of the 25th Dynasty, though Manetho ignores him and gives that honor to his successor. He styled himself after the title of Thutmose III in the Amon temple at Gebel Barkal:[43] "Strong Bull Appearing [i.e., Crowned] in Thebes" and "Strong Bull Appearing in Napata." A sandstone stela erected in his third year has this declaration: "Amon of Napata has granted me to be ruler of every foreign country. He to whom I say, 'You are chief!' he is to be chief. He to whom I say, 'You are not chief!' he is not chief."[44]

His famous conquest of Egypt in his twentieth year (728 B.C. or possibly 732 B.C.)[45] is described in splendid fashion on a stela found in 1862 in his Amon temple.[46] It is nearly 6 feet high, 4 feet 7 inches wide, and contains 159 lines of text. Scholars are effusive in their praise for the composition and the details contained in this Triumphal Stela. Török declares: "The text of the Stela represents also as a literary document an exceptional achievement. Its style, the monumental proportions and balance of the composition, the wide spectrum and refinement of literary quotations, the sophistication of certain essential passages."[47] According to J. H. Taylor: "The various incidents of the expedition are described with exceptional candour and vividness on a stela erected in the Temple of Amon at Gebel Barkal."[48] Adams comments: "The commemorative stela of Piankhi . . . is one of the masterpieces of ancient literature."[49] J. Leclant describes it as "one of the longest and most detailed texts of Ancient Egypt."[50] According to S. M. Burstein, this "commemorative inscription is the finest extant example of Egyptian historical writing."[51] K. Myśliwiec declares: "It is one of the most important historical documents bequeathed to us by pharaonic Egypt."[52]

43. At Gebel Barkal, Amon was depicted as criocephalic, that is, with a ram's head; at Thebes, he is depicted as anthropomorphic.

44. Eide et al., Fontes Historiae Nubiorum, no. 8.

45. As the stela was inscribed in the king's twenty-first year, most scholars date his campaign to his twentieth year. See Lichtheim, Ancient Egyptian Literature, 3.68. Morkot (Black Pharaohs, 184) prefers year four or twelve. For the various dates proposed for this invasion, see Morkot, Black Pharaohs, 316. The extremely late date of 712 or 709 offered by Depuydt, "Date of Piye's Egyptian Campaign," must be rejected.

46. Eide et al., Fontes Historiae Nubiorum, 47–51. An army officer found this stela and sent a copy of it to Auguste Mariette, who ordered it brought to Cairo. It took two years for the transport of the 2.25-ton monument. The definitive study of the stela is Grimal, La stèle triomphale de Pi(ʿank)y.

47. Török, Kingdom of Kush, 162.

48. Taylor, Egypt and Nubia, 38.

49. Adams, Nubia, 248.

50. Leclant, "Empire of Kush," 161.

51. Burstein, Ancient African Civilizations, 7.

52. Myśliwiec, Twilight of Ancient Egypt, 73. For a detailed commentary on the campaign, see Spalinger, "Military Background."

The text begins by describing the aggressive actions of Tefnakht of Sais, who in alliance with Nimlot (an alternative spelling is Namart) of Hermopolis marched south against the city of Heracleopolis. Piankhy ordered his troops to march north from Thebes, whereupon Tefnakht withdrew to Hermopolis. After the new year, Piankhy departed from Napata to Thebes, where he celebrated the Opet festival.[53] He then attacked the walled city of Hermopolis with wooden towers from which archers and slingers operated. According to A. Kuhrt, "The description of the siege and fall of Hermopolis, as recounted by Piye in his victory stela, is one of the most vivid pieces of Egyptian historical writing."[54]

When Nimlot offered his wives and daughters to him, Piankhy claims that he "did not direct his gaze at them." What is particularly striking is his reaction to horses that were starving: "His majesty proceeded to the stable of the horses and the quarters of the foals. When he saw they had been [left] to hunger he said: 'I swear, as Re loves me, as my nose is refreshed by life: that my horses were made to hunger pains me more than any other crime you committed in your recklessness!'"[55] The finest horses in the Near East were bred in Kush and exported even to Assyria, with personnel to accompany them.[56] These horses are described at Nineveh as *kusaya*, that is, horses from Kush. According to S. Dalley: "The earliest mention of Nubians in Assyrian administrative records is probably that of the Nimrud Wine List No. 9, which has been redated, following collation, to 732 B.C., during the reign of Tiglath-pileser."[57] Thus the practice of importing horses from Nubia must have begun then.[58] L. A. Heidorn adds: "It is clear, however, that the Sudan was known as a horse-breeding region in recent centuries and that the Dongola Reach—the area of ancient Kush—had a long tradition as the home of the country's finest breed."[59]

Piankhy proceeded to capture the key city of Memphis. He offered his respects to the god of Memphis, Ptah, and also to the god of Heliopolis, Re. At Athribis only Nimlot was allowed to enter the palace, because the others "were uncircumcised and fish-eaters." Piankhy then withdrew to

---

53. The Opet festival at Thebes celebrated the triad of Amon, his consort Mut, and their son Khonsu, whose statues were carried in boat shrines between the temples of Karnak and Luxor. A contemporary boat festival celebrated by Muslims in the same area may retain some recollections of that celebration. See Wachsmann, "Sailing into Egypt's Past."

54. Kuhrt, *Ancient Near East*, 2.629.

55. Lichtheim, *Ancient Egyptian Literature*, 3.73.

56. Neo-Assyrian texts also mention Kushite eunuchs and Kushite women workers.

57. Dalley, "Foreign Chariotry and Cavalry," 44.

58. In 716 King Shlkanni of Musri (i.e., Osorkon IV of Egypt) sent a gift of twelve large horses to Sargon II. Morkot, "There Are No Elephants," notes that Assyrian kings as early as Ashurnasirpal II were receiving ivory, probably procured from elephants in Nubia.

59. Heidorn, "Horses of Kush," 114.

his home in Napata and set up his victory stela in the temple at the base of Gebel Barkal.[60]

The relief on the top of the stela shows Piankhy facing the seated Amon, with the goddess Mut behind. Behind the king are Nimlot and his wife, who has her hand raised lifting a sistrum. Below them are the defeated rulers Osorkon IV, Iuput II, Petubast, and Pediese and four chiefs of the Libyan Meshwesh, prostrating themselves.[61] Kendall comments on the irony of the Kushite's triumph:

> Here is Piye, a foreigner, whose ancestors were once depicted being trodden beneath the sandals of the pharaoh, who has now become the pharaoh himself, a brother king to a Thutmose or a Ramesses, who has employed his sculptors, probably all Egyptian, to depict his conquest over Lower Egypt just as one of the Egyptian kings of an earlier age might have depicted a victory over Asiatics, Libyans, Hittites, Sea Peoples, or even Kushites.[62]

Piankhy was buried at el-Kurru in a pyramid grave. Though he may have been inspired by the sight of the great pyramids at Giza near Memphis, his and later Kushite pyramids were much smaller and had steeper slopes, resembling more the New Kingdom tombs near Thebes.[63] The base of his pyramid was only 8 meters square.[64] An offering chapel was added on the eastern face. He also was the first to adopt the Egyptian practice of enclosing *shawabti*, or substitute figurines, though in contrast to Egyptian custom, these were uninscribed. Another Egyptian practice was the placement of the major internal organs in canopic jars. Hereafter the royal dead were mummified and laid in anthropoid wooden coffins.[65] Though the original treasures were looted, a large bronze offering tray was recovered from the tomb of his wife Khensa at el-Kurru.[66]

A most un-Egyptian practice that Piankhy initiated was to have some of his horses buried upright in pits. Some scholars believed that they had been decapitated. Kendall suggests instead that their heads were probably removed by looters since the horses must have been richly capari-

---

60. Grimal, *History of Ancient Egypt*, 339.

61. For an illustration of this relief, see Morkot, *Black Pharaohs*, 17.

62. Kendall, *Gebel Barkal Epigraphic Survey*, 18.

63. According to O'Connor (*Ancient Nubia*, 69), the average diameter of the Kushite pyramids was 13.5 meters. Of the later pyramids at Nuri, Reisner ("Preliminary Report," 62) reports: "Leaving aside the great pyramid of Tirhaqa, who possessed unusual wealth and power, there is one pyramid of 32 meters square, fourteen of 27–28 meters, and five of 10–12 meters."

64. That is, the base was but one-tenth that of the Great Pyramid. See Edwards, *Pyramids of Egypt*, 256; Brier, "Other Pyramids."

65. On the Egyptian cult of the dead, see Yamauchi, "Life, Death, and the Afterlife."

66. Morkot, *Black Pharaohs*, 177.

Figure 4.2. Offering table of
King Piankhy (bronze,
Nubian, reign of Piankhy,
747–716 B.C.) (©2002
Museum of Fine Arts,
Boston).

soned.[67] Welsby notes: "Recent work has showed that fragments of skulls
were found, indicating that the animals had not been decapitated before
burial as had previously been thought."[68]

Shabako

Shabako was a younger son of Kashta and brother of Piankhy. His
reign, which had been dated to 716–702, must now be redated four to
five years earlier according to some scholars.[69] In his second year he
traveled north to establish border security in the Sinai.[70] As Vercoutter
observes: "One thing at least is certain, Shabaka did not interfere with
the Apis cult, but on the contrary paid his tribute to the god as soon as
he reached Memphis by seeing that his name was inscribed in the burial

67. Kendall, *Gebel Barkal Epigraphic Survey*, 43–44.
68. Welsby, *Kingdom of Kush*, 290.
69. Frank Yurco, letter to author, November 2002.
70. Eide et al., *Fontes Historiae Nubiorum*, 125.

chamber of the animal god and so ensuring that he should benefit by the god's blessing."[71]

It is perhaps because Shabako remained in Egypt that Manetho considered him the founder of the 25th Dynasty. Remains of his buildings are found at Bubastis, Athribis, Memphis, Abydos, Dendera, Esna, Edfu, and Thebes. At Karnak he constructed the Treasury of Shabako. Near the sacred lake he erected a portico of twenty columns, and at the fourth pylon at Karnak he redecorated the gate called "Amon-Re is Awesome" with gold.[72] He revived the office of the chief priest of Amon, installing his son Horemakeht in that post.[73] As he was still the ruler of Kush, he commanded an enormously long if narrow stretch of territory. According to Welsby: "Shabaqo went far beyond the brief [sic] of Piye and carved out for himself a massive empire extending at least 3,379 km along the Nile, which was only surpassed in size on the conquest of the Sudan by Mohammed Ali in 1819–20."[74]

The only military activity of Shabako himself is a reference in a scarab, which reports that he massacred rebels in Upper and Lower Egypt. Shabako's commander, Re'u, fought the Assyrians near Raphiah at the southern border of Palestine, where he was defeated by them. When Osorkon IV of Bubastis in 716 contacted the Assyrian king Sargon II, he was deposed by Shabako. Tefnakht's successor at Sais, Bocchoris (Bakenrenef), rebelled against Kushite rule. Manetho claims that Shabako burned Bocchoris alive.

Yamani, a rebel leader of Ashdod, whose name possibly means "The Greek,"[75] rebelled in 712 against the Assyrians[76] and then fled through Egypt to the border of Kush. It had been thought earlier that Shabako was the ruler who extradited him to the Assyrians, "loading him down with chains, fetters, and iron bands." But an inscription of Sargon II found in the Zagros Mountains reveals that Shebitku extradited Yamani (see under "Shebitku," below).

It thus appears that cordial relations were established with the Assyrians for a time. According to Morkot: "In these early years, the Kushites

---

71. Vercoutter, "Napatan Kings and Apis Worship," 67. On the alleged stabbing of the Apis bull by King Cambyses of Persia, who conquered Egypt in 525 B.C., see Yamauchi, *Persia and the Bible*, 115–22; on the honoring of the Apis by Alexander the Great and his successors, see 523–24.

72. Yoyotte, "Un porche doré."

73. Grimal, *History of Ancient Egypt*, 344.

74. Welsby, *Kingdom of Kush*, 64. In sharp contrast to Shabako's many buildings in Egypt, little from his reign has been uncovered in his homeland.

75. Some scholars doubt such an identification. On Greeks in the Near East, see Yamauchi, *Persia and the Bible*, 382–84.

76. Spalinger, "Year 712 B.C."

seem to have maintained friendly relations with Assyria, and seals from
Kuyunjik (i.e., Nineveh) suggest that Sargon and Shabako exchanged diplomatic correspondence."[77]

One very important religious document from Shabako's reign is a large
granite stela now entitled "The Theology of Memphis," exalting the city's
main god, Ptah.[78] Ptah is hailed as "he who made all and brought the
gods into being." Shabako claimed that he copied the text from an ancient
worm-eaten document. The stone unfortunately was greatly damaged
when it was later used by farmers as a millstone! Although Myśliwiec believes that the text reflects the theology of the Old Kingdom,[79] other scholars now date it to the late New Kingdom. According to R. A. Fazzini:
"Once attributed to the Old Kingdom or even earlier, the Memphite Theology is now considered no earlier than Ramesside in origin, and some
would interpret it as a kind of pious and political archaizing 'forgery' of
D[ynasty] XXV."[80]

Shabako died at Memphis. His corpse was taken up the Nile and buried at el-Kurru. His tomb was once surmounted by a pyramid, 36 feet on
each side, with a funerary chapel on its east side.

Herodotus correctly reports that the "Ethiopians" ruled Egypt for fifty
years (2.137) and portrays Shabako (whom he calls Sabacos) as a ruler
who, instead of executing criminals, forced them to reinforce embank-
ments around their towns.[81] Herodotus also hails him as a "great archi-
tect," and Diodorus Siculus remembers him as a righteous and pious
king.

Shebitku

Shebitku was the son[82] or nephew[83] of Shabako. His highest attested
reign in Egyptian documents is only year three. It is certain that his successor Taharqa began his reign in 690. Kitchen assigns Shebitku twelve
years and dates his reign to around 702–690, partly on the rationale that
hostile relations between the new Assyrian king, Sennacherib, who invaded Judah in 701, may have been caused by the accession of a more ag-

77. Morkot, *Black Pharaohs*, 208.

78. *ANET* 4–6.

79. Myśliwiec, *Twilight of Ancient Egypt*, 89.

80. Fazzini, *Egypt*, 7.

81. On the mixed value of Herodotus for Egypt and other areas, see Yamauchi, "Herodotus—Historian or Liar?"

82. A relationship favored by Török, *Kingdom of Kush*, 169; cf. Eide et al., *Fontes Historiae
Nubiorum*, 127.

83. That is, the son of Piankhy, a relationship favored by Kitchen; see also Russmann,
"Egypt and the Kushites," 118; Redford, *Egypt, Canaan, and Israel*, 354.

gressive Kushite king.[84] But already in the reign of Sargon II reliefs show
the Assyrians in 720 attacking fortified cities in southwestern Palestine,
which are being defended by ambidextrous Kushite soldiers.[85] This forms
the background of Isaiah 20:1: "Sargon king of Assyria sent his com-
mander-in-chief [*tartān* = Akkadian *turtannu*] to Ashdod, and he took it
by storm," which led to the prophet's warning in 20:5: "All men shall be
dismayed, their hopes in Cush and their pride in Egypt humbled" (New
English Bible).[86]

In 1999 a new inscription of Sargon II, found in the Zagros Mountains of
western Iran at Tang-i Var, was published. Concerning a rebel leader from
Ashdod, it reports that "he fled to the region of the land of Meluḫḫa[87] and
lived (there) stealthfully (lit. like a thief)." "Šapataku' (Shebitku), king of
the land of Meluḫḫa heard of the mig[ht] of the gods Aššur, Nabû, (and)
Marduk. . . . He put (Iamani) in manacles and handcuffs. . . . He had him
brought captive into my presence."[88] The new Tang-i Var inscription of
Sargon II thus establishes that Shebitku extradited Yamani; since Sargon II
died in 705, Shebitku was thus ruling by 706.[89] Some, therefore, argue that
his reign must now be redated to 706–690.[90] Kitchen, however, understands the Akkadian word *šarru* in the more general sense of a subordinate
ruler, that is, of Kush and not of Egypt, under Shabako, and holds that a re-
vision of dates is not necessary.[91]

Sennacherib's Invasion of 701

Speaking of the wealth of biblical and extrabiblical sources for Sennacherib's invasion of 701, which involved Judah's resistance under

---

84. Kitchen, *Third Intermediate Period in Egypt*, 385, 583. He assumes a two-year coregency.

85. Franklin, "Room V Reliefs at Dur-Sharrukin," 265. For other reliefs of Kushites in
Assyrian sculptures, see Reade, "Sargon's Campaigns"; and Albenda, "Observations on
Egyptians."

86. Three fragments of Sargon's monumental stela were found at Ashdod. See Hestrin et
al., *Inscriptions Reveal*, 32 (English section), 58 (Hebrew section).

87. Originally Meluḫḫa designated a country to the east of Mesopotamia, such as Iran or
the Indus River Valley. See Jaritz, "Tilmun-Makan-Meluḫḫa"; Gelb, "Makkan and Meluḫḫa." In this period, Meluḫḫa designated Kush (Nubia).

88. Frame, "Inscription of Sargon II," 40.

89. Unless the Assyrian document is interpreted to mean that Shebitku was king of the
area of Kush, while Shabako was still the king of Egypt, as Kitchen maintains. Morkot, *Black
Pharaohs*, 316: "The Tang-i Var inscription indicates that Shebitqo was ruling in Kush *before*
his accession as pharaoh in Egypt. Yurco had attempted to posit a co-regency between the
two kings, but no explicit evidence of such an arrangement has been found." See Yurco,
"Shabaka-Shebitku Coregency."

90. See Kahn, "Inscription of Sargon II."

91. Kitchen, "Regnal and Genealogical Data," 50–51.

Figure 4.3. Shebitku's tomb at el-Kurru (Derek A. Welsby).

Hezekiah and the attempted intervention of the Cushite/Egyptian army, Peter Machinist comments:

> Not only are the biblical texts for it extensive and varied, bespeaking its importance for the ancient Judaeans, but they can be supplemented and coordinated, more than for any other event in Israelite history, by a range of extra-biblical evidence, both written and non-written. In fact, the existence of Assyrian annalistic accounts of the campaign and of a detailed Assyrian palace relief sequence of one of its episodes, the siege of Lachish, allows the rare chance to look at the event from two sides, Assyrian as well as Israelite.[92]

After his accession in 704 upon the untimely death of his father Sargon II on the battlefield in eastern Turkey,[93] Sennacherib first had to deal in 703 with the troublesome Chaldean rebel, Merodach-Baladan, who proclaimed himself king in Babylon.[94] He then reasserted his domination of

---

92. Machinist, "*Rab Šâqêh* at the Wall of Jerusalem," 153. For a general summary, see Gallagher, *Sennacherib's Campaign to Judah.*

93. The death of Sargon II took place in Tabal; his body was not recovered. See Yamauchi, *Foes from the Northern Frontier,* 25–27, 52–53.

94. Merodach-Baladan had already engaged the Assyrians under Sargon II in 720 and 710–709. Isaiah 39:1–8 (//2 Kings 20:12–19) depicts his embassy to Hezekiah as a solicitous inquiry after the Judean king's health; in addition, it was no doubt an attempt to enlist him as an ally against the Assyrians. See Yamauchi, "Chaldea, Chaldeans."

the Levant, after numerous revolts took place there. Revolts were led in
Sidon by Lule and in Ashkelon by Sidka.[95] As the Assyrians advanced,
Lule fled to Cyprus but Sidka was carried off to Assyria. The nobles of Ek-
ron rebelled against their ruler Padi and the Assyrians. A five-line inscrip-
tion discovered at Ekron names both Padi and his son Achish.[96] Rulers of
Sidon, Byblos, Ashdod, Moab, and Edom proffered their submission.

The biblical records and the Assyrian documents agree that Hezekiah
paid considerable tribute to the Assyrians. Sennacherib boasts that
Hezekiah surrendered a tribute of "30 talents of gold, 800 talents of silver,
precious stones, . . . elephant-hides, ebony-wood, box-wood (and) all
kinds of valuable treasures, his (own) daughters, concubines, male and female musicians."[97] Sennacherib also claims that he deported 200,150 persons from Judah.[98]

The Siege of Lachish

The successful siege of the southern Judean fortress of Lachish is well
attested by both Assyrian texts and reliefs[99] and by the excavations there.
Excavations in 1978–89 by D. Ussishkin confirm that the destruction of
level III can be ascribed to the Assyrian invasion.[100] Especially striking is
the siege ramp, which was constructed with 13,000–19,000 tons of rubble.
Sennacherib's famous Lachish reliefs portray five siege vehicles with bat-
tering rams ascending the ramp. The defenders attempt to set fire to the
vehicles and turn away the rams with chains, one of which was found at
the site. Archers fire arrows and slingers hurl stones. Hundreds of arrowheads were found, but as Ussishkin notes, "Significantly, three-pronged
'Scythian' bronze arrowheads, which were later used by the Babylonian

95. Grimal, *History of Ancient Egypt*, 346.

96. Dothan, Gitin, and Naveh, "Royal Dedicatory Inscription from Ekron"; Dothan, "Ekron's Identity Confirmed"; Naveh, "Achish-Ikausu." For a general survey of the archaeological evidence, see Stern, *Archaeology of the Land of the Bible*, vol. 2.

97. *ANET* 288. Thomas, *Documents from Old Testament Times*, 67, revises the number of silver talents to 300 to correspond to the amount listed in 2 Kings 18:14.

98. On this controversially large number, see Stohlmann, "Judaean Exile"; Millard,
"Large Numbers"; Younger, "Deportations of the Israelites"; cf. Yamauchi, "Archaeological
Background of Ezra"; idem, "Eastern Jewish Diaspora."

99. Sixty feet of the reliefs from Sennacherib's palace in Nineveh depicting the siege of
Lachish are now in the British Museum.

100. The site of Lachish was excavated initially by J. L. Starkey from 1932 until his murder in 1938. For a long time there was a dispute as to whether the destruction level was to be
attributed to the Assyrian attack of 701 or to the Babylonian attack of 597. Scholars such as B.
Mazar, R. Amiran, and O. Tufnell (Starkey's successor) favored the former, while W. F. Albright, G. E. Wright, K. Kenyon, and Y. Yadin favored the latter. See Ussishkin, "Answers at
Lachish"; idem, *Conquest of Lachish by Sennacherib*; idem, "Assyrian Attack on Lachish."

army, are completely missing here."[101] The excavations also uncovered a mass grave of 1,500 victims.

Jerusalem Besieged

Judah was ruled by Hezekiah, a pious worshiper of Yahweh,[102] who was advised by the prophet Isaiah to defy the Assyrians.[103] In preparation for the anticipated siege, Hezekiah had two teams of workers start from the Gihon spring at one end and the Siloam pool at the other end and dig the famous Siloam tunnel in Jerusalem (2 Chron. 32:1–8). An inscription found at the pool describes the meeting of the two teams.[104]

Critical scholars discern two accounts in the biblical text: A = 2 Kings 18:13–16 and B = 2 Kings 18:17–19:37//Isa. 36:2–37:38, with A regarded as accurately corresponding to the Assyrian annals, whereas B is regarded by many scholars as a later account or one relating to a second invasion (see below).[105]

The Assyrian official known as Rab-shaqeh (NIV: "field commander") spoke before the walls of Jerusalem (Isa. 36:11) in Hebrew, rather than in Aramaic[106] as requested by the Jewish leaders, taunting the Jews with the evidence of the invincibility of the Assyrian army and the failure of Yahweh to deliver the towns that had already been captured.[107] But it is quite clear that despite the Assyrian king's boasts, he did not capture Jerusalem; nor did he require Hezekiah to appear at Nineveh.[108] According to

101. Ussishkin, "Assyrian Attack on Lachish," 75. On the Scythian arrowheads used in the siege of Jerusalem by the Babylonians and their implications for the use of Scythian mercenaries, who may possibly be identified with the "foes of the north" in Jeremiah's prophecies, see Yamauchi, *Foes from the Northern Frontier*, chap. 5.

102. Na'aman, "Debated Historicity of Hezekiah's Reform."

103. See Childs, *Isaiah and the Assyrian Crisis*.

104. Thomas, *Documents from Old Testament Times*, 209–11; ANET 321. The inscription, which was found in 1880 during the Ottoman Empire's control of Palestine, is in the Istanbul Museum.

105. The most comprehensive critical study comparing the biblical accounts and the Assyrian sources is Gonçalves, *L'expédition de Sennachérib en Palestine*. For a succinct summary, see Dion, "Sennacherib's Expedition to Palestine." See also Seitz, "Account A and the Annals of Sennacherib." Clements, *Isaiah and the Deliverance of Jerusalem*, is dismissive of account B. For an account that integrates the biblical evidence, the Assyrian texts, and the archaeological data, see Millard, "Sennacherib's Attack on Hezekiah"; idem, "On Giving the Bible a Fair Go."

106. Some deduce that the Rab-shaqeh may have been a deported Israelite who knew Hebrew. See Ben Zvi, "Who Wrote the Speech of Rabshakeh?" On the development of Aramaic as a lingua franca from the Neo-Assyrian period on, see Yamauchi, "Aramaic."

107. There are many striking parallels to Rab-shaqeh's speech in Assyrian documents. See, e.g., Saggs, "Nimrud Letters," 55.

108. See Cogan, "Sennacherib's Siege of Jerusalem."

W. R. Gallagher: "Finally Sennacherib's account ends abruptly. There is no return march to Nineveh; Sennacherib just appears there at the end of the account. It raises the suspicion that Sennacherib's scribes concealed something."[109] A. Spalinger expresses a similar suspicion:

> Therefore, it would appear that there is something concealed in this official account of Sennacherib. The two great victories that the Assyrian monarch boasts of occurred in quite small places (Timnah and Elteqeh). Sennacherib was unable to conquer Jerusalem and the "tribute" that Hezekiah is supposed to have sent him actually occurred some time after 701 B.C. The main instigator of the revolt, Hezekiah, was not in the least way harmed.[110]

According to A. R. Millard, "Hezekiah was treated lightly in comparison with many. Loyal vassal kings were normally allowed to retain their thrones under Assyrian suzerainty, with considerable independence, but Hezekiah had not been loyal."[111] Nor was Judah turned into an Assyrian province.

The biblical account attributes the victory to the intervention of the Lord's angel of death; scholars speculate that a possible plague may have devastated the Assyrian army. Herodotus (2.141) reports that a legion of mice gnawed the Assyrian weapons, suggesting the possibility of rats, who may have borne the fleas that transmitted the plague. Berossus also reports a potential sickness. Gallagher observes:

> How vulnerable was Assyria to epidemic diseases? The eponym lists show that epidemics broke out in Assyria in 802, 765 and 759. Another epidemic occurred in Sargon's 15th year, i.e. 707 B.C. It was perhaps one reason why Sargon undertook no campaign in 706. Eighth-century Assyria was thus vulnerable to epidemics, and in 701 the danger of diseases may have been especially great.[112]

Lord Byron in his memorable poem "The Destruction of Sennacherib" described the disaster to the Assyrian army thus:

> The Assyrian came down like the wolf on the fold,
> And his cohorts were gleaming with purple and gold;
> And the sheen of their spears was like stars on the sea,
> When the blue wave rolls nightly on deep Galilee.
>
> Like the leaves of the forest when Summer is green,
> That host with their banners at sunset were seen;

109. Gallagher, *Sennacherib's Campaign to Judah*, 141.
110. Spalinger, "Foreign Policy of Egypt," 35.
111. Millard, "Sennacherib's Attack," 71.
112. Gallagher, *Sennacherib's Campaign to Judah*, 247.

Like the leaves of the forest when Autumn had blown,
That host on the morrow lay withered and strown.

For the Angel of Death spread his wings on the blast,
And breathed in the face of the foe as he passed;
And the eyes of the sleepers waxed deadly and chill,
And their hearts but once heaved and for ever grew still![113]

Simply reading the biblical narrative (2 Kings 19:36–37) one might get the impression that an immediate judgment from Yahweh was the murder of Sennacherib by his sons. This did not take place, however, until 681 B.C. Cuneiform sources confirm that Esarhaddon's brothers were responsible for their father's death.[114]

The Reference to Tirhakah

What is of particular interest to the subject of this book is the biblical reference to Tirhakah, the brother of Shebitku, as leading an Egyptian army that momentarily distracted the Assyrians (2 Kings 19:9//Isa. 37:9). The biblical text refers to Tirhakah as "king," when it is certain that he began his reign only in 690 B.C., which causes some scholars[115] to simply dismiss the biblical reference as unhistorical.[116] According to Spalinger: "It is better to view the mention of 'Taharqa, King of Kush' in verse 19.9 as an anachronism."[117]

Other scholars suggest that Sennacherib conducted *two* campaigns against Judah. This was first proposed by G. Rawlinson in 1858 and followed by scholars such as E. A. W. Budge, H. R. Hall, and W. F. Albright. It is presented in Bright's *History of Israel* and by A. K. Grayson in the *Cambridge Ancient History* and defended by S. H. Horn.[118] The most persistent and vigorous advocate of two campaigns is W. H. Shea, who raises various arguments in its favor.[119]

According to this scenario, the first invasion of Sennacherib resulted in a battle with an Egyptian army at Eltekeh, followed by a siege of Jerusa-

113. Morrison, *Masterpieces of Religious Verse*, 63.

114. See Shea, "Murder of Sennacherib."

115. Gallagher, *Sennacherib's Campaign to Judah*, 222: "I shall postulate that 19:9 is wrong and Taharqa was not involved in the war of 701."

116. Redford (*Egypt, Canaan, and Israel*, 353 n. 163) holds that the author of 2 Kings 19 was simply mistaken.

117. Spalinger, "Foreign Policy of Egypt," 40.

118. Bright, *History of Israel*, 298–309; Grayson, "Sennacherib and Esarhaddon," 111; Horn, "Did Sennacherib Campaign Once or Twice?"

119. Shea, "Sennacherib's Second Palestinian Campaign"; idem, "New Tirhakah Text"; idem, "Jerusalem under Siege"; idem, "Murder of Sennacherib."

lem and Hezekiah's agreement to pay tribute. Then a second campaign around 689 resulted in the capture of Lachish, a second siege of Jerusalem, and the intervention of the Egyptian army led by Taharqa, after he had become king in 690.

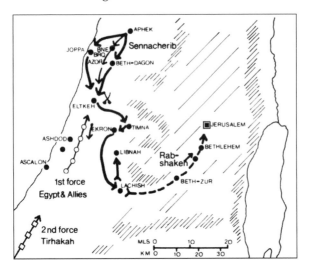

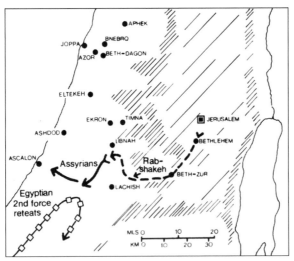

Figure 4.4. Movements of Assyrian and Egyptian forces in 701 B.C. (Kenneth A. Kitchen).

One Campaign

Kitchen argues convincingly for only one Assyrian campaign under Sennacherib and shows that as Taharqa was about twenty in 701, he could well have led the army then.[120] The reference to Taharqa as "king" is then to be taken as a proleptic designation, inasmuch as the account was certainly written after he had become king. Another possibility is mentioned by Shea (who does not himself favor it): "If Shebitku was the king of Nubia as early as 712 B.C. then perhaps Taharqa could have been the king of Nubia as early as 701 B.C., even though he did not take the throne in Egypt until 690 B.C."[121]

Shebitku summoned his brother Taharqa from Nubia to Egypt, according to the former's Kawa inscription: "For whom His Majesty, King Shebitku, justified, had sent to Bow-land (Nubia), in order that he (Taharqo) might be there with him (Shebitku), because he (Shebitku) loved him (Taharqo) more than all his (other) brothers."[122] According to the Kawa IV Stela, Taharqa brought an army with him.

The Assyrian annals locate the clash with Taharqa's army at Eltekeh in Philistia, northwest of Judah, while the Assyrian army was on its way from Joppa to Ekron. According to the Assyrian annals, Sennacherib boasted:

> In the plain of Altaqu, their ranks were drawn up before me, they sharpened their weapons. Upon a trust (= inspiring) oracle (given) by Assur, my lord, I fought with them and brought about their defeat. The Egyptian charioteers and princes, together with the charioteers of the Kushite king, my hands took alive in the midst of the battle.[123]

Since the biblical account (2 Kings 19:8–9) indicates that Sennacherib was already at Libnah in Judah when he heard of the approach of the Egyptian army, Kitchen postulates two battles at Eltekeh.[124]

Török optimistically characterizes the Kushite intervention as follows: "The battle at Eltekeh could be interpreted as a victory for the double

---

120. See Kitchen, *Third Intermediate Period in Egypt*, 383–86, 553–57; cf. also idem, "Late-Egyptian Chronology"; idem, "Further Thoughts on Egyptian Chronology"; idem, "Egypt, the Levant and Assyria." According to Yurco ("Shabaka-Shebitku Coregency," 36): "Most have tended to favor strongly only one—namely, the Third Campaign, conducted in 701 B.C. . . . Most Israeli biblical archaeologists likewise have opted for one campaign, dated 701 B.C., because that is the situation indicated by the stratigraphy of sites such as Lachish and Ekron." See also Gallagher, *Sennacherib's Campaign to Judah*, 8; Cogan and Tadmor, *II Kings*, 248–50. Kitchen's position is supported by Bates, "Could Taharqa Have Been Called?" By analogy, while crown prince, Alexander played a strategic role in commanding the cavalry at the battle of Chaeronea when he was but eighteen. See also Hoffmeier, "Egypt's Role in the Events of 701 B.C."

121. Shea, "Murder of Sennacherib," 38. Cf. Redford, "Note on the Chronology," 60.

122. Eide et al., *Fontes Historiae Nubiorum*, 139, 144.

123. Cited by Dion, "Sennacherib's Expedition to Palestine," 24.

124. Kitchen, *Third Intermediate Period in Egypt*, 384–85, 556.

kingdom."[125] Going even further, H. T. Aubin in a highly imaginative tour
de force credits the Kushite army with the "rescue of Jerusalem."[126]

On the contrary, the biblical account describes Taharqa's intervention
as a failure, thus confirming Isaiah's frequent warnings (18:1–4; 30:1–8;
31:1–3) about the folly of relying upon the "splintered reed" of Egypt (Isa.
36:6; cf. Ezek. 30:14–16). According to N. Na'aman, "Isaiah's warnings
were not vain words."[127]

Taharqa's Family and Accession

Taharqa was the son of Piankhy and the younger brother of Shebitku,
whom he succeeded.[128] He claimed to be the descendant of Senusret III,
the Egyptian conqueror of Kush.[129] He married several of his sisters and
had at least three sons; his most important daughter was Amenirdis II,
who became the God's Wife of Amon.[130]

Taharqa, who reigned for twenty-six years from 690 to 664, was without question the most important pharaoh of the 25th Dynasty.[131] After his
accession, he spent most of his time in Egypt: in Tanis according to the
Hintzes and Welsby,[132] in Memphis according to Myśliwiec and Russmann.[133] When he became pharaoh, Taharqa called his mother from Kush
to be with him in Lower Egypt:

> [Now my mother] was in Bow-land (Nubia);
> Namely, the king's sister, sweet of love, the king's mother, Abar,
>   may she live.
> Moreover, I had departed from her as a recruit of twenty years
> when I came with His Majesty [i.e., Shebitku] to North-land.
> Then she came sailing north to see me after a period of years.
> She found me appearing on the throne of Horus,
> after I had received the diadems of Rê
> and was wearing the uraei on my head
> all the gods being the protection of my body.
> She was exceedingly joyful.[134]

125. Török, *Kingdom of Kush*, 170.
126. Aubin, *Rescue of Jerusalem*.
127. Na'aman, "Hezekiah and the Kings of Assyria," 243.
128. Livingston's thesis in "Tirhaka: King of Ethiopia," is unfounded.
129. Leclant, *Recherches sur les monuments Thébains*, 394.
130. Eide et al., *Fontes Historiae Nubiorum*, 131.
131. An extensive bibliography on Taharqa may be found in Leclant, "Taharqa."
132. Hintze and Hintze, *Civilizations of the Old Sudan*, 18; Welsby, *Kingdom of Kush*, 64.
133. Myśliwiec, *Twilight of Ancient Egypt*, 93; Russmann, "Egypt and the Kushites," 118.
134. Eide et al., *Fontes Historiae Nubiorum*, 153–54.

Taharqa's Athleticism

In 1977 a remarkable stela was found in the area west of Memphis on a desert road about three miles west of the pyramid of Pepi II. This reveals the athleticism of the pharaoh and of his troops:[135]

> (When) he ran with them on the back of the desert of White-wall (Memphis)
>   in the ninth hour of the night.
> They reached the Great Lake (Lake Qarun) in the first hour of the day
> and (then) returned to the Residence in the third hour of the day.
> He [distinguished] the first of them
> and let them eat and drink with the elite force.
> [He] (also) distinguished [those who] (came) after them
> and rewarded them with every (kind of) thing—
> for, you see, His Majesty (really) liked the work of battle that was given to
>   him.[136]

That is, "a part of this well trained army was able to run at long distances to reach the Faiyûm from Memphis after 5 hours, having covered a distance of about 50 km. (30 miles)."[137] This means that they averaged one mile every ten minutes—for five hours![138]

Taharqa's Piety

What is most striking about the piety of Taharqa and the other Kushite pharaohs of Dynasty 25 was their complete allegiance to the pantheon of Egyptian gods. This may be seen from the inscriptions that Taharqa engraved and the buildings he erected. For example, from the unique temple that he built by the Sacred Lake at Karnak, we learn details of the ceremonies that the king would have observed there.[139]

After Taharqa arrived, he would be presented to the gods, for whom he would slaughter four animals and offer incense to the solar gods Harakhty and Atum. He would offer a second series of offerings to Amon-Re and Mut. Taharqa claimed that Re had given him the authority to judge people and to purify a world threatened by Apophis. Taharqa is shown with baboons, who represent the god Thoth, adoring Re, the sun god, at dawn.

135. Altenmüller and Moussa, "Die Inschriften der Taharkastele," 57.
136. Eide et al., *Fontes Historiae Nubiorum*, 161.
137. Moussa, "Stela of Taharqa," 337.
138. For other examples of athleticism in the ancient Near East, see Yamauchi, "Athletics in the Ancient Near East."
139. Parker, Leclant, and Goyon, *Edifice of Taharqa*, 80: "In the archaeology and history of Egypt, the edifice of Taharqa by the Sacred Lake of Karnak remains even now a monument of a unique type, puzzling, and because of this, often ignored."

Figure 4.5. Kneeling
Taharqa, from Kawa
(©British Museum).

Herodotus, borrowing from Hecataeus, described Egypt as "the gift of
the Nile." The annual and predictable flood of the Nile not only irrigated
the land but also provided nutrients for the soil's fertility. A Nile that was
too low would not irrigate enough land; on the other hand, too high a Nile
could produce damage to the irrigation system. In year six of Taharqa's
reign, he gave thanks to an especially beneficial flood, which he interpreted as the manifestation of divine favor for his piety toward Amon-Re:

> Now His Majesty is one who loves god,
> so that he spends his time by day and lies by night
> seeking what is of benefit for the gods,
> (re)building [their] temples if they have fallen into decay,
> "giving birth" to their statues as on the first occasion,
> building their storehouses, endowing their altars,
> presenting to them endowments of every kind,
> making their offering-tables of fine gold, silver, and copper.[140]

As a result, the king claimed: "This land has been overflowed (with abundance) in his time as it was in the time of the Lord-of-all, every man sleeping until dawn, without saying, 'Would that I had!,' at all, Ma'at being introduced throughout the countries, and Inequity being pinned to the ground."[141]

An unusual text inscribed on the back of a stela of Thutmose III, previously ascribed to Shoshenq I, is now interpreted by P. Vernus as a plea of Taharqa to his god, after some setback in the land of Khor (i.e., Palestine) about 677 B.C., which had cut off offerings for the god.[142] Though Taharqa does not blame his god for the setback, neither does he himself take responsibility for the disaster.[143] As Amon does not leave things half done, the god must now take charge. Shea uses this text to support his view of a second campaign by Sennacherib.[144] F. J. Yurco demurs: "For all of the ambiguity in this text, caused in no small part by Taharqa's attempt to explain trouble in Philistia without blaming either himself or his deity, Amun, the main thrust is clear. . . . There is nothing in Taharqa's text nor in Spalinger's analysis of any suggestion that Taharqa's mysterious debacle was a military defeat suffered in a clash with Assyrian troops."[145]

Depictions of Taharqa

Russmann comments: "Representations of Taharqa confront us with almost an embarrassment of riches. In stone, in bronze, and in relief, far more remains of this king than of any other in his dynasty."[146] In addition to the Negroid features,[147] a number of distinctive Kushite details

140. Eide et al., *Fontes Historiae Nubiorum*, 148.

141. Cited in Török, *Kingdom of Kush*, 280.

142. Vernus, "Inscriptions de la troisième intermédiaire"; see Eide et al., *Fontes Historiae Nubiorum*, 186; Kitchen, *Third Intermediate Period in Egypt*, 558.

143. Spalinger, "Foreign Policy of Egypt," 22.

144. Shea, "Sennacherib's Second Palestinian Campaign," 413–14; idem, "Murder of Sennacherib," 37–38.

145. Yurco, "Shabaka-Shebitku Coregency," 43.

146. Russmann, *Representation of the King*, 16.

147. Myśliwiec, *Twilight of Ancient Egypt*, 85: "The Kushite kings are always represented as broad-shouldered persons with short, thick necks. Their faces display African features, in particular, fleshy lips and broad, flat noses."

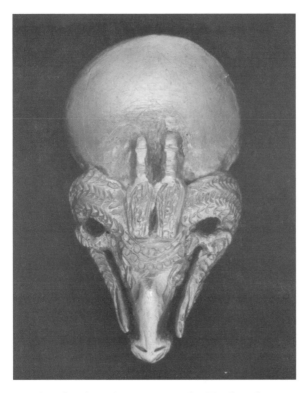

Figure 4.6. Gold ram-
head earring (Nubian,
sixth century B.C.)
(©2002 Museum of Fine
Arts, Boston).

are also displayed. Unique to the Kushite kings is the double uraei, that
is, the two serpents on the forehead, representing their rule over both
Egypt and Kush. The majority of scholars believe that the Kushite kings
wore a skullcap.[148] Russmann disagrees: "However, closer examination
strongly suggests that it was, in fact, a bare head with close-cropped
hair."[149]

Particularly striking is a granite lion with Taharqa's head, now in the
British Museum. Bronze figurines depict him striding or kneeling. In his
tomb at Nuri, Taharqa deposited more than 1,070 *ushabti* (*shawabti*) figurines of varying sizes.[150] As this was more than twice the number placed
in New Kingdom tombs, Myśliwiec wonders: "Was this to provide two
huge work forces to serve the Lord of the Two lands who ruled over such
a great empire?"[151] The *ushabtis* were made of varied stones: serpentine,
granite, limestone, calcite, alabaster, syenite, and ankerite.

148. Török, *Royal Crowns of Kush*, 4–14.
149. Russmann, "Egypt and the Kushites," 122.
150. Welsby, *Kingdom of Kush*, 87. Some are nearly two feet high.
151. Myśliwiec, *Twilight of Ancient Egypt*, 105.

Figure 4.7. Taharqa as a
sphinx, from Kawa
(©British Museum).

A stela of Esarhaddon towering over two captives is interpreted by
some scholars (e.g., Kuhrt) as a statue of the groveling Taharqa.[152] This is
more probably the statue of his son, the crown prince Ušanaḫuru, who
was captured in the Assyrian invasion.[153]

Taharqa's Buildings

Taharqa built on a lavish scale in Egypt, especially in Memphis and
Thebes. Adams observes: "The surviving monuments of Taharqa, both in
Egypt and in Nubia, outnumber those of all the other XXV Dynasty pharaohs combined."[154] Taharqa built splendid colonnades at the four entrances to the temple at Karnak and, within each, small chapels dedicated
to Amon and Osiris. We have already mentioned his unique building by
the Sacred Lake, which was partly underground.[155]

152. Kuhrt, *Ancient Near East*, 2.634.
153. Redford, *Egypt, Canaan, and Israel*, 360: "He is next to Ba'al of Tyre, as he had the te-
merity to revolt."
154. Adams, *Nubia*, 265.
155. Fazzini, *Egypt*, 22.

Figure 4.8.
Taharqa's
ushabtis,
from his
pyramid at
Nuri
(©British
Museum).

Besides his buildings in Lower Egypt and Upper Egypt, Taharqa was
the first in many centuries to build upriver from the First Cataract. At
Qasr Ibrim, a site not inundated by Lake Nasser because it stood on a
high bluff, Taharqa built a mud-brick temple, which was later converted
into a Christian church. He also erected a mud-brick temple on Semna Island, together with an altar dedicated to Senusret III, the Egyptian conqueror of Kush![156]

Downstream from Kerma and the Third Cataract at Sedeinga, Taharqa
erected a small pyramid, 32 feet on a side, made of blocks of slate. Its
function is unclear; perhaps it was a cenotaph (i.e., a memorial tomb without a burial).

Upstream from Kerma at Kawa, Taharqa established a major religious
sanctuary to the god Amon. Its earlier Egyptian name, Gem-[p]-Aten, indicates that it was established in the Amarna period. Between 1930 and
1936, scholars from Oxford University, including F. L. Griffith, M. F. L.

156. Dunham and Janssen, *Second Cataract Forts,* 1.12.

Figure 4.9. Esarhaddon towering over two captives, including Taharqa's kneeling son (Staatliche Museen zu Berlin—Preussischer Kulturbesitz, Vorderasiatisches Museum).

Macadam, and L. P. Kirwan, excavated only the central part of the city. Morkot comments: "But the evidence from those excavations shows that it was a city of great religious importance from the Napatan period until its destruction in the later years of the Meroitic kingdom."[157] Taharqa employed artisans from Memphis, who replicated the style of Old Kingdom statuary. Three stelae from this sanctuary are among the most important

157. Morkot, *Black Pharaohs*, 136.

inscriptions for Taharqa's reign. They reveal that in year 10 of his reign (ca. 680 B.C.), he was able to import cedar wood from Lebanon.[158] And "Asiatics" (i.e., Semites) were brought there to care for the gardens of the temple.

Figure 4.10. View of Gebel Barkal, the holy mountain, from the southeast (December 21, 1916) (©2002 Museum of Fine Arts, Boston).

At Gebel Barkal, Taharqa carved two chapels in the side of the mountain; one of them has Hathor columns and images of Bes, a grotesque dwarfish deity who protected women in childbirth. An inscription states that it was built for the goddess Mut and was to function as a birth house.

In 1987 Kendall, in a daring feat, built a scaffold to examine the isolated pinnacle of Gebel Barkal, because on an earlier visit he had detected an inscription high up. The text was placed by Taharqa at a height of over 200 feet above the plain. Kendall reports: "It is carved near the top of the southwest pinnacle, a massive turret-like rock shaft separated from the cliff edge by a deep gorge about 11 meters (36 feet) across."[159] The badly worn inscription reports a victory of Taharqa over the Libyans. Kendall's report created a great sensation at the Fifth International Congress of Egyptologists at Cairo, because it revealed the extraordinary engineering

158. Eide et al., *Fontes Historiae Nubiorum*, 176.
159. Kendall, *Gebel Barkal Epigraphic Survey*, 3.

that the Kushites must have employed in order to engrave the inscription.[160] According to Myśliwiec:

> The interpretation of the needle of rock at Gebel Barkal as a giant uraeus finds its confirmation in an as yet unpublished relief at Abu Simbel from the reign of Ramesses II. It depicts Gebel Barkal, and the part of the Pure Mountain that interests us is represented as a huge uraeus-serpent wearing the white crown of Upper Egypt. It is emerging from a throne on which Amun is seated inside the mountain. There can be no doubt that the entire rock massif was regarded as a huge and unique seat of this god.[161]

Esarhaddon's Invasions of Egypt

After the murder of Sennacherib, Esarhaddon (680–669 B.C.) ascended to the Assyrian throne after punishing his brothers. He was at first very concerned about the incursions of Cimmerians and Scythians on his northern frontier, as his queries to the diviners reveal.[162] In contrast to his father's hostile policy toward Babylon, Esarhaddon helped to rebuild the ravaged city.[163] He forced the Medes to swear "vassal treaties" to safeguard the accession of his sons.[164]

Because Taharqa was stirring Phoenician cities to rebel against the Assyrians, Esarhaddon mounted a series of campaigns against him. In 678 Esarhaddon took the town of Arza on the border of Egypt, but in 673 he suffered a defeat, which understandably is not noted in Assyrian records but is reported in the more objective Babylonian Chronicle: "The troops of Assyria were defeated in the land of Egypt."[165] He mounted a successful invasion in 671, defeating Taharqa. In his inscriptions, Esarhaddon boasts:

> I conquered Tyre, which is in the midst of the sea; its king Baal, who trusted upon Taharqa (*Tar-qu-ú*) he trusted, I took away all his city and its harbor.
> I conquered Egypt, Patros,[166] and Kush, its king Taharqa I wounded five times with my arrow, his entire land I took possession of and ruled.[167]

160. Kendall, "Kingdom of Kush."
161. Myśliwiec, *Twilight of Ancient Egypt*, 104. See also Russmann, "Egypt and the Kushites," 122.
162. See Yamauchi, *Foes from the Northern Frontier*, chaps. 3–4.
163. See Yamauchi, "Babylon."
164. See Wiseman, *Vassal-Treaties of Esarhaddon*.
165. Spalinger, "Esarhaddon and Egypt," 301.
166. Patros is derived from the Egyptian *p3 t3 rsy* (the Southern Land) and may mean all the area south of Memphis or the area of Upper Egypt from Aswan southward.
167. Borger, *Die Inschriften Asarhaddons*, 86.

In his journey across the northern Sinai, Esarhaddon was aided by Arabs who carried water for him, just as they did later for the Persian conqueror of Egypt, Cambyses, in 525 B.C. The Assyrian king boasted that he captured Memphis in a half day: "His wife, his concubines, his crown prince, Ušanaḫuru (i.e., Nes-Anhuret) and his other sons and daughters, their possessions, horses,[168] cattle and small flocks I led in innumerable numbers to Assyria." He proclaimed: "The root of Kush I tore out of Egypt."[169] Other captives included archers, shield bearers, animal physicians, singers, bakers, carpenters, and snake charmers.[170] He then appointed officials to collect tribute from the Egyptians. He was preparing a new campaign against Egypt when he died en route in 669.

Ashurbanipal's Invasion of Egypt

Ashurbanipal (668–ca. 627 B.C.) was the last great ruler of the Assyrian Empire. He is famed for his great library at his capital, Nineveh.[171] When the Egyptians rebelled upon the death of his father, Ashurbanipal captured Memphis in 669. When he later learned of plots involving rulers from the Delta and Taharqa, he pursued the latter all the way upriver to Thebes in 664.[172] According to Ashurbanipal, Taharqa "heard of the approach of my expedition (only when) I had (already) set foot on Egyptian territory. He left Memphis and fled into Thebes to save his life."[173] Afterward Taharqa retreated to his homeland, where he died during the same year.

One of the Delta rebels, Necho I (Akkadian *Niku*), was pardoned by the Assyrians and reinstalled at Sais. He became the founder of the 26th Dynasty. His son, Psammetichus I, was placed on the throne of Athribis, another Delta city.

The Tomb of Taharqa

After fleeing to his homeland, Taharqa died in 664. He was buried in a new cemetery at Nuri, about five miles upstream from Gebel Barkal and on the opposite bank. With few exceptions, all of the subsequent Napatan

168. A tablet from Nineveh records that 50,000 horses were removed from Egypt. See Török, *Kingdom of Kush*, 181.
169. Ibid., 99. See also *ANET* 293.
170. Some critics object to the use of Hebrew *ḥartummîm* (magician) in Dan. 1:20; 2:2; et al. as highly suspect because it is derived from Egyptian. Yet Akkadian documents from Mesopotamia indicate the presence of such Egyptian specialists in Babylon. See Yamauchi, "Archaeological Background of Daniel," 9–10.
171. Yamauchi, "Nineveh."
172. See *ANET* 295.
173. *ANET* 295.

Figure 4.11. Pyramids at Nuri (Derek A. Welsby).

pharaohs until the fourth century B.C. were buried here under about sixty royal pyramids. The base of Taharqa's large pyramid was 28.5 meters square. Reisner, who dug here in 1916–1918, found no trace of the king's burial.

Tantamun

The last ruler of the 25th Dynasty was Tantamun (also called Tanwetamani), who ruled from 664 to 656. He was the younger brother of Shebitku (i.e., the son of Shabako) and the nephew of Taharqa.[174] In a "Dream Stela," Tantamun claims that he was given a divine mission to win back Egypt:

> In the year 1, or his coronation as king . . . his majesty saw a dream by night: two serpents, one upon his right, the other upon his left. . . . Then they answered him saying: "Thine is the Southland; take for thyself also the North-land." The Two Goddesses shine upon thy brow, the land is given to thee, in its length and breadth. No other divides it with thee.[175]

After stopping at Elephantine, where he sacrificed to Khnum, and at Thebes, where he sacrificed to Amon, he proceeded to Memphis,

174. Leahy, "Tantuamon, Son of Shabako?" See also Eide et al., *Fontes Historiae Nubiorum*, 209.
175. Breasted, *Ancient Records of Egypt*, 4.469.

where he paid homage to Ptah. He then defeated Necho of Sais.[176] Ashurbanipal, upon hearing the news, counterattacked and forced Tantamun to flee south to Thebes and, when that city was captured, to escape to Napata. Ashurbanipal claimed: "I made Egypt (Masur) and Nubia feel my weapons bitterly and celebrated my triumph. With full hands and safely I returned to Nineveh, the city (where I exercise) my rule."[177]

The sack of Thebes by the Assyrians in 663 was a memorable event. Massive booty was taken from Thebes, including "silver, gold, gems, costumes, chattels, and even obelisks!"[178] Before the fall of Nineveh in 612, the prophet Nahum used the sack of Thebes by the Assyrians as a warning to the Assyrians themselves (Nah. 3:8–9 NIV; cf. Jer. 46:25):

> Are you better than Thebes,[179]
>   situated on the Nile,
>   with water around her?
> The river was her defense,
>   the waters her wall.
> Cush and Egypt were her boundless strength;
>   Put and Libya were among her allies.

Unlike Taharqa, Tantamun was buried in the older cemetery of el-Kurru in tomb 16. From the sack of Thebes until the death of Tantamun, the historical situation remains unclear. Even though Tantamun, who still claimed the title *pharaoh*,[180] never returned to Egypt, "events in Thebes continued to be dated in terms of the years of his reign."[181] At the same time, even after Psammetichus I (664–610 B.C.) of Dynasty 26[182] was recognized in Thebes, officials who had been installed by the Kushites—such

---

176. According to Spalinger, "Assurbanipal and Egypt," 323, Necho probably died during this conflict.

177. *ANET* 295.

178. Redford, *Egypt, Canaan, and Israel*, 364.

179. The King James Version reads "No" after the Hebrew loanword *Nōʾ ʾāmôn*, from Egyptian *n.t* (city). See Huddleston, "Nahum, Nineveh, and the Nile."

180. Adams, *Nubia*, 249, observes: "As late as the third century A.D. Nubian rulers still called themselves by the pharaoh's traditional titles, 'Lord of the Two Lands' (i.e., Upper and Lower Egypt), 'Beloved of Amon,' and so on, though none of them had set foot in Egypt for nearly a thousand years." On the tomb of Tantamun, see Albers, "Pyramid Tomb of Tanutamen."

181. Grimal, *History of Ancient Egypt*, 352.

182. The 26th Dynasty ruled Egypt until the Persian Cambyses conquered the country in 525 B.C. See Yamauchi, *Persia and the Bible*, chap. 3. In contrast to Török (*Kingdom of Kush*, 187), Spalinger ("Psammetichus, King of Egypt") argues that the king's Ionian and Carian mercenaries sent by King Gyges of Lydia were used not against the Assyrians but against the other Delta rulers.

Figure 4.12. Mask of
Queen Malakaye (gilt
silver, Nubian, reign of
Tantamun, 664–655
B.C.) (©2002 Museum of
Fine Arts, Boston).

as Shabako's grandson, Harkhebi, the high priest of Amon of Thebes (ca. 660–644 B.C.)—continued to retain their offices.[183]

Adams summarizes the significance of the Kushite 25th Dynasty as follows:

> The achievements of the "Ethiopian" pharaohs during the three generations of their rule in Egypt had not been inconsiderable. They restored the northern country to unity, however, temporarily, for the first time in more than three hundred years. Their building activities in and around Thebes, though modest by New Kingdom standards, were nevertheless more extensive than those of any ruler since Ramesses IV. . . . Their aim was nothing less than the restoration of Egyptian culture and religion to their original "purity."[184]

Mentuemhet

Quite amazingly through all the dynastic changes, including the sack of Thebes by the Assyrians, a rather remarkable individual, Mentuemhet,

183. Eide et al., *Fontes Historiae Nubiorum*, 193.
184. Adams, *Nubia*, 267.

Figure 4.13. Relief of Mentuemhet
approaching Anubis (Egyptian)
(Nelson-Atkins Museum of Art).

held his position and power for twenty-six years. At his height he controlled the area extending from Aswan north to Hermopolis. Russmann
marvels:

During a career that spanned the last part of the Kushite Twenty-fifth Dynasty and the Assyrian sack of Thebes, an eight-year interregnum during which southern Egypt was politically autonomous, and finally the re-establishment of royal control by the Twenty-sixth Dynasty, Mentuemhat was the most powerful official in Upper Egypt, and sometimes its *de facto* ruler.[185]

His third wife Wedjarenes was a Kushite, the granddaughter of Piankhy.[186] He himself was not a Kushite, but was from a well-established Theban family.[187] He held numerous titles, including Prince of the City (i.e., of Thebes),[188] Governor of Upper Egypt, and Fourth Prophet (of Montu). He is mentioned in the annals of Ashurbanipal as Manti-me-(an)-ḫê.

According to the famous Adoption Stela of Nitocris, the daughter of Psammetichus I, Mentuemhat still held his offices in the ninth year of the new dynasty. Judging from the size of his donations to Nitocris[189] and his splendid tomb, one of the largest and most elaborate private monuments in Egypt, he was a very wealthy man who played a key role in a peaceful transition during a time of great turmoil.

Figure 4.14.
Relief of a divine
votaress and the
goddess Hathor
(sandstone,
Egyptian,
Dynasties 25–26,
ca. 760–525 B.C.) (©2002
Museum of Fine Arts, Boston).

185. Russmann, "Relief Decoration," 1.
186. Russmann, "Mentuemhat's Kushite Wife," 26, describes her as follows: "The corresponding image shows her as a Kushite, with the thick, columnar neck characteristic of Twenty-fifth Dynasty kings, and her hair closely cropped, in the Kushite manner."
187. Leclant, *Montouemhat*, 261–68.
188. He succeeded a Kushite Kelbasken as mayor of Thebes.
189. Caminos, "Nitocris Adoption Stela."

Figure 4.15. Amenirdis I, daughter of
Kashta (Joslyn Art Museum, Omaha,
Nebraska).

The God's Wife

An important institution at Thebes, which also helped to unify Egypt
through changes of dynasty, was the office of the "God's Wife," that is, the high
priestess of Amon.[190] During Dynasties 25 and 26, this position was held by a
celibate royal princess. According to Leclant: "Under the XXVth dynasty in ef-
fect, the Theban region was essentially the domain of the Divine Adora-
trices."[191] The God's Wife controlled great wealth and power and built shrines
for her funerary cult in the Theban area across the river near Medinet Habu.
The God's Wife is even portrayed in activities once reserved for kings.[192]

190. See Gitton and Leclant, "Gottesgemahlin"; Troy, *Patterns of Queenship*, 97–99.
191. Leclant, *Recherches*, 353.
192. Fazzini, *Egypt*, 24.

About 760 B.C. Osorkon III had his daughter, Shepenwepet I, appointed God's Wife of Amon. When Piankhy came to power, he had Shepenwepet I adopt Amenirdis I, the daughter of Kashta, as her successor.[193] Amenirdis I in turn about 720 B.C. adopted Shepenwepet II, daughter of Piankhy, during Taharqa's reign. Shepenwepet II served for fifty years in this office. Later (about 690 B.C.) Taharqa had his own daughter, Amenirdis II, adopted in this office. When Psammetichus I came to power, he had the last two Kushite priestesses adopt his daughter, Nitocris, as a successor in 656 B.C. According to Török: "This manner of appointment was chiefly intended to support the legitimacy of the Adoratrice's father both on a cultic and a practical political level."[194]

The Adoption Stela of Nitocris from the ninth year of Psammetichus I (656 B.C.) was discovered in 1897. This is regarded as one of the most important documents of the Saite Period (26th Dynasty). Psammetichus says explicitly that he determined not to expel Taharqa's daughter, but decided instead to present his own daughter, Nitocris, to be adopted by her. According to R. Caminos: "Nitocris must have been very young at the time, since she is known to have died seventy years later, in 586 B.C."[195] The adoption stela of her daughter, Ankhnesneferibre, was discovered in 1904. She was to hold this office for over sixty years.[196] The striking longevity of some of these God's Wives indicates how well fed and cared for they must have been. Even for the royalty in Egypt, the average life span was about forty years, although there were many exceptions to this average.[197]

Psammetichus II

For reasons that are not clear, in his third year (593 B.C.) Psammetichus II launched a major campaign southward against the Kushites. The Tanis version of this campaign has it ending at the island of Sai, between the Second and Third Cataracts. Another version found in 1964 at Shellal near Aswan has the campaign reaching Pnubis, south of the Third Cataract.[198] Adams (relying on Herodotus 2.30–31) believes that the expedition reached Napata near the Fourth Cataract.[199] J. Yoyotte and S. Sauneron speculate that some advanced units may have reached the Fifth Cataract.[200] On their way back the army vandalized some of the Kushite inscriptions. What is most fascinating

---

193. Alara, an earlier Cushite ruler, dedicated his sister as a sistrum player to Amon. See Török, *Kingdom of Kush*, 234.

194. Ibid., 149.

195. Caminos, "Nitocris Adoption Stela," 99.

196. Leahy, "Adoption of Ankhnesneferibre," 148.

197. See Adamson, "Human Diseases and Deaths."

198. Eide et al., *Fontes Historiae Nubiorum*, 279.

199. Adams, *Nubia*, 268.

200. Yoyotte and Sauneron, "La campagne nubienne," 190.

are the graffiti of Greek and Carian mercenaries, who inscribed their names
on the leg of one of the colossi of Ramesses II at Abu Simbel.[201] Psammetichus
II claimed to have brought back 4,200 prisoners.[202] After his victory over
Kush, the pharaoh made a triumphal tour of the Levant in 591, which may
have influenced the Jews to turn once again toward Egypt for help, this time
against the Babylonians, despite the warnings of Jeremiah.

The Napatan king at the time of the 593 invasion was Aspelta (593–568
B.C.). The Election Stela of Aspelta recounts his descent from seven generations of female ancestors.[203] Reisner's excavations at Nuri discovered two
huge stone sarcophagi of Aspelta and of his predecessor, Anlamani. Aspelta's
sarcophagus was brought to the Museum of Fine Arts in Boston, while Anala-
mani's remained in the Sudan at Khartoum.[204] Aspelta built temples at Meroe
and at Defeia near Khartoum. Though the Kushites did not worship their
kings during their lifetime, the Coronation Stela of Aspelta describes the de-
ceased king as a god.[205] After Aspelta, there is a gap of about 150 years in our
historical knowledge. By the fourth century B.C. the center of Kushite power
had shifted farther south to Meroe, between the Fifth and Sixth Cataracts.

Cushi, the Father of Zephaniah

Zephaniah prophesied during the reign of Josiah (640–609 B.C.).
Rather unusually his genealogy is traced back for four generations: he is
listed as "son of Cushi, son of Gedaliah, son of Amariah, son of
Hezekiah" (1:1). Does this mean that his father was a Cushite? R. L.
Smith answers "probably not," because "the fact that the three ancestors
before Cushi have good Hebrew names indicates that Zephaniah's family was Judean even though there might have been some intermarriage
in or foreign influence on the family."[206] R. D. Haak allows this possibility: "It does not seem unlikely that a person of Ethiopian descent could
become part of the political entity of 'Judah' and even be the father of a
prophet."[207] G. Rice argues that the prophet's interest in Cush (2:12; 3:10)
may be indirect evidence that Cushi was indeed a Cushite.[208] This identi-

201. See Yamauchi, *Greece and Babylon*, 64–66.
202. Manuelian, *Living in the Past*, 330.
203. Török, *Kingdom of Kush*, 236.
204. Doll, "Texts and Decoration"; idem, "Day Hour Texts"; idem, "Identification and
Significance."
205. Welsby, *Kingdom of Kush*, 79.
206. Smith, *Micah–Malachi*, 125.
207. Haak, "'Cush' in Zephaniah," 250.
208. Rice, "African Roots," 29. According to Adamo ("Images of Cush," 67), "one important aspect of this long genealogy is that it makes known to the readers that this prophet is a
black man or has an African ancestry."

fication is also accepted by R. W. Anderson: "Textual references to the presence of Cushites in Syria-Palestine, then, would seem to indicate that at least Jehudi, Zephaniah ben Cushi, Cush of Benjamin and probably Cushi (or several people with this name or designation) were accepted as members of Judean society."[209]

Jehudi and Ebed-Melech

Two Cushite individuals who played different roles in the life of Jeremiah are Jehudi and Ebed-Melech.[210] They were both officials in the court of the Judean king Jehoiakim, who was disturbed by the prophecies of Jeremiah recorded and read by Baruch the scribe.[211] Jehudi son of Nethaniah, son of Shelemiah, son of Cushi (Jer. 36:13–14), was sent to demand Baruch's scroll. This represented a series of sermons that Jeremiah had preached during the fourth year of Jehoiakim (36:1), that is, in 605 B.C., which was the same year that Nebuchadnezzar ascended the throne and attacked Jerusalem (Dan. 1:1; cf. Jer. 46:2).[212]

Ebed-Melech's name literally means "Slave of the King," but this phrase is used honorifically of royal officials to mean "Servant of the King."[213] In Jeremiah 38:7 he is described as a *sarîs*, a word that can be translated "eunuch" in certain contexts.[214]

Since Jeremiah had encouraged the people of Judah to surrender to Nebuchadnezzar, who was the Lord's instrument (Jer. 21:9; cf. 38:1–28), he was accused of treason and arrested (37:11–15). Some of the princes took matters into their own hands and had him placed into a waterless but muddy cistern (38:1–6). By this time Jeremiah was an old man, since he had begun his ministry forty years before, and he would have perished in a short time. At this critical juncture Ebed-Melech informed Zedekiah of what had befallen Jeremiah (38:8–9), whereupon the king ordered Ebed-Melech to take thirty men to rescue Jeremiah (38:10). Ebed-Melech made a rope of rags and worn-out clothes to lift Jeremiah out of the miry pit

209. Anderson, "Zephaniah Ben Cushi," 69.

210. Molin, "'Ebed-Melek."

211. The association of Baruch's seal impression (bulla) with that of Jerahmeel, the king's son, suggests that Baruch was originally a royal scribe. He dared to defy the king's wrath by serving as Jeremiah's secretary. See Avigad, "Baruch the Scribe"; Shanks, "Jeremiah's Scribe and Confidant."

212. This initial attack of Nebuchadnezzar is not explicitly mentioned in Akkadian texts. The apparent discrepancy between Jehoiakim's "third year" and "fourth year" of Jehoiakim for the battle of Carchemish (605 B.C.) may be explained by the fact that there were two dating systems, an antedating and a postdating system. See Wiseman, "Some Historical Problems," 16–18.

213. See Yamauchi, "Slaves of God."

214. Tadmor, "Was the Biblical *Sarîs* a Eunuch?"

(38:11–12). For this act of mercy and courage, Jeremiah prophesied that the Lord would spare Ebed-Melech's life (39:15–18), even when the Babylonians captured the city. In contrast, Zedekiah was captured, made to witness the execution of his sons, and then blinded and taken captive to Babylon (39:1–7). J. D. Hays observes: "Theologically it is significant that a foreigner acted to save the prophet of the Lord. Ebedmelech's Cushitic nationality is mentioned four times (Jer. 38:7, 10, 12; 39:16). While the entire nation of Judah was disobedient to the Lord, it was a black Cushite who confronted the king and delivered Jeremiah."[215]

---

215. Hays, "Cushites," 405; idem, *From Every People and Nation,* 130–38. Cf. Rice, "Two Black Contemporaries," 101: "Indeed, is this not the reason why Ebed-melek is so expressly and emphatically identified as 'the Ethiopian' (four times! 38:7, 10, 12; 39:16)—to emphasize the prophet's utter abandonment by his fellow countrymen?"

5

ROME AND MEROE

Meroe

Meroe, the capital of a Nubian kingdom that flourished for a millennium from around 650 B.C. to A.D. 350,[1] was situated about 960 miles south of the Mediterranean and 600 miles from Aswan.[2] It was located on the east bank of the Nile, between the Fifth and Sixth Cataracts, 145 miles north of Khartoum, the capital of Sudan. Herodotus (2.28–31) was the first classical writer to refer to Meroe.

After the Meroitic civilization declined in the fourth century A.D., Herodotus's account of Meroe was dismissed as legendary until the site was rediscovered by James Bruce in 1772. A French traveler, F. Cailliaud, visited Meroe in 1821 and published his account as *Voyage à Méroé*. In 1830 an Italian, Giuseppe Ferlini, destroyed the top of the impressive pyr-

An earlier version of this essay, titled "The Romans and Meroe in Nubia," appeared in *Itali-Africa: Bridging Continents and Cultures*, ed. Sante Matteo (Stony Brook, N.Y.: Forum Italicum Publishing, 2001), 38–46. Used by permission.

1. The first inscriptional reference to Meroe as a capital does not appear until the Kawa inscription of Irike-Amanote from the second half of the fifth century B.C.

2. For general accounts, see Shinnie, *Meroe*; Millet, "Meroitic Nubia"; Edwards, *Archaeology of the Meroitic State*; Burstein, "Kingdom of Meroe."

amid of Queen Amanishakheto (first century B.C.) and recovered an extraordinary treasure trove of jewelry.[3] Because the jewelry was unique,
Ferlini had a difficult time selling it.[4]

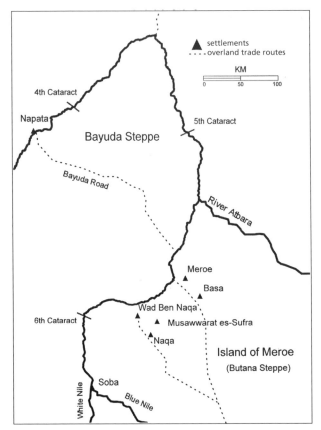

Figure 5.1. Meroitic
sites (S. Mutiti).

Excavations were directed at Meroe from 1911 until 1916 by John
Garstang.[5] These excavations were poorly conducted and only partially
published. Garstang uncovered a great temple of Amon almost 500 feet in
length. He also identified a temple on the outskirts with the Table of the
Sun described by Herodotus (3.17). The Sun Temple discovered by
Garstang dates to the first century A.D., however, and should not be
equated with the Sun Temple described by Herodotus.[6] The wall of the te-

3. Priese, *Gold of Meroe.*
4. Wildung, "Meroitic Treasure," 301.
5. Garstang, *Meroë.* See Török, *Meroe City.*
6. Burstein, "Herodotus and the Emergence of Meroe," 3.

menos surrounding the temple is a square 336 feet on each side. The temple itself is little more than 30 feet long and is surrounded by an ambulatory.[7]

On the south wall of this temple are some detailed battle scenes depicting life-sized Meroitic soldiers armed with swords, lances, and battle axes, defeating enemies who are depicted in miniature size. The enemies are armed with bows and arrows and are sometimes adorned with feathers. They may be native tribes from either the east or the west of the Nile.[8]

Important archaeological work was accomplished in Nubia by George Reisner from 1916 to 1925 in the excavations of the royal cemeteries at Napata and Meroe.[9] Some of Reisner's interpretations, however, are vitiated by his bias that Napata and Meroe are simply debased offshoots of Egyptian civilizations rather than legitimate indigenous cultures.

Excavations were conducted more recently at Meroe by P. L. Shinnie and A. Hakem for the University of Khartoum.[10] Shinnie describes the town as well laid out, with palaces, temples, and ordinary houses, as well as a manufacturing area with iron-smelting furnaces.[11] He also observes: "On the very bottom level of excavation were found traces of postholes showing that some of the inhabitants were living in huts very similar to those used by some of the present-day inhabitants of the area."[12] T. Kendall describes the magnitude of the site as follows:

> Today Meroe is the largest archaeological site in sub-Saharan Africa. Lying about a half a mile from the river, the city ruins alone cover about a square mile in area. Most prominent among these ruins is the huge stone-walled enclosure containing the rubble remains of the palace and government buildings, several small temples (one with painted frescoes), and a so-called "Roman bath" or nymphaeum. Immediately behind it sprawls another walled compound enclosing the Amun Temple, a near copy of the one at Barkal.[13]

A French excavation at Wadi ben Naqa on the Nile south of Meroe uncovered a first-century A.D. royal palace.[14] Storerooms contained timber, ivory, and storage jars. Two temples bore the names of Netekamani and Amanitare in both Egyptian and Meroitic hieroglyphs, which proved to be the key to deciphering the phonetic values of the latter.

7. Hinkel, "Meroitic Architecture," 404–5.
8. Hofmann, "Notizen zu den Kampfszenen."
9. Reisner's assistant, Dows Dunham, published the results in five volumes: *Royal Cemeteries of Kush*.
10. Shinnie and Bradley, *Capital of Kush*, vol. 1.
11. Shinnie, *Ancient Nubia*, 108.
12. Ibid., 110.
13. Kendall, *Proposal to Excavate the "Sun Temple,"* 13.
14. Vercoutter, "Un palais des 'Candace.'"

From 1960 to 1970 the major site of Musawwarat es-Sufra was excavated by F. Hintze for Humboldt University.[15] Shinnie calls this "perhaps
the most remarkable group of buildings in Nubia."[16] This impressive site
includes three major temples, stone ramps, and an elephant statue. A large
enclosure was interpreted as a center for the training of elephants. Just
south of Musawwarat is the site of Naqa, with a temple to Apedemak that
contains important reliefs of Netekamani and Amanitare. Nearby is the so-
called Roman Kiosk, because it reflects influence from Roman prototypes.

J. M. Plumley and W. Y. Adams conducted fruitful excavations at Qasr
Ibrim, which is the only site of Nubia not inundated. Once on a high bluff,
it is now an island. Originally a Ptolemaic fortress, the site was occupied
by the Romans in 30 B.C. and then by the Meroites. A great quantity of
written material in many languages was recovered from the site, including Greek papyri and a Latin letter from the period of the Roman occupation. Upon the signing of the treaty with Augustus, the Meroites were in-
sistent that this key site be returned to them, more for its religious than its
military significance. The Meroite temple became a place of pilgrimage, as
indicated by the carving of numerous feet depressions around the temple.
It is possible that the statue of Isis was carried up the Nile to this site from
Philae annually.

In recent excavations (1996–97) at Doukki Gel, a site near Kerma,
Charles Bonnet and his colleagues uncovered important remains of a
first-century A.D. palace and temple. The large palace was about 130 feet
long and 114 feet broad; unfortunately, it is badly preserved.[17] The temple,
which is as long, is better preserved. In a later season excavators found a
sandstone plaque of a king offering his cartouche to the ram-headed god
Amon.[18] What surprised the excavators was evidence below this temple
of a still-earlier sanctuary from the Napatan period. Associated with this
level was a workshop that made statuettes of Osiris. In the most recent
season (2000–2001) excavators found a further surprise: a temple from the
time of Akhenaten (ca. 1350 B.C.), which replaced a still-earlier temple
from the time of Amenhotep II or Thutmose IV, thus indicating a remarkable continuity of religious sanctity at the site, which lasted a millennium
and a half! The excavators used 70,000 bricks to partially restore the
Meroitic temple.[19]

15. Hintze and Hintze, *Civilizations of the Old Sudan*.

16. Shinnie, *Ancient Nubia*, 111.

17. Bonnet, "Kerma: Rapport préliminaire sur les campagnes de 1995–1996 et 1996–
1997," 110.

18. Bonnet, "Kerma: Rapport préliminaire sur les campagnes de 1997–1998 et 1998–
1999," 72.

19. Bonnet, "Kerma: Rapport préliminaire sur les campagnes de 1999–2000 et 2000–
2001," 205–10.

The Area under the Persians

When the Persian king Cambyses invaded Egypt in 525 B.C., he sent an expedition against the Nubians.[20] Later Darius and Xerxes counted Kush (*Kusa*) as part of the Persian Empire. Kushite troops, wearing leopard skins and lion skins, served in Xerxes' army (Herodotus 7.69). Darius used ivory from Kush for his palace of Susa. Biennial gifts of gold, ebony, and ivory were sent to the Persians from Kush. On the Apadana stairway at Persepolis, the Kushite delegation leads a long-necked animal, which looks like an okapi but may have been intended to represent a giraffe— the tallest animal in the world and therefore a spectacular trophy.

Figure 5.2. Dorginarti (A. Hoerth).

At Dorginarti near the Second Cataract, the University of Chicago under Richard Pierce and James Knudstad uncovered a fort, which was at first identified as coming from either the Middle or New Kingdom. Reexamination of the materials by Lisa Heidorn indicates that the fort should be dated to the Saite and the Persian eras. Heidorn concludes: "Herodotus's account (3.25) concerning the Ethiopian campaign of Cambyses is now lent support by the archaeological evidence from Dorginarti; and when Herodotus mentions gifts given by the Ethiopians to Darius I (3.97),

20. See Yamauchi, *Persia and the Bible*, chap. 3.

Figure 5.3. Dorginarti excavation (A. Hoerth).

it would seem that the Persians exerted some sort of control over at least part of Nubia/Kush during the reign of Darius I."[21]

Ptolemaic Relations with Aithiopia

Ptolemy I marched against Aithiopia (as Kush was called in Greek) in 319–318 B.C., as did Ptolemy II in 274. Thereafter peaceful relations developed for nearly a century, as attested by the presence of Greek luxury goods in Meroitic tombs. Ergamenes I, a Meroitic king contemporary with Ptolemy II (285–247 B.C.), received a Greek education according to Diodorus (3.6). Diodorus also reports that Ergamenes I dared to defy the powerful priesthood. Ergamenes I was the first major king to build his tomb at Meroe. Ergamenes II (218–200 B.C.) later built temples at Philae.

Contacts with Ptolemaic Egypt were frequent in the third century B.C., which has been called the period of the "early Meroitic miracle." S. M. Burstein comments: "Greeks of all sorts—diplomats, intellectuals, artisans, and most important, Ptolemaic elephant hunters—travelled freely throughout Meroitic territory."[22] Kendall notes: "One Simonides was said to have lived there five years and to have written a book about his

21. Heidorn, "Saite and Persian Period Forts," 209.
22. Burstein, *Agatharchides of Cindus*, 7.

adventures."[23] An inscribed drum with the Greek alphabet was found at Meroe.[24] All of these indications freely explain why the Ethiopian eunuch (see chap. 6) could read the Book of Isaiah in the Septuagint version.

Figure 5.4. Cemetery at Meroe (Derek A. Welsby).

Meroitic Civilization

After withdrawing permanently from Egypt about 590 B.C., the Kushites still maintained a remarkable kingdom for about a thousand years until about A.D. 350. About 250 B.C. the royal cemetery was transferred from Napata to Meroe.[25] With the exception of a few pyramids near Gebel Barkal, Meroe remained the royal cemetery for six hundred years. Shinnie notes: "The cemeteries, consisting of pyramids with burial chambers below them, are found in three groups—the southern, northern and western cemeteries."[26] The numerous pyramids at Meroe are smaller and steeper than the Egyptian pyramids; they also do not come to a point but were capped by a level platform. They were built of sandstone, and stood 33 to

23. Kendall, *Kush*, 12.
24. Burstein, *Graeco-Africana*, 111–13.
25. There is evidence that Meroe had been settled since the eighth century B.C.
26. Shinnie, *Ancient Nubia*, 108.

Figure 5.5. Pyramids at Meroe (Steven E. Sidebotham).

98 feet high.[27] The burial chambers were below the surface of the earth. Small chapels were erected on the east side of the pyramids.

The famous Lion Temple built by Arnekhamani (ca. 220 B.C.) at Musawwarat es-Sufra was dedicated to the chief god of the Meroites, Apedemak.[28] Herodotus mistakenly claimed that at Meroe only Zeus (Amon) and Dionysus (Osiris) were worshiped. The Meroites adopted many deities from the Egyptians. Amon of Thebes was called Aman, and they built large temples to him both at the foot of Gebel Barkal and at Meroe. Isis was called Wosi. Her first temple was built only in the time of Harsiyotef (ca. 350 B.C.). Meroites made yearly pilgrimages north to the temple of Isis at Philae, an island near Aswan. Meroitic graffiti from the first century A.D. indicate that Meroitic priests held permanent positions there. Like the Egyptians, the Meroites believed in the divine origin of their rulers as the sons of Amon.

Ergamenes II built an early temple to Mandulis, the local god of Kalabsha. Later a great temple was built at Kalabsha during the time of Augustus. This god was given a guest status at Philae. Not until the Meroitic period (ca. 300 B.C.) do we learn the names of indigenous gods, such as Apedemak, instead of Egyptian gods. Another native god was Sebiumeker, who was the lord of Musawwarat. He is not attested in Egypt.[29]

27. Lehner, *Complete Pyramids*, 199.
28. See Žabkar, *Apedemak*.
29. Wildung, "Meroitic Pantheon," 265.

Figure 5.6. Lion Temple at Musawwarat es-Sufra (Steven E. Sidebotham).

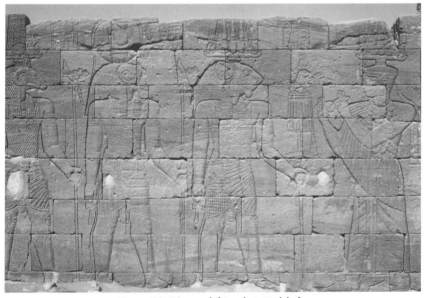

Figure 5.7. Lion god (Derek A. Welsby).

Figure 5.8.
Meroitic offering
table from Faras,
with the deities
Nephthys and
Anubis (©British
Museum).

Except for some very early burials at the Kushite site of Kerma,[30] the sacrifice of retainers to accompany the masters was not normally practiced in Egypt, but magical means of substitute *ushabti* figures, models, and paintings sufficed to ensure sufficient help in the afterlife.[31] However, the sacrifice of retainers is widely attested in Meroitic burials.[32] This may have been accomplished with the aid of aconite, a poisonous bark.[33]

The Roman Intervention into Meroe

After his decisive victory at Actium in 31 B.C. over the naval forces of Antony and Cleopatra, Octavian pursued the couple to Egypt. When Antony and Cleopatra committed suicide, Octavian (renamed Augustus in 27 B.C.) made Egypt his personal province and installed as governor Cornelius Gallus, a poet who was a friend of Virgil.

30. Trigger, *Nubia under the Pharaohs*, 93.
31. Yamauchi, "Life, Death, and the Afterlife."
32. Burstein, *Graeco-Africana*, 33.
33. Dunham, *Two Royal Ladies*, 15.

Excavations at Qasr Ibrim recovered a papyrus copy of a poem composed by Gallus.[34] In 29 B.C. he pushed south past Philae, probably to secure access to the gold mines in the region. At Philae he set up a trilingual (hieroglyphic, Latin, Greek) inscription.[35] The kingdom of Meroe was declared a Roman protectorate, under obligation to pay an annual tribute. A governor (*tyrannus*) was appointed over the Triakontoaschoinos, a stretch of the Nile Valley, 30 schoinoi (240 miles) in length south of Aswan.[36]

Upon recalling Cornelius, Augustus replaced him with Aelius Gallus. Aelius was sent by the emperor to conquer Meroe, a commission that he did not accomplish, despite Augustus's boast in his *Res Gestae* (26): "At my command and under my auspices two armies were led almost at the same time into Ethiopia and Arabia Felix; vast enemy forces of both peoples were cut down in battle and many towns captured. Ethiopia was penetrated as far as the town of Nabata, which adjoins Meroë."[37]

In 25 B.C., taking advantage of the withdrawal of soldiers to provide troops for Aelius Gallus's campaign in Arabia, the Meroites—under the leadership of Queen Amanirenas—launched an attack on Syene (Aswan) and on the islands of Philae and of Elephantine by the First Cataract.[38] It was no doubt on this occasion that they carried off a magnificent bronze head of Augustus that the excavators later found buried under the threshold of a temple at Meroe, so that all who entered would tread over the enemy's head. Some remarkable frescoes were recovered from this temple. One figure represents a light-skinned Roman, the second figure a black Negro, and the third figure a brown-skinned prisoner.[39]

In 24 B.C. Augustus's new commander, C. Petronius, launched a punitive expedition that reached as far south as Napata. He pursued the treacherous Akinidad, who had been appointed by the Romans as *tyrannus*, and the queen, whom he described as "a masculine sort of woman, and blind in one eye." A later Meroite attack upon the Roman garrison at the fortress of Primis (Qasr Ibrim) was unsuccessful. Petronius returned to Primis and left four hundred soldiers there with two years' supplies.

Through diplomacy, peace between the Romans and the Meroites was established. The Meroites obtained very favorable terms in a treaty signed at Samos in 20 B.C. The Romans withdrew from Qasr Ibrim, and the

34. Smith, "Nubia," 135.
35. The Greek version is milder than the Latin version in its assertion of Roman authority. See Burstein, "Cornelius Gallus and Aethiopia."
36. Kirwan, *Rome beyond the Southern Egyptian Frontier*; Desanges, "Les relations de l'empire romain"; Török, "Geschichte Meroes."
37. Brunt and Moore, *Res Gestae Divi Augusti*, 33.
38. Jameson, "Chronology of the Campaigns."
39. Shinnie, "Murals from the Augustus Temple."

Figure 5.9. Head of Augustus found at
Meroe (©British Museum).

Meroites were no longer required to pay tribute. The frontier was established at Hiera Sycaminos (Maharraqa), 68 miles south of Aswan.

This era of peace and prosperity enabled the so-called Ethiopian eunuch to travel to Judea, perhaps on a diplomatic mission (see chap. 6).
Shinnie observes: "The amount of building shows that the first century
A.D. was one of wealth and power in the Meroitic kingdom, but, after the
early part of the century, we have very little information other than the
names of rulers. The presence of imported objects in the tombs shows that
commercial contact with Roman Egypt was maintained."[40]

The peaceful relations established between the Romans and the Meroites were maintained for three centuries, with a garrison of only three co-
horts (about 1,500 soldiers) stationed at Syene, until Diocletian in 297
withdrew the garrison and entrusted the allied Nobades with defending
the area against the marauding Blemmyes.[41]

40. Shinnie, *Ancient Nubia*, 116.
41. Speidel, "Nubia's Roman Garrison," 768–75.

6

WHY THE ETHIOPIAN EUNUCH WAS NOT FROM ETHIOPIA

To understand the New Testament properly, we need to broaden our vision to encompass not only chronological and historical but also geographical data, inasmuch as names over time come to refer to different places.[1] As a historian of the ancient world, I find that many New Testament scholars are confined by tunnel vision to the immediate text, with little awareness of its broader background. Let us take the passage about the "Ethiopian eunuch" in Acts 8:26–40 as an example.

1. For example, the name *Asia*, derived from Hittite *Assuwa*, once designated the area around Ephesus (Acts 19:10). Later the phrase *Asia Minor* corresponded to Turkey; today *Asia* refers to countries such as China and Japan. See Yamauchi, *Archaeology of New Testament Cities*, 15. Another example is the term *India*, which in different texts could mean India, northeast Africa, or South Arabia. See Mayerson, "Confusion of Indias," 171.

The Belief That the Ethiopian Eunuch Was from Ethiopia

Ethiopian Orthodox Christians view the conversion of the eunuch as the foundation of their church.[2] In a major reference work, an Ethiopian scholar states: "The local cultural situation of the first century, identified by Aksum, then the country's capital, does not conflict—what little evidence exists is, in fact, in harmony—with the story of the Ethiopian eunuch's conversion by the apostle Philip (Acts 8)."[3]

The medieval Ethiopian epic *Kebra Negast* not only claimed that the Queen of Sheba, who visited Solomon, was from Ethiopia but also identified this queen as Candace, ignoring the chronological distance of the episodes and thus associating the envoy of the latter with Ethiopia.[4]

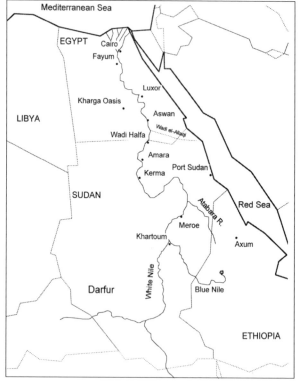

Figure 6.1. Northeast Africa (Michael Lucas).

2. Isaac, *Ethiopian Church*, 18.
3. Haile, "Ethiopian Orthodox Church," 77.
4. Ullendorff, "Candace (Acts 8.27)," 53–54; idem, *Ethiopia and the Bible*, 9.

Modern Ethiopia Was Until Recently Abyssinia

Though some later church fathers may have referred to the kingdom of Aksum as Aithiopia,[5] this area was generally known—the Arabic designation of the country was al-ḥabaša[6]—as Abyssinia[7] from the fourth century until after the Second World War.[8] Aksumite coins from the fourth century bear the legend "King of the Habashat,"[9] and medieval texts speak of the "Queen of the Habasha."[10] King Menelik II (d. 1913) laid the groundwork for the modern country of Ethiopia by expanding his control southward and establishing the new capital of Addis Ababa.[11] It was his great nephew Tafari Makonnen, the Ras or "chief" of the province of Harar, who in 1928 assumed the name of Haile Selassie (Might of the Trinity)[12] and was crowned Negus (emperor) in 1930, only to see his country invaded by the Italians in 1934 under the order of Mussolini.[13]

Afrocentric Bibles

With the laudable aim of interesting African Americans in recognizing the presence of Africans in the Bible, two Bibles were recently published under the influence of Afrocentric scholars:[14] *The Original African Heritage Study Bible* (1993) and *Holy Bible: African American Jubilee Edition* (1999). Rather surprisingly, these reference Bibles do little to enlighten their readers as to the location and nature of the Ethiopia mentioned in Acts.

The Original African Heritage Study Bible contains a rather polemical note on Acts 8:27:

> This is the longest passage in the New Testament that explicitly and unambiguously deals with black Africa in relation to the Holy Land in the New Testament. In some ways it has been a thorn in the flesh of those interpreters who

5. The first Greek writer to designate the kingdom of Axum as Aithiopia was church historian Philostorgius (died ca. 440), according to Dinkler, "Philippus und der ἀνὴρ αἰθίοψ," 90.

6. Wehr, *Dictionary of Modern Written Arabic*, 154.

7. Cf. Buxton, *Abyssinians*.

8. Silverman, "Ethiopia," 75: "Ethiopia was known to the Western world through classical literature as Abyssinia until the end of World War II."

9. Munro-Hay, *Aksum*, 81.

10. Andersen, "Queen of the Habasha."

11. Marcus, *Life and Times of Menelik II*.

12. An influential Caribbean movement known as the Rastafarians regards Selassie as God, much to his displeasure during his lifetime. See Spencer, *Dread Jesus*.

13. Hardie, *Abyssinian Crisis*. For a comprehensive history, see Pankhurst, *Ethiopians*.

14. Afrocentrism tends to exaggerate the black presence in Africa, so that every inhabitant of the continent, including Cyreneans and Egyptians, is viewed as black. See chap. 8.

have harbored a definite racial bias against blacks. Some of them have refused to accept the idea that Ethiopians are to be considered black people and have gone as far as locating biblical Ethiopia as far away as in Mesopotamia.

The Original African Heritage Study Bible contains an essay by Maggie Peebles entitled "African Edenic Women and the Scriptures," in which she makes this unfounded statement about Candace: "She is credited for bringing Christianity to her country by sending her high treasurer the Eunuch to Jerusalem to seek information concerning the teaching of Christ" (p. 1811). *The Original African Heritage Study Bible* also reprints a long sermon by Edward W. Blyden delivered in 1882 entitled "Philip and the Eunuch," in which the preacher asserts: "The eunuch returned to his country . . . and became the founder, it is believed, of the Abyssinian Church, which through various trying vicissitudes, continues to this day" (p. 1835). The more recent *Holy Bible: African American Jubilee Edition* fails in any note on Acts 8 or in two essays to inform its readers about the location and background of the Ethiopia mentioned in this passage.[15]

New Testament Scholars on Acts 8:26-40

Contrary to the diatribe on Acts 8 found in *The Original African Heritage Study Bible*, biblical scholars have long recognized that the reference to Candace identifies Aithiopia[16] as the kingdom of Meroe. All the studies and the score of commentaries on Acts that I examined correctly recognize that Candace was the title of the ruler over the "black" kingdom of Meroe. Most of them cite well-known classical references to this kingdom.[17] But what is rather striking is that with few exceptions[18] there is little awareness of the growing body of scholarship on Meroe.[19]

15. Ntintili, "Presence and Role of Africans," 106; Felder, "Presence of Blacks in Antiquity," 122.

16. In this chapter, I use the word *Aithiopia* to distinguish the ancient country from modern-day Ethiopia.

17. These classical references were known long ago (cf. Grohmann, "Kandake") and were exploited by Lösch, "Der Kämmerer der Königin Kandake." For a more recent exposition, see Bruce, "Philip and the Ethiopian."

18. Exceptions are Martin, "Function of Acts 8:26–40"; idem, "Chamberlain's Journey"; Crocker, "City of Meroe"; Smith, "Do You Understand?" But even these studies hardly do justice to the available scholarship on Meroe.

19. Even in the comprehensive *Anchor Bible Dictionary*, articles by Witherington, "Candace," and Gaventa, "Ethiopian Eunuch," show little awareness of Meroitic studies. For general introductions, see Shinnie, *Meroe*; Hintze and Hintze, *Civilizations of the Old Sudan*; Hintze, "Kingdom of Kush"; Burstein, *Ancient African Civilizations*; idem, "Kingdom of Meroe"; Welsby, *Kingdom of Kush*.

The Location of Meroe

C. J. Martin perceptively notes one major reason for the ignorance of most Bible readers about the location of Aithiopia = Meroe: "Of the useful atlases recommended by Joseph A. Fitzmyer in his excellent reference work, *An Introductory Bibliography for the Study of Scripture*, the majority do not include Meroë (or Nubia) in their maps of the world of the New Testament."[20]

What is little appreciated is the enormous distance that the eunuch traveled and the formidable obstacles that he overcame. Meroe lies nearly one thousand miles south of the Mediterranean coast. Travel within Egypt proper was easy enough: in traveling from south to north, one floated down the Nile; in traveling in the reverse direction, one was aided by the prevailing winds. But at Aswan the traveler encountered a formidable series of cataracts—granite outcroppings that created rapids in the rivers—beginning with the First Cataract and proceeding upstream to the Sixth Cataract.[21]

The Sixth Cataract is 45 miles north (downstream) from the modern capital of the Sudan, Khartoum, where the Blue Nile from Ethiopia joins the White Nile from central Africa. Meroe is located 75 miles northeast of Khartoum. The triangle formed between the White Nile, the Blue Nile, and the Atbara River was the Island of Meroe, well known to classical authors.

Diplomatic and Cultural Exchanges

Meroe's strategic position commanded trade routes into inner Africa, which gave access to highly desirable objects such as ivory and ebony.[22] In the excavation at Wad ben Naga by Jean Vercoutter from 1958 to 1960 a great store of ivory and ebony was found.[23] The Meroites also had gold,[24] slaves, leopard skins, and incense to offer. Despite the great distances involved, archaeological finds at Meroitic burial sites, even after the inevitable looting by tomb robbers, indicate the presence of fine imported jewelry, vases, and wine from Rhodes, the west coast of Asia Minor, and southern France and olive oil from North Africa.[25] These objects came from diplomatic and trade missions.[26]

20. Martin, "Chamberlain's Journey," 121.
21. Kees, *Ancient Egypt*, chaps. 12–13; Baines and Málek, *Atlas of Ancient Egypt*; Vandersleyen, "Des obstacles."
22. Kirwan, *Rome beyond the Southern Egyptian Frontier*, 17.
23. Vercoutter, "Un palais des 'Candace.'"
24. Priese, *Gold of Meroe*.
25. Hofmann, "Der Wein- und Ölimport," 234–35.
26. Török, *Economic Offices and Officials*.

Figure 6.2. Head of a black youth (marble, 2d century B.C.) (Brooklyn Museum of Art).

As F. J. Snowden Jr. observes: "Ethiopian diplomats were not uncommon, since Ethiopian relations with the Ptolemies and Romans involved diplomatic exchanges. Diodorus (3.11.3) interviewed Ethiopian ambassadors resident in Egypt."[27] Many inscriptions of individuals contain the Meroitic titles *apote-leb Arome-li-s* (envoys to Rome) or *apote qor-s* (ambassador of the king).[28] The eunuch had, no doubt, been in Alexandria, where he would have learned about Judaism from the large Jewish population there. And he may have traveled to Judea to establish economic and diplomatic ties with Herod Agrippa I, the new king of the Jews (A.D. 37–44).[29] Like many other foreign tourists, he would have wanted to see Herod's magnificently rebuilt temple.

Meroitic Inscriptions

For a long time the Kushites simply used Egyptian hieroglyphs for their monumental inscriptions. In the late second century B.C. a dis-

27. Snowden, "Ethiopians and the Graeco-Roman World," 27.
28. Török, *Kingdom of Kush*, 65.
29. See Perowne, *Later Herods*, chap. 10.

Figure 6.3. Funerary stela (sandstone, Nubian, 2d–3d century A.D.) (©2002 Museum of Fine Arts, Boston).

tinctive Meroitic script, based on Egyptian, was introduced.[30] The twenty-three Meroitic hieroglyphic signs were borrowed from Egyptian hieroglyphs; the twenty-three Meroitic cursive signs are related to Egyptian hieratic (including fifteen consonantal signs, four syllabic signs, and four vowel signs). The corpus consists of about three hundred texts, many of them funerary texts,[31] from about the second cen-

30. Török, *Kingdom of Kush*, 62.
31. Griffith, *Meroitic Inscriptions*, part 2.

Figure 6.4. Stela of King Tanyidamani (granite gneiss, Nubian, A.D. 160–180) (©2002 Museum of Fine Arts, Boston).

tury B.C. to the third/fourth century A.D. Thanks to a bilingual Meroitic-Egyptian text from the reign of Natakamani (12 B.C.–A.D. 12), F. L. Griffith deciphered the phonetic values of the script in 1910. Since his decipherment, however, almost no further progress has been made. This means that we can read the names of the kings and queens, but we know the meaning of only twenty-six words, among them *ato* (water), *at* (bread), *wi* (brother), *sem* (wife), *kdi* (woman), *mk* (deity), *annata* (priest), *plamusa* (leader), and *qore* (ruler). The variants *kdke*, *ktke*, and *kdwe*, which became the basis of Greek *Kandake* (Candace), may have originally meant king's sister.[32] The Meroitic script outlasted the Meroitic kingdom, as the last inscription is dated to the fourth–fifth century A.D.[33]

Meroitic Chronology

The remarkable Aithiopian kingdoms of Napata and Meroe extended about 1,100 years (from 750 B.C. to A.D. 350).[34] The relative chronology of about seventy kings was established by George Reisner, who between 1916 and 1925 dug at the cemeteries near Napata (Kuru, Nuri, Gebel Barkal) and at Meroe (Begrawiyeh North and South).[35] Reisner divided pyramids into groups and then assigned each one the name of a king or queen known from inscriptions.[36]

The uncertainties of the details of this chronology are underlined by F. Hintze:

> We know only a few fixed points for a period of more than 600 years, and some of these points are not fully reliable. The succession of the pyramids within the groups established by Reisner on the basis of archaeological traits is in many instances still rather uncertain; most of the pyramids have no names so that it is hypothetical and often problematical to associate them with certain rulers. On the other hand, we know many names of kings without being able safely to associate certain pyramids with them. Besides, some pyramids were destroyed or pulled down. . . . Another uncertain factor in reconstructing the Meroitic chronology is the respective length of reign of individual rulers, which can be estimated only in terms of the size and decoration of the pyramids.[37]

32. Török, *Kingdom of Kush*, 63.

33. Priese, "Meroitic Writing and Languages," 255, notes: "Three Meroitic signs were adopted into the otherwise Greek script of Old Nubian."

34. O'Connor, *Ancient Nubia.*

35. The cemeteries at Meroe are in the village of Begrawiyeh.

36. Reisner, "Meroitic Kingdom of Ethiopia," 34–79, 157–60.

37. Hintze, "Meroitic Chronology," 142. See also Gadallah, "Meroitic Problems."

Figure 6.5. Meroitic queen enthroned and protected by Isis
(2d century B.C.) (©British Museum).

Figure 6.6. Statue of
Meroitic queen and two
goddesses (sandstone,
Nubian, early first
century B.C.) (©2002
Museum of Fine Arts,
Boston).

Candace as a Title

After the third century B.C. we see the remains of large pyramids and
buildings bearing the names of queens exclusively, who seem to have
ruled in their own right. The title *Candace* is first mentioned by Bion in

book 1 of his *Aithiopika*. Most scholars believe that the word *Candace* is a title for the queen mother.[38]

According to S. M. Burstein, "Candace was the title of the mother of the Meroitic king. During the late first century B.C. and first half of the first century A.D. several Candaces appear to have functioned as ruling queens."[39] The practice of naming such figures Candace comes to an end after the kings Natakamani, Amanitare, and Sherakarer in the first half of the first century.

W. Y. Adams notes complicating factors in reconciling classical sources with Meroitic inscriptions:

> It must have been the prestige and behind-the-scenes power enjoyed by the Nubian queens which gave rise to the Roman tradition that Kush was governed by a hereditary line of female rulers, all named Candace. The name seems in fact to be a corruption of a Meroitic title (*kdke*) which was borne by all the royal consorts or queen-mothers of Kush; it does not specify a queen-regnant. There were indeed at least five queens regnant during the later centuries of the Kushite dynasty, but no two of them reigned in succession, and it is not certain that they bore the title *kdke*.[40]

Only four queens used the Meroitic title *qore* (ruler):

1. Queen Amanirenas ruled during the last third of the first century B.C.; she is called both *qore* and *kdke* (Candace). Her burial may be in the Barkal pyramid 4.

2. Queen Amanishakheto ruled in the late first century B.C. and early first century A.D. She is also called *qore* and *kdke*. According to L. Török: "The prosperity of her reign is indicated by her building activity at Kawa and Wad ben Naqa, and attested to by the splendid collection of jewels discovered by Ferlini (1837) in a recess on the front side of the pyramid of Beg[rawiyeh] N[orth] 6."[41]

3. Queen Amanitare was coregent with King Natakamani. She is buried in Begrawiyeh North 1. Earlier scholars identified the Candace of Acts 8 as Amanitare, whose reign was dated by Dows Dunham to A.D. 25–41, but her reign is now dated to 12 B.C.–A.D. 12 by F. Hintze.

38. Hintze, "Kingdom of Kush," 98; Welsby, *Kingdom of Kush*, 26. See also Trigger, "La Candace." But Hofmann, "Kleopatra-Kandake," 34, comments: "Ich möchte an dieser Stelle nicht wieder darauf eingehen, dass ich für eine Interpretation Kandake = Königsmutter keinen einzigen Beleg haben und dass ich deshalb das meroitische *kdke*, *ktke*, *kdwe* für den Titel halte, den die neben dem König fungierende Frau (*kdi*) trägt."

39. Burstein, *Ancient African Civilizations*, 140 n. 17.

40. Adams, *Nubia*, 260.

41. Török, *Kingdom of Kush*, 456.

4. Queen Nawidemak ruled in the first half of the first century A.D.; she is called *qore*. Her burial is in Bar. 6. She is probably the Candace mentioned in Acts 8.[42]

Figure 6.7. Meroitic queen with triple-headed lion god (after R. Lepsius, *Denkmäler aus Ägypten und Äthiopien*).

According to T. Kendall, Meroitic queens are portrayed as "powerful figures, enormously fat, covered with jewels and ornament and elaborate fringed and tasseled robes. Their huge frames tower over their diminutive foes, whom they are shown grasping brutally by the hair with one hand and to whom they deal the *coup de grace* with the other."[43] He also observes: "By Meroitic times, with the decline of Egyptian influence, extreme corpulence had again become the fashion in the Sudan, at least among the ladies at court, and a remarkable succession of massive queens and princesses appears in monumental art from the third century B.C. to the fourth century A.D."[44]

The Ethiopian Eunuch in Later Tradition

The Ethiopian eunuch eventually went home and presumably testified about his newfound faith. According to Irenaeus's *Against Heresies* 3.12.8, written about A.D. 180, the eunuch was "sent into the regions of Ethiopia, to preach what he had himself believed." According to Eusebius's *Ecclesiastical History* (2.1.13–14), written in the early fourth century A.D.:

42. The dating of these queens is based on the latest determinations by Török in his 1997 summary. An earlier study by Wenig, "Bemerkungen zur Chronologie," 43, dates Nawidemak to 70–60 B.C. and Amanitare to around A.D. 20.
43. Kendall, *Kush, Lost Kingdom of the Nile*, 14.
44. Kendall, "Ethnoarchaeology in Meroitic Studies," 655.

Tradition says that he, who was the first of the Gentiles to receive from Philip by revelation the mysteries of the divine word, and was the firstfruits of the faithful through the world, was also the first to return to his native land and preach the gospel of the knowledge of the God of the universe and the sojourn of our Savior which gives life to men, so that by him was actually fulfilled the prophecy which says, "Ethiopia shall stretch out her hand to God" [Ps. 68:31].

The Kingdom of Aksum

In Ethiopia from 700 to 300 B.C., the kingdom of Daamat flourished on the Tigrean plateau, influenced by elements from South Arabia. This was succeeded by a new kingdom centered at Aksum, which was situated on the strategic road between the Nile Valley and the port of Adulis on the Red Sea.[45] It grew wealthy as an entrepôt in the trade of exotic objects such as ivory, incense, gold, hides, horn, and slaves from Africa, which were exported to Rome. The first reference to Aksum is found in *Periplus of the Erythraean Sea*, a late-first-century A.D. sea captain's guide to ports on the Red Sea.[46]

Aksum expanded its power on the plateau in the first and second centuries A.D. and by the third century extended its influence west toward Meroe and east across the Red Sea to South Arabia. Mani, founder of the Manichean religion (third century A.D.), reckoned the four great kingdoms of the world in his day as Rome, Parthia (Persia), China, and Aksum.

Visible monuments of the rulers are immense granite stelae, which represent the façade of palaces. Excavations by Neville Chittick in 1972–74 established that these stelae were markers over royal tombs.[47] Unfortunately, none of the stelae bears any names. Today the stelae are found in four areas of the present town of Aksum. The largest stela, almost 100 feet high, has fallen. Its weight is estimated to be about 300 tons. The Italians, who under Mussolini occupied Ethiopia from 1939 to 1945, removed a 78-foot stela from Aksum, estimated to weigh 200 tons, and erected it in Rome between the Capena Gate and the Palatine Hill. Though the United Nations brokered an agreement in 1947 for the Italians to return the stela, the stela still remains in Rome.[48]

45. Bard and Fattovich, "Some Remarks on the Processes of State Formation." Adulis is now in the independent country of Eritrea.
46. Burstein, *Ancient African Civilizations*, 79–82.
47. Munro-Hay, *Excavations at Aksum*.
48. Harris, "Ethiopia Demands Its Ancient Stela," 13. Cf. Anonymous, "Message from the Gods?"

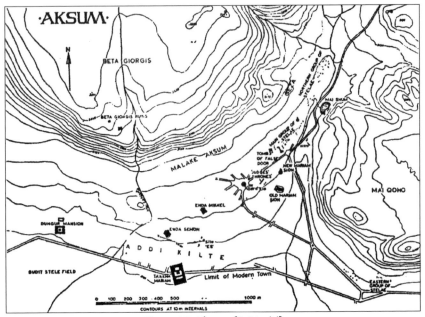

Figure 6.8. Aksum (S. Mutiti).

Figure 6.9. Stelae of Aksum (M. Fuller).

Figure 6.10. Stela of Aksum
(M. Fuller).

The Conversion of Aksum to Christianity

If the Ethiopian eunuch—who actually came from Nubia—did not re-ally evangelize the area today called Ethiopia, when did Christianity come there? It arrived in a most unusual way in the fourth century during the heyday of the Aksumite kingdom. According to Rufinus, a Syrian named Meropius landed at Adulis. He and his companions were killed by the natives, who had been incensed by the violation of a treaty. Two young brothers, Edesius and Frumentius, were spared and brought to the court of Ella Amida at Aksum. As they grew, the king made Edesius his cupbearer and Frumentius his archivist. They used their political power and influence to further the spread of Christianity in the country. When Ella Amida died and was succeeded by his son, Ezana, Edesius and Frumentius were allowed to leave.

Frumentius visited Bishop Athanasius of Alexandria to report on the status of Christianity in the Aksumite kingdom and requested him to send a missionary there. Rufinus then reports:

> Then Athanasius (for he had recently assumed the episcopate), having carefully weighed and considered Frumentius' words and deeds, declared in a council of the priests: "What other man shall we find in whom the Spirit of God is as in you, who can accomplish these things?" And he consecrated him and bade him return in the grace of God whence he had come.[49]

Frumentius returned as Abba Salama, setting the precedent whereby the *abuna* (head) of the Ethiopian Orthodox Church would be consecrated by the Egyptian Coptic Church.

Ezana, the new king, was at first still loyal to pagan gods such as Mahrem, Astar, Beher, and Meder.[50] We have several important inscriptions of this vigorous king in Ge'ez, Greek, and South Arabian, recording his conquests over the Bega (descendants of the Medjayu, who occupied the Red Sea Hills) and most significantly over Nubia and Meroe. It is probable that the Aksumite incursion brought an end to the kingdom of Meroe around A.D. 360. Fragments of Aksumite inscriptions have been found at Meroe. One Ge'ez text reads as follows:

> By the power of the Lord of Heaven, Who in heaven and upon earth is mightier than everything which exists, Ezana, the son of Ella Amida, a native of Halen, king of Axum and of Himyar, . . . of Kasu (i.e. of Kush), King of Kings. . . . By the might of the Lord of heaven, Who has made me Lord, Who to all eternity, the Perfect One, reigns, Who is invincible to the enemy, no enemy shall stand before, and after me no enemy shall follow. By the might of the Lord of all, I made war upon Noba, for the peoples had rebelled and had made a boast of it.[51]

A Greek text published in 1970 makes Ezana's Christian faith explicit: "In the faith of God, and the power of the Father and Son and Holy Spirit, who saved for me the kingdom by the faith of his son Jesus Christ, who helped me and always does help me, I, Azanas, king of the Axomites and Homerites . . . Son of Elle-Amida, servant of Christ, give thanks to the lord my God."[52] The conversion of Ezana to Christianity has been com-

49. Burstein, *Ancient African Civilizations*, 96.
50. Ibid., 90.
51. Ibid., 96.
52. Horsley, *New Documents*, 1.143–44. Some scholars, however, contend that Ezana I was not converted and that a later Ezana II (fifth century A.D.) was the king who turned to Christianity. See Horsley, *New Documents*, 2.209–11. See also Kaplan, "Ezana's Conversion Reconsidered."

pared to the conversion of Constantine, the Roman emperor, about forty years earlier, in 312.

A century later nine saints (monks from Syria) arrived, established monasteries, and translated some of the Scriptures into Gecez. The Ethiopian Church embraced a very broad canon, listing eighty-one books, including Old Testament apocryphal and pseudepigraphical works.[53] Such important works as Enoch are preserved complete only in an Ethiopic version.

Figure 6.11. Ethiopian depiction of the Virgin Mary (M. Fuller).

Ethiopian Christianity has retained many Jewish elements, such as circumcision, the Sabbath, purity laws, and fasting. Their churches are arranged in three areas of holiness, corresponding to the model of the Jew-

53. Mikre-Sellassie, "Bible and Its Canon."

Figure 6.12. Ethiopian book written in Geᶜez (M. Fuller).

ish temple, with the *tabot* (ark) resting in the innermost sanctuary. As noted in chapter 3, Ethiopian Christians believe that in their cathedral at Aksum they have the original Solomonic ark of the covenant, recovered by Menelik, the son of the Queen of Sheba.[54]

Figure 6.13. Cathedral at Aksum (M. Fuller).

54. See Master, "Origin of Jewish Elements."

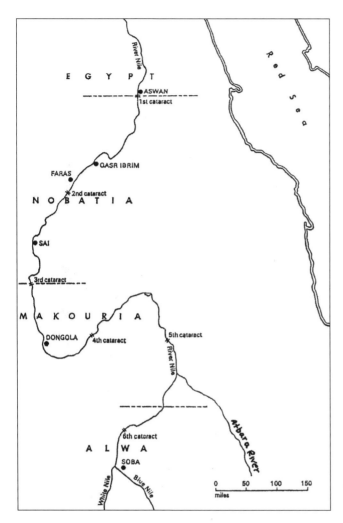

Figure 6.14. Three Nubian kingdoms (S. Mutiti).

The Three Kingdoms of Nubia

After the withdrawal of Roman troops by Diocletian in the late third century downriver to Aswan, two tribal groups from the east and the west came to occupy areas of the Nile. The Blemmyes from the east were constantly attacking monasteries and gained a foothold in the Nile Valley. But they were eventually overturned by the Nobadians from the west, who were recruited by the Romans as allies. Excavations indicate that Qasr Ibrim became a Nobadian settlement.[55] The Nobadians evidently

55. Adams, "Ballaña Kingdom and Culture," 172.

brought the Nubian language with them, though their kings wrote inscriptions in a kind of pidgin Greek. The culture called the X-Group by
Reisner is now known as the Ballana people, from impressive royal tombs
uncovered by W. B. Emery at Ballana and Qustul.[56]

Figure 6.15. Nubian text of
Revelation found at Qasr
Ibrim (©British Museum).

The Christianization of Nubia

Though there are some indications of Christianity in tombs of the fifth
century and reports of monks from Egypt moving into Nubia at this time,
the official conversion of the rulers did not occur until the reign of the
great Byzantine rulers Justinian and Theodora. Justinian, a vigorous
champion of orthodox Christianity, closed the famous pagan temples at
Philae. Justinian favored the Chalcedonian formula, but Theodora was
sympathetic to the Monophysite cause, so much so that she hid Monophysite monks in the palace at Constantinople.[57]

In the Byzantine era (after the fourth century) three different kingdoms
arose in the area of Nubia: (1) Nobatia between the Second and Third Cataracts with its capital at Faras, (2) Makouria between the Third and
Fourth Cataracts with its capital at Dongola, and (3) Alwa below the Sixth
Cataract with its capital at Soba.

56. Emery, *Nubian Treasure*.
57. See Clouse, Pierard, and Yamauchi, *Two Kingdoms*, 190–94.

When Theodora learned that her husband was sending Melkite (i.e., Chalcedonian) missionaries to Silko (a Nobadian king), she outwitted him by hastily sending a rival Monophysite mission that arrived first and in 543 converted the ruler of Nobatia. Julian, who led this mission, could not stand the heat of the area and spent seven hours a day nearly naked, soaking in puddles of water in a cave to keep cool! After the death of Theodora in 547 and the death of Justinian in 565, another Monophysite missionary named Longinus came to Nobatia in 568 to establish churches and train clergy. Avoiding the hostile middle kingdom of Makouria,[58] Longinus succeeded in converting the ruler of Alwa in 575.

Polish excavations at Faras uncovered a cathedral that contained 160 frescoes and 400 wall inscriptions in Greek, Coptic, and Old Nubian, including lists of bishops from 707 to 1169. Archaeological evidence of the conversion of these kingdoms to Christianity is quite dramatic. According to P. L. Shinnie,

> The missions seem to have been remarkably successful and within a short period Christianity had become the religion of both rulers and ruled. The evidence is to be seen in the rather sudden change of burial customs from those of post-Meroitic (X-Group or Ballana) style with their abundance of grave goods, and for the chiefly burials the custom of human and animal sacrifice, to a strictly Christian one in which, with few exceptions, the body was buried without any accompanying objects.[59]

Adams concurs:

> Another point of consensus is that the evangelization of the Nobadians proceeded very rapidly, and was complete well before the end of the sixth century. . . . There is no transition from pagan to Christian burial ritual. On the contrary the use of funerary offerings, of contracted burial, and of aboveground tumuli seem to have disappeared as if overnight. . . . The Christian period is symbolized by the longest peace in Nubian history, and by countless representations of a heavenly king, but no single monument nor tomb of any earthly king.[60]

58. Makouria was converted to Melkite Christianity, before being absorbed by its neighbors.

59. Shinnie, *Ancient Nubia*, 122–23.

60. Adams, "Ballaña Kingdom and Culture," 176–77. For further details, see Shaw, *Kingdom of God in Africa*; Shenk, "Demise of the Church"; Vantini, *Christianity in the Sudan*; idem, "Remotest Places"; Godlewski, "Christian Nubia."

7

CYRENE IN LIBYA

Names for Libyans

The dominance of Egypt in the northeastern part of Africa in the world of the Old Testament is well known. More peripheral parts of Africa, though little noticed, appear in a surprising number of both Old and New Testament texts. These include areas that are now incorporated into the modern country of Libya.[1] The most important part of ancient Libya was known as Cyrenaica, after the Greek colony at Cyrene.

The name *Libya* ultimately goes back to Egyptian *Rbw* = *Libu*, a tribe mentioned in Egyptian texts of the thirteenth–twelfth centuries B.C. In Hebrew the name occurs as *Lûbîm* and in the Septuagint as *Libyēs*. Their troops appear in the armies of Shoshenq I (2 Chron. 12:3) and of Zerah (16:8). The Lubim could not protect No-Amon (Thebes) from the Assyrians (Nah. 3:9). Daniel 11:43 states: "He will gain control of the treasures of gold and silver and all the riches of Egypt, with the Libyans and Nubians in submission" (NIV).

An earlier version of this essay appeared in *Archaeology in the Biblical World* 2 (1992): 6–18. Used by permission.

1. The British Society for Libyan Studies has an informative website: http://www .britac.ac.uk/institutes/libya.

The Egyptians also had other names for the various tribes that lived west of the Nile River: (1) *ṯmḥ* (Tjemhu), attested in the 6th Dynasty (by the 19th–20th Dynasties this became the main designations of the Libyans); (2) *ṯḥnw* (Tjehnu), who lived on the coast west of the Delta; and (3) *mšwš* (Meshwesh), who gradually infiltrated into the Delta.[2]

Another Hebrew word for Libya is *pûṭ* (Put), which may be derived from Egyptian *pd* (foreign archers). Put is the name of the third son of Ham (Gen. 10:6; 1 Chron. 1:8). The word, which occurs as Babylonian *puta* and Old Persian *putaya*, signifies Libya (Jer. 46:9; Ezek. 27:10; 30:5; 38:5).[3] It occurs together with *lûbîm* in Nahum 3:9.

In passages where they are associated with Egypt (Gen. 10:13–14; 1 Chron. 1:11) and other North African areas (Jer. 46:9; Ezek. 30:5), the *Lûdîm* are identified with Lybians rather than with Lydians.[4]

The Greek word *Libyēs* became the term for the area west of Egypt.[5] The Romans used the name *Libya* either in a general sense to describe the whole of North Africa or later in an administrative sense as an official name for the regions between Alexandria and Cyrenaica. Under Diocletian the province was subdivided into Libya Inferior (between Egypt and Cyrenaica) and Libya Superior (Cyrenaica).[6]

New Testament References to Cyreneans

The New Testament has a number of references to Cyreneans, including Mark 15:21[7] (cf. Luke 23:26; Matt. 27:32): "A certain man from Cyrene, Simon, the father of Alexander and Rufus, was passing by on his way in

---

2. Zibelius, *Afrikanische Orts und Völkernamen*, 129–31.

3. The Septuagint usually renders Put with Libya (Jer. 46:9 MT = 26:9 LXX; Ezek. 27:10; 30:5; 38:5; Nah. 3:9). According to Josephus (*Antiquities* 1.6.2 §132), Put colonized Libya. Though a few scholars suggest for Put a location in Punt or in Yemen, Mitchell, "Where Was Putu-Iaman?" 77, on the basis of a text from the thirty-seventh year of Nebuchadnezzar, states: "I conclude therefore that Putu-Iaman is likely to have been the Greek colony in Cyrene, north-east Libya in modern terms, and that any connection with Yemen may be ruled out."

4. Baker, "Lud."

5. We have relatively little archaeological information on the native inhabitants of Libya. We have one Punic-Libyan bilingual dated to 138 B.C.; see Galand, "Le Libyque." Linguists assume that the Libyan language was related to that of the Berbers, who dominated North Africa. On the Berbers, see Bullard, "Berbers of the Maghreb and Ancient Carthage." The one possible native deity that has been identified is called *Gobba* in a Greek inscription, which was found in the Cave of the Birds southwest of Teucheira; see Reynolds, "Libyans and Greeks," 383. White, "Archaeological Survey of the Cyrenaican and Marmarican Regions," 215, reports that he found the first assemblage of Libyan cultural artifacts on an island in a lagoon at Marsa Matruh.

6. Cornell and Matthews, *Atlas of the Roman World*, 173.

7. See Gundry, *Mark*, 953–54.

from the country, and they forced him to carry the cross" (NIV). Since Mark was probably writing to Christians in Rome, this reference implies that Alexander and Rufus were well known to the believers there, whereas their father Simon was not. Simon is a Jewish name, Alexander a Greek name, and Rufus a Latin name meaning "red." Some identify Simon's son Rufus with the Rufus mentioned in Romans 16:13.[8]

A first-century ossuary from the Kidron Valley in Jerusalem bears the name "Alexander, the son of Simon."[9] This Alexander also bears in Hebrew the nickname *Qrnyt*, possibly a rendering of *qireniyah* (Cyrenean). P. W. Van der Horst concludes: "If indeed they were from Cyrene, there is at least a good chance that we have here the ossuary of the son of the man who carried Jesus' cross."[10] In some later docetic texts (e.g., the Nag Hammadi Second Treatise of the Great Seth), Simon is a substitute who died on the cross instead of Jesus. In other Christian texts and depictions, he became a symbol of an eyewitness and pilgrim.[11]

The Book of Acts has several references to Cyrene. Among the crowd of Jewish pilgrims in Jerusalem at Pentecost were some from "the parts of Libya near Cyrene" (2:10). Opposition to Stephen arose "from members of the Synagogue of the Freedmen (as it was called)—Jews of Cyrene and Alexandria as well as the provinces of Cilicia and Asia" (6:9). Some of the believers who were scattered from Jerusalem by persecution included "men from Cyprus and Cyrene, [who] went to Antioch and began to speak to Greeks also, telling them the good news about the Lord Jesus" (11:20—all quotations from the NIV).

Simon of Cyrene = Simeon Niger?

In Acts 13:1, we read: "In the church at Antioch there were prophets and teachers: Barnabas, Simeon called Niger, Lucius of Cyrene, Manaen (who had been brought up with Herod the tetrarch) and Saul" (NIV). Some speculate that Simeon Niger may be another name for Simon of Cyrene. The Latin nickname *Niger* means black, referring no doubt to his complexion.[12] It was commonly used of Aithiopians.[13] Simon and Simeon

8. Bruce, *Commentary on the Book of the Acts*, 260.

9. In 1941 a first-century A.D. tomb was discovered in the Kidron Valley, which yielded over a dozen Cyrenean names, eight of which were Greek. See Avigad, "Depository of Inscribed Ossuaries"; Powers, "Treasures in the Storeroom."

10. Van der Horst, "Jewish Funerary Inscriptions," 57. See also Evans, "Jesus and the Ossuaries," 29–30; idem, *Jesus and the Ossuaries.*

11. Müller, "Simon von Kyrene."

12. The term *Niger* gave rise to the word *Negro* and its pejorative corruption *Nigger*, as well as to the names of two countries in Africa: Niger and Nigeria.

13. See Snowden, *Blacks in Antiquity*, 3–5; Thompson, *Romans and Blacks*, 30–31.

are indeed variants of the same name. But this identification is not likely, because Luke uses the name *Simon* in his Gospel (Luke 23:26)—not the name *Simeon* as in Acts. Moreover, he identifies Lucius—and not Simeon—as Cyrenean. D. J. Williams comments: "If Luke had intended that identification, it is odd that he has spelled the name differently. It may be, then, that 'Niger' was added precisely to distinguish this Simon from the Cyrenean, as indeed from all the other Simons known to the church (e.g., 10:5f.)."[14]

The Original African Heritage Study Bible, which equates Simeon Niger with Simon of Cyrene (pp. 1815–16), also has this comment (pp. 1594–95) on Acts 13:1:

> Two persons of Africa are included, namely Simeon who was called "Niger" (a Latinism for "the black man") and Lucius of Cyrene, which is in northern Libya. Only two others are mentioned. This would suggest that 50 percent of the prophets and teachers in the first "Christian" church were Africans and thus by modern legal racial standards, Blacks.

This betrays a common misperception among Afrocentric scholars: the assumption that all Africans were blacks. In the case of Cyrene, the city was a Greek colony; Simon was no doubt a member of the Jewish community there. The native Libyans of the countryside were not blacks, but Berbers.

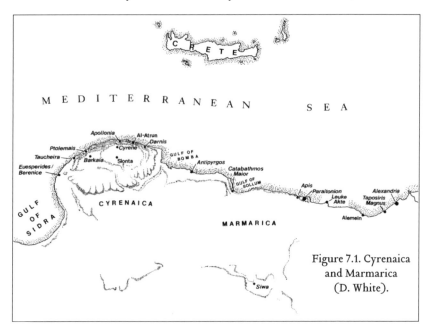

Figure 7.1. Cyrenaica and Marmarica (D. White).

---

14. Williams, *Acts*, 209.

The Geography of Cyrene

Cyrene is located in eastern Libya in an area named after it: Cyrenaica. It was a Greek colony placed on an especially fertile coast below a tree-covered limestone mountain, the Jebel Akhdar (Green Mountain), which rises 2,000 feet. The city is located 15 miles from its port of Apollonia on the sea. A perennial spring flows from the base of the mountain. Annual rainfall of about 600 millimeters and the presence of dew enabled the Cyreneans to grow three harvests.

As a Greek-speaking city, Cyrene was oriented east toward Alexandria and Egypt. To the west is the barren 300-mile coast known as the Syrtis. Paul and his fellow travelers were afraid of drifting into the shoals of the Syrtis during their storm-driven voyage (Acts 27:17). Western Libya contains the other major Libyan city: Tripolis. Tripolitania was more influenced by Latin-speaking Carthage in the west. These geographical divisions still persist in modern Libya, which is the fourth-largest country in Africa.

The area to the east of Cyrene is known as the Marmarica, after the tribe who lived in that region.[15] Just across the modern Egyptian-Libyan border is the famed oasis of Siwa, with its oracle to Zeus-Ammon, visited by Alexander the Great. The oracle was probably first founded by Libyans.[16]

The Early History of the Libyans

Early Egyptians had sporadic problems with a variety of Libyan tribes, including the Libu, Tjehnu, and Meshwesh. The latter two are described by V. Beltrami "as fair and blue eyed, tall, Mediterranean in physical appearance, wearing their hair long in tresses adorned with feathers."[17] Further to the south, tribes like the Tjemhu are attested. The latter wore characteristic feathers and penis sheaths. Attempts to discover archaeological remains of these Late Bronze tribes in their homelands have not been successful.

Though contacts with the Libyans are attested as early as the Old Kingdom, it was during the New Kingdom that contacts became more common in the 18th Dynasty. "Under Akhenaten, however, they are assigned a prominent place at the tribute ceremony, offering typical semi-desert products—ostrich feathers and ostrich eggs."[18] Isolated references to the infiltration of Libyans as far south as Heracleopolis and Thebes were noted on papyrus texts from the late 20th Dynasty.[19]

15. See White, "Archaeological Survey of the Cyrenaican and Marmarican Regions."
16. See Yamauchi, *Persia and the Bible,* 110–13.
17. Beltrami, "Population of Cyrenaica," 141.
18. O'Connor, "Egyptians and Libyans," 36.
19. Haring, "Libyans in the Theban Region."

During the 19th Dynasty sharp conflicts arose when Seti I (1294–1279 B.C.) and Ramesses II (1279–1213 B.C.) built a series of forts in the western Delta and along the Marmarican coast as far west as Marsa Matruh. Seti I fought against the chiefs of the Tjehnu and drove out Libyan squatters from the Delta. Ramesses II also came into conflict with the Tjehnu, Tjemhu, and Libu (the earliest reference to this name). The Libyan Meshwesh attacked in concert with the so-called Sea Peoples during the reigns of Merenptah (1213–1204 B.C.) and Ramesses III (1185–1154 B.C.). In scenes on Ramesses III's temple at Medinet Habu, the Libyans are portrayed with narrow beards, sidelocks of hair, and their characteristic penis sheaths. Merenptah fought a massive invasion in his fifth year, and Ramesses another invasion in his fifth year. In both cases the Libyans reached the Sebennytic branch of the Nile ("the Great River"). Merenptah claims he killed over 9,300 Libyans; Ramesses III claims to have killed 28,000!

The 22d Dynasty (945–715 B.C.) and the 23d Dynasty (818–715 B.C.) during the Third Intermediate Period were Libyan dynasties that ruled Egypt for over two centuries. The founder of the 22d Dynasty, Pharaoh Shoshenq I (945–924 B.C.)—called Shishak in the biblical text—came from a Libyan background.[20] He is called the Great Chief of the Meshwesh, a Libyan tribe. Shoshenq received Jeroboam when he fled from Solomon (1 Kings 11:40), and later he invaded Palestine during Rehoboam's fifth year (1 Kings 14:25–26; 2 Chron. 12:2–10).[21] Shoshenq's raid mentioned in the Bible reflects only a small part of the campaign recorded in his own monument at Karnak.[22]

Although these rulers had been settled in Egypt for generations and were Egyptianized, A. Leahy argues that their Libyan backgrounds became evident in the decentralization of the political system, in certain conventions in language and script, and in the cessation of the elaborate preparations for the afterlife during their reign in Egypt.[23]

The Colonization of Cyrene

Herodotus (4.150–58), who visited Cyrene after 440 B.C., preserves a detailed account of the colonization of Cyrene by the Greeks. Dorians came from the island of Thera (70 miles north of Crete), impelled by a se-

---

20. Kitchen, *Third Intermediate Period in Egypt*, 287–302, 432–47.

21. See Yamauchi, "Shishak."

22. See Kitchen, *Third Intermediate Period in Egypt*, 294–300; idem, "Shishak's Military Campaign." Kitchen, "Shoshenqs of Egypt and Palestine," refutes the revisionist suggestion of Clancy, "Shishak/Shoshenq's Travels," who wishes to redate Shoshenq I to 800 B.C. See also the posthumous essay of Ahlström, "Pharaoh Shoshenq's Campaign."

23. Leahy, "Libyan Period in Egypt."

vere drought to seek more fertile land.[24] According to Pausanias (3.14.3), one of the colonists was a Lacedaemonian, Chionis, who had been a victor in the stade races at Olympia in 664, 660, and 656. About 639 B.C. the Theraeans first landed east of Cyrenaica on an offshore island, Platea, and then landed on the coast at Aziris. They were led by natives to the plateau of Cyrene around 630 B.C. The Greek men took native wives.[25]

Early Laconian pottery confirms the traditional date of the city's founding. Herodotus (4.159) indicates that a second wave of settlers came around 580 B.C. This led to a division of the citizens into three *moirae* or tribes: (1) the Theraeans and *perioikoi* (dwellers around), (2) Cretans and Peloponnesians, and (3) Islanders. G. Schaus suggests that the *perioikoi* may have been Spartan *perioikoi* rather than Libyans dwelling around Cyrene.[26]

Though these initial contacts between the Greek colonists and the natives were friendly, as the Greeks acquired more land and as the later Romans penetrated further inland, tensions and even conflicts arose from time to time. The native tribes sometimes joined forces with the enemies of Cyrene, such as the Ptolemies.[27]

Figure 7.2. Silphium plant, displayed on a fifth-century B.C. silver hemidrachma struck by Cyrene (D. White).

The leader of the colony and the eponymous founder of the Battiad monarchy was Battus I. The Battiad kings also served as priests of Apollo.

24. If Marinatos's interpretation is correct, contact between Thera and the Libyan coast occurred in the Late Bronze Age. See "'Libya Fresco.'"

25. Boardman, *Greeks Overseas*, 153–57. Herodotus 4.181–85 also preserves a valuable account of the trans-Saharan route. See Liverani, "Libyan Caravan Road."

26. Schaus, "Evidence for Laconians."

27. Abdelaim, "Libyan Nationalism."

In a series of eight kings, the names *Battus* and *Arcesilas* alternate. From the sixth century B.C. a famous Laconian cup depicts Arcesilas II supervising the weighing of silphium, a plant that was the chief object of exportation conducted under royal auspices.[28] Used as a vegetable in pickles and sauces, as an antiseptic, and as an aphrodisiac, this plant was soon rendered extinct in Cyrenaica, perhaps by the grazing of sheep.[29]

When Cambyses conquered Egypt in 525 B.C., Arcesilas III sent gifts to the Persian king.[30] The country of Libya (i.e., *Putaya*) is included in Darius's Canal Stela. Leading a twisted-horned antelope, the twenty-second delegation on the eastern stairway of Darius's Apadana at Persepolis is identified by most scholars as Libyans.[31] They appear to have a tuft of hair over their foreheads, a characteristic of the Tjehnu. A Persian expedition around 515 B.C. seems to have damaged the temple of Demeter outside the walls of the city.

Figure 7.3. Bronze head of Libyan male, perhaps King Arcesilas IV, the last of the Battiad monarchs (D. White).

The last Battiad monarch was Arcesilas IV, whose victorious races at the Pythian Games at Delphi (462 B.C.) were praised by Pindar. A democratic revolution in 440 B.C. overthrew the monarchy and established a

28. See Chamoux, "Du Silphion."
29. El-Athram, "Silphium Plant in Cyrenaica."
30. See Yamauchi, *Persia and the Bible*, chap. 3; Mitchell, "Cyrene and Persia."
31. Yamauchi, *Persia and the Bible*, 355–56.

council of generals, a senate of 101, and an assembly of 500. The franchise
was limited to 10,000 property owners. Forty years later (401 B.C.) a democratic faction under Ariston executed 500 oligarchs. Many of the wealthy
fled west to the city of Euhesperides.

When Alexander conquered Egypt, Cyrenean envoys went to greet
him with gifts, which included three hundred warhorses and five four-
horse chariots. Using an aristocratic revolution in 322 B.C. as a pretext,
Ptolemy I seized Cyrene. His *diagramma* stipulated, "Whoever breaks the
decrees of Ptolemy which Ptolemy established for the peoples of Cyrene
shall be sentenced to death." Ptolemy I captured 100,000 prisoners of war
from Palestine and employed 30,000 of them in garrisons, including a
number of Jews who were sent to Cyrene. Some of their descendants distinguished themselves, such as Jason of Cyrene, who composed the work
on which 2 Maccabees is based (2 Macc. 2:23).[32]

Under Ptolemaic rule many Cyreneans migrated to Egypt, where they
enlisted in the armed services. They served as far south as Wadi Halfa
and Elephantine. Their greatest concentration was in the Faiyûm area. M.
von Habsburg notes: "Cyrenaica was the only African region to furnish
large numbers of men to the Egyptian military in Hellenistic times."[33]

Berenice II, the wife of Ptolemy III, was born in Cyrene. Statues of this
beautiful queen were found at the site in 1915 and in 1976. From the Hellenistic period, distinguished Cyreneans included Theodore the geome-
ter, Callimachus the poet, Carneades the philosopher, and Eratosthenes
the scientist. Philip Ward declares: "Cyrene is the Athens of Africa. So too
it excelled all African cities except Alexandria in the number and greatness of its ancient writers and scientists."[34]

Cyrene under the Romans

Upon the death of Ptolemy Apion in 96 B.C., his will bequeathed
Cyrene to Rome. Rome accepted the royal estates but left the key cities
their independence. The Roman general Lucullus, who visited Cyrene in
87–86 B.C., found the Jews at odds with the Greeks (Josephus, *Antiquities*
14.7.2 §114). Finally, in 74 B.C. the Roman senate decided to annex Cyrenaica, probably because the Romans needed its grain and were also concerned about pirates off the Libyan coast.[35]

Pompey, who was entrusted with extraordinary powers to deal with
pirates in the eastern Mediterranean, resettled some of the pirates at

32. Goldstein, *II Maccabees*, 4–5, 19–22.
33. Habsburg, "Egyptian Influence in Cyrenaica," 358.
34. Ward, *Touring Libya*, 57.
35. Braund, "Social and Economic Context."

Ptolemais in Cyrenaica. At least eight inscriptions found in Cyrenaica refer to either Pompey or his legate, Cn. Cornelius Lentulus Marcellinus.[36] Rome combined Cyrenaica with Crete as a single province in 67 B.C. Cyrene rejoiced with Octavian in his triumph at Actium over Antony and Cleopatra in 31 B.C. and began its official dating from that year.

Edicts of Augustus, dated 7–4 B.C. and found in the Agora, reveal that the Cyreneans were still considered under Greek laws. These inscriptions, which are among the most important from the reign of Augustus, were first published in 1927.[37] The first decree stipulates that capital charges against a Greek should be decided by a mixed jury of Roman citizens and Greeks. The second requires the governor to send to Rome under guard any individual who claims to have information concerning the well-being of the emperor. The third decrees that recently created Roman citizens must still fulfill the civic duties of the cities of their birth. The fourth stipulates that for noncapital crimes between Greeks, the jurors should be Greeks, unless the defendant prefers Romans. The fifth permits plaintiffs to obtain a legal representative to present their cases, so that they would not personally have to spend long periods in Rome waiting for their cases to be heard.[38]

From the reign of Augustus we have evidence for the year A.D. 3/4 of Jewish graduates from the gymnasium of Cyrene. S. Applebaum notes among the ephebes such Jewish names as Barthubas, Elazaros, Iēsoutos, and Simōn. From other periods we have such Jewish names as Iouda and Dōsitheos.

Under Augustus, Agrippa wrote on behalf of the Cyrenean Jews:

> Marcus Agrippa to the magistrates, council and people of Cyrene, greeting. The Jews in Cyrene, on whose behalf Augustus has already written to the former praetor of Libya, Flavius, and to the other officials of the province to the effect that the sacred monies may be sent up to Jerusalem without interference, as is their ancestral custom, now complain to me that they are being threatened by certain informers and prevented (from sending these monies) on the pretext of their owing taxes, which are in fact not owed. I therefore order that these monies be restored to the Jews, who are in no way to be molested, and if sacred monies have been taken away from any cities, the persons in charge of these matters shall see that amends are made to the Jews there. (Josephus, *Antiquities* 16.6.5 §§169–70)

The proconsuls who governed Cyrene were often from the province of Africa (i.e., Tunisia). At some time during the reign of Augustus, P. Sulpi-

36. Reynolds, "Cyrenaica, Pompey."
37. Anderson, "Augustan Edicts from Cyrene"; LaRonde, "Cyrènaïque romaine."
38. Lewis and Reinhold, *Roman Civilization*, 2.36–42.

cius Quirinius, under whom the Christmas census was enacted, vanquished the rebellious Mararidas and Garamantes tribes.[39] The proconsuls were assisted by quaestors. One quaestor who served before A.D. 38 became the emperor Vespasian.[40]

From the early reign of Nero (A.D. 56) we have an inscription of donors who contributed to the repair of a synagogue in Berenice, near Cyrene.[41] Applebaum suggests that the remains of a building outside the walls on the southern height of Wadi Bel Gadir may have been a synagogue.[42]

The Jewish revolt in Palestine, which began under Nero in 66 and was suppressed by Titus under Vespasian in 74, led to catastrophic consequences for the Jews in Cyrene. According to Josephus (*Jewish War* 7.11.1 §§437–42):

> The madness of the Sicarii further attacked, like a disease, the cities around Cyrene. Jonathan, an arrant scoundrel, by trade a weaver, having taken refuge in that town, won the ear of not a few of the indigent class, and led them forth into the desert, promising them a display of signs and apparitions. His knavish proceedings escaped detection in general; but the men of rank among the Jews of Cyrene reported his exodus and preparations to Catullus, the governor of the Libyan Pentapolis. . . . On being brought before the governor, he [Jonathan] contrived to elude punishment himself, while affording Catullus a handle for injustice, by falsely asserting that he had received his instructions in the scheme from the wealthiest of the Jews.

The Roman governor took advantage of Jonathan's false accusations to take vengeance against some of his wealthy Jewish enemies: "After them he slew all the well-to-do Jews, three thousand[43] persons in all; a step which he thought that he could safely take, as he confiscated their property to the imperial exchequer" (Josephus, *Jewish War* 7.11.1–2 §§445–46). Jonathan tried to deflect blame from himself onto the Jews of Alexandria and Rome, including Josephus, but was condemned to death under Vespasian.

Under the reign of Trajan in 115 the Jews of Cyrene were led to rebel under a certain Lucuas:[44]

> For both in Alexandria and in the rest of Egypt and especially in Cyrene, as though they had been seized by some terrible spirit of rebellion, they rushed

39. LaRonde, "Cyrènaïque romaine," 1021. On Quirinius and the problems of the Christmas census, see Schürer, *History of the Jewish People*, 1.399–427; Lawrence, "Publius Sulpicius Quirinius."

40. LaRonde, "Cyrènaïque romaine," 1016.

41. Ibid., 1044.

42. See Applebaum, "Lamp and Other Remains"; idem, "Jewish Status at Cyrene."

43. In his *Life* 76 §424 Josephus gives the number of those condemned as two thousand.

44. Applebaum, "Jewish Revolt in Cyrene."

into sedition against their Greek fellow citizens, and increasing the scope of the rebellion in the following year started a great war while Lupus was governor of Egypt. In the first engagement they happened to overcome the Greeks, who fled to Alexandria and captured and killed the Jews in the city, but though thus losing the help of the townsmen, the Jews of Cyrene continued to plunder the country of Egypt and to ravage the districts in it under their leader Lucuas. The Emperor sent against them Marcius Turbo with land and sea forces including cavalry. He waged war vigorously against them in many battles for a considerable time and killed many thousands of Jews, not only those of Cyrene but also those of Egypt who had rallied to Lucuas, their king. (Eusebius, *Ecclesiastical History* 4.2.2–4)

Orosius (*Adversus Paganos* 7.12.6) wrote (cf. Dio Cassius 68.32.1–2):

[The Jews] waged war on the inhabitants throughout Libya in the most savage fashion, and to such an extent was the country wasted that its cultivators having been slain, its land would have remained utterly depopulated, had not the Emperor Hadrian gathered settlers from other places and sent them thither, for the inhabitants had been wiped out.

The Jews of Cyrenaica went on a rampage, destroying pagan temples and massacring Gentiles. A number of Greek and Latin inscriptions explicitly refer to the damage and destruction wreaked by the Jews during their revolt (Greek *tarachōs*; Latin *tumultus*) under Trajan.[45] Archaeologists discovered evidence of these devastations in four areas of Cyrene: (1) the sanctuary of Apollo and the Acropolis, (2) the Agora, (3) the Caesareum area, and (4) the temple of Zeus. Applebaum concludes: "It may be doubted whether there ever arose in the early Roman Empire any movement which so imperilled Roman authority as did the Jewish Diaspora revolt in the reign of Trajan."[46] The revolt of the Jews in Cyrene caused Jews elsewhere, including those on Cyprus, to rebel against the Romans from 115 to 117.[47]

The Archaeology of Cyrene

Hostile Senusi tribes deterred Europeans from visiting the area of Cyrene until the eighteenth century. The first European to visit the site was Claude Lemaire in 1706. In 1792 W. G. Browne reached the famous oasis of Siwa, which is in Egypt just across the border from Libya. The

45. See Applebaum, *Jews and Greeks in Ancient Cyrene*, 272–73.
46. Ibid., 341.
47. On the possible consequences of this revolt on disillusioned Jewish intellectuals, who may have contributed to the origins of Gnosticism, see Smith, *No Longer Jews*.

sketches of these and other European travelers are both striking and invaluable.[48]

Figure 7.4. The Valley Road (H. Budek and F. Sear).

T. Burton conducted a small excavation in the northern necropolis in 1947. In 1951 Libya achieved its independence. Alan Rowe dug extensively among the tombs in 1952 and 1956. From 1957 Italian efforts were conducted under the direction of Sandro Stucchi. From 1957 to 1960 part of the Valley Road and adjoining buildings were excavated. In the period up to 1966 the Odeon and the house of Hesychius were cleared. Much restoration work has also been conducted. Prior to the excavations, not a single column stood upright.[49]

From 1969 until 1981 Donald White of the University Museum of the University of Pennsylvania worked at Cyrene in the area of the Demeter sanctuary, located in Wadi Bel Gadir outside the southeastern walls of Cyrene. The area of five terraces was traced from 600 B.C. until the temple was destroyed by an earthquake in A.D. 262. The expedition recovered 724 pieces of sculpture, many made of imported marble.[50] Particularly significant was a rare portrayal of a bearded young Libyan with curly hair and

48. White, "Illustrations by the Early Travelers."
49. Goodchild, *Kyrene und Apollonia*, 63.
50. Kane, "Sculpture from the Cyrene Demeter Sanctuary."

beard.[51] White found votive offerings in favissae and a massive deposit of 4,000 sherds. Of these about 22% were imports from Athens.[52]

Archaeological Sites of Cyrene

The Caesareum was a large public area (315 ft. by 280 ft.) dedicated to the deified Julius Caesar. This was cleared and excavated by G. Oliverio and G. Caputo between 1935 and 1938.[53] Approached by entrances in the southwest and southeast, the square was surrounded on three sides by columned porticos. On the fourth side a basilica was raised by Trajan. In the center was a temple to Bacchus.

West of the Caesareum was a Roman theater, one of four in Cyrene. Oliverio thinks that this building functioned as a *bouleutērion* (civic auditorium) for officials. Nearby was the temple of Venus.

One of the magnificent structures at Cyrene was the double block of the house of Jason Magnus, so called after an inscription found in the temple of Hermes within the block. The buildings in this area had rich mosaic floors. There was a colossal statue of Heracles in the atrium of the house of Jason Magnus, and statues of the Muses in the peristyle of the west wing. P. Mingazzini interprets the buildings as a gymnasium,[54] but R. G. Goodchild objects that the complex does not have the baths that normally accompanied Roman gymnasiums.[55] He came to the conclusion that the buildings served as the official residence of the gymnasiarch.

The long stoa of the Hermes, which extends 328 feet and is 60 feet wide, connects the Caesareum and the Agora. It was decorated with fifty-six busts of Heracles and Hermes. The stoa was cleared by Oliverio in 1936 and reconstructed between 1957 and 1961 under the direction of Stucchi, who interprets it as a roofed dromos or running track.[56] The date of its original construction is uncertain, but it may date from after the Jewish revolt.

The Agora, or public square of the Greek city, contained an area extending 230 feet by 164 feet. This was cleared between 1917 and 1925 and contained the so-called tomb of Battus, the founder of the colony. On the north was erected a great stoa in the fourth century B.C. The springhouse was transformed into an Augusteum under the first Roman emperor. This contained various dedications to gods such as Apollo and Diana. It was in

51. White et al., "Seven Recently Discovered Sculptures," 27–28.
52. Elrashedy, "Attic Imported Pottery," 206.
53. Goodchild, *Kyrene und Apollonia*, 61.
54. Mingazzini, *L'insula di Giasone Magno a Cirene*.
55. Goodchild, *Kyrene und Apollonia*, 84–85.
56. Bacchielli et al., *L'Agorà di Cirene*.

Figure 7.5. Stoa of Hermes at Cyrene (H. Budek and F. Sear).

Figure 7.6. The Agora at Cyrene (H. Budek and F. Sear).

one of the rooms of the Bouleutērion that the famous edicts of Augustus were found.

In the Agora stands the capitolium or temple of Hadrian and Antoninus Pius, from which came the colossal statue of Jupiter found by Italian soldiers. Nearby was the Nomophylakeion, which served as the official archive building. It contained inscriptions referring to the *nomophylakes* (official in charge of the archives) and a great number of *cretulae* (clay sealings). This was one of the buildings burned during the Jewish revolt.

Figure 7.7. Statue of Nike at Cyrene (H. Budek and F. Sear).

The statue of Nike on a boat's prow has been reerected in the Agora, like the Victory of Samothrace in the Louvre, commemorating some naval victory—perhaps that of Pompey over the pirates in 67 B.C. or of Augustus over Antony at Actium in 31 B.C.

On the acropolis, where the earliest settlement must be located, much remains to be uncovered. This was where the American expedition led by Richard Norton dug in 1910–11. Among the buildings found here is a temple to Serapis and Isis, cleared in 1935.

The Stratēgeion was built in the fourth century B.C. in honor of three generals who defeated the Nasamonean tribe in the Syrtis to the west. The building must have been restored in the reign of Tiberius, as indicated by an inscription found in it.

Figure 7.8. The fountain of Apollo in the sanctuary of Apollo at Cyrene (D. White).

The earliest town was established on the height overlooking a spring called Apollo's Fountain. The sacred sanctuary of Apollo rises above the Agora near the sacred spring. The most important building is the great temple of Apollo, which was cleared from 1925 to 1934. The first Apollonion was built around 550 B.C. This went through four more phases, the last in the third century A.D. Like many other buildings, it was destroyed in the earthquake of A.D. 365. In the sanctuary area is another temple to Isis, built under Hadrian. Carved into the mountainside is a sacred grotto that served as a triclinium or as a room for ceremonial lustrations.

The Greek theater nearby, which is the oldest, was transformed into an amphitheater by the Romans. The Romans under Trajan built extensive baths in A.D. 98; these were destroyed seventeen years later by the Jews. Along the Valley Road are some unusual Greek baths carved out of the cliff.

Before the end of the sixth century B.C. the temple of Zeus—an immense Doric building, 230 feet by 105 feet, which was larger than the Parthenon—was built on the northeast heights. This building was restored under Augustus or Tiberius. During their revolt under Trajan, the Jews

Figure 7.9. The temple of Apollo (left) and the much smaller temple of Artemis
(right) as they appear in their Roman development phases in the sanctuary
of Apollo at Cyrene (D. White).

must have expended enormous efforts to attack this central temple of the
Gentiles. They overthrew the huge peristasis columns, which measured
nearly 7 feet in diameter and 30 feet in height, by inserting wedges of
wood, which were set on fire, to crack the stone.[57]

The temple was restored under Marcus Aurelius (ca. A.D. 175). This
later temple housed a gigantic statue of Zeus, eight times life-size, mod-
eled after the Zeus of Olympia, which was later smashed into such small
pieces by Christian zealots that only its fingers and toes remain intact.

On the outskirts of the town was a temple to Demeter, which especially
attracted women devotees, as noted in a poem by Callimachus. Excavations reveal that the building was reconstructed in the Hellenistic era. The
campaign of 1971 uncovered a statue of Octavia, the sister of Augustus
and the wife of Mark Antony. A very beautiful head, found elsewhere on
the site, is identified as either Agrippina the elder (the wife of Germani-
cus) or Agrippina the younger (the wife of Nero).

White observes: "No evidence has been brought to light to suggest that
the Demeter Sanctuary suffered directly at the hands of the Jewish rebels.
The likelihood is that its sheltered location south of the formidable barrier of the wadi saved it from the ravages that destroyed the temples of

57. Goodchild, "Temple of Zeus at Cyrene," 33.

Figure 7.10. Cyrene's temple of Zeus, first built in the sixth century B.C. and rebuilt on several later occasions, including the late second century A.D. For many years this great structure, seen here as it appeared in 1975, has been undergoing reconstruction under the supervision of the Italian Mission (D. White).

Zeus and Apollo, along with a good deal else of the walled city."[58] After the severe damage caused by the Jewish revolt under Trajan, the city of Cyrene was furnished with extensive buildings under Hadrian and the later Antonines.[59]

Along the Valley Road in temple F was found an inscription from the second or third century, with the symbolic word ICHTHYS, which is the earliest evidence of Christianity in Cyrene.[60] The most important Christian structure is the East Church, which was cleared in 1955–57. The church, which was not built before the fifth century, is about 130 feet by 98 feet and contains a well-preserved baptistery.

The city of Eusperides to the west of Cyrene was founded by Greek settlers from Cyrene shortly before 515 B.C. The remains of this port city, which was renamed Berenice in 247/246 B.C., are within the limits of the modern city of Benghazi.[61] Eventually the Pentapolis of Cyrenaica came to include the following cities: (1) Cyrene, (2) its port Apollonia (modern

58. White, "Cyrene's Suburban Expansion," 116; idem, "Cyrene's Sanctuary of Demeter"; idem, *Extramural Sanctuary of Demeter*.

59. Reynolds, "Hadrian"; Walker, "Architecture of Cyrene."

60. Goodchild, *Kyrene und Apollonia*, 142.

61. See Lloyd, "Some Aspects of Urban Development."

Marsa Suza), (3) Berenice (*Benghazi*), (4) Tauchira (*Tocra*), and (5) Ptolemais (*Tolmaide*). After the Jewish revolt, a sixth city, Hadrianapolis, was built by Hadrian.[62]

Christianity in Cyrenaica

A late tradition in Eusebius ascribes the beginning of Christianity in Egypt to Mark.[63] An even less reliable Coptic tradition claims that Mark was a Cyrenean Jew, which leads a scholar from Egypt to assert: "Indeed, the apostle of Egyptian Christianity was a native Jew of Cyrene, St Mark the Evangelist, who came to Alexandria by way of the Pentapolis and, after planting the new faith in Egypt, himself returned to Cyrene to work on his fellow citizens on more than one occasion."[64]

Eventually many Christian churches were established in Cyrenaica, but we have recovered relatively few Christian inscriptions.[65] Goodchild reports on the archaeological evidence at Cyrene for the occupation of former pagan temples by Christians:

> That the triumphant Christians deliberately slighted the surviving monuments of paganism is proved at Cyrene, by recent excavations in other parts of the city. During 1956–1957 a group of three adjacent temples was uncovered in the Valley Street adjoining the "Casa Parisi" museum. Two of them had been deliberately stripped of their fittings and burned out, after which a blocking was built across their fronts.[66]

The province's first recorded bishop was Ammonas of Berenice, who took office in A.D. 260. The Council of Nicea in A.D. 325 was attended by bishops from Tauchira, Ptolemais, Barca, and Boreum. Epiphanius reports that Arius was born in Libya, as was Sabellius, the theologian who promoted the heresy of Modalism.

One of the most remarkable clergy in late antiquity was Synesius, who became bishop of Ptolemais. Born into a wealthy pagan Alexandrian family about 370, he became a student of the Neoplatonist Hypatia, a woman who was killed by a Christian mob. Synesius, who also studied at Athens, was as much a Platonist as he was a Christian in his convictions. He believed that the soul was immortal by nature and refused to believe that the world would be destroyed by fire. His collection of 156 letters (A.D.

---

62. On these other sites, see Boardman and Hays, *Excavations at Tocra*; Nasgowitz, *Ptolemais Cyrenaica*; Lüderitz, *Corpus jüdischer Zeugnisse*.

63. See Smith, "Mark the Evangelist."

64. Atiya, *History of Eastern Christianity*, 433.

65. Reynolds, "Christian Inscriptions of Cyrenaica."

66. Goodchild, *Kyrene und Apollonia*, 44.

399–413) is a rich source of information about the attacks of Berber marauders.[67]

A. S. Atiya makes a telling observation on Christianity in Cyrenaica:

> One fact remains clear about Cyrenaican Christianity. It seemed to be almost entirely concentrated amongst the Greek population, who fought the Berbers from the southern Sahara as a race of marauders whom they never truly cared to convert or civilize. Thus the Berbers remained outside the pale of the Church with their own pagan practices. When the Arabs came on the scene, the Greeks emigrated, and the two remaining nomadic races met with better understanding. This in part accounts for that sudden disappearance of Christianity from the Pentapolis and the spread of Islam after the advent of the Arabs.[68]

Unfortunately, centuries later a similar attitude of cultural superiority and paternalism among European and American missionaries denied positions of leadership to black African Christians until the post-colonial period of independence allowed the emergence of vigorous indigenous leaders.

67. Bregman, *Synesius of Cyrene*.
68. Atiya, *History of Eastern Christianity*, 435.

8

AFROCENTRIC BIBLICAL INTERPRETATION

On October 12, 1994, the *New York Times* carried an article concerning Warner Sallman, whom it called the "best-known artist of the century" for his painting of the head of Christ, which has been reproduced more than half a billion times. Our earliest descriptions of the appearance of Jesus come from the Middle Ages. In an alleged report by Lentulus, which dates from the twelfth century, Jesus is described with "wavy hair, rather crisp of the colour of wine, and glittering as it flows down from His shoulders, with a parting in the middle of the head after the manner of the Nazarenes. . . . He has a beard abundant and of the same hazel-colour as His hair, not long, but forked. His eyes are blue and very bright."[1] This is quite obviously an imaginative Eurocentric portrait of Jesus.

An earlier version of this essay appeared in the *Journal of the Evangelical Theological Society* 39 (1996): 397–409. Used by permission.
    1. Farrar, *Life of Christ*, 664. According to Jensen, "Two Faces of Jesus," early Christian artists portrayed Jesus as either a handsome, bare-faced youth or as a mature, bearded figure.

Contrast this imagery with the recent portrayal of a black Jesus from *The Original African Heritage Study Bible*, a new Afrocentric Bible that represents in photographic illustrations and textual commentary the conviction that all the biblical figures from Moses to Jesus were black. The image of Christ as black appeared as early as 1700, when a Congolese girl, Beatrice Kimpa Vita, taught that "Christ appeared as a black man in Sao Salvador and that all his apostles were black. He was a Christ who identified himself with the Africans, who threw in his lot with that of the suffering, oppressed blacks as opposed to the white exploiters and oppressors."[2] In a 1963 interview Malcolm X declared: "Christ wasn't white. Christ was a black man."[3] The March 1969 issue of *Ebony* magazine depicted a kinky-haired, broad-nosed black Christ.[4]

These diverse representations raise the issue of Eurocentric versus Afrocentric interpretations of ancient history in general and of the Bible in particular.

Eurocentric Interpretations

One could cite many examples of interpretations of African history by white scholars that are transparently racist and condescending. In *Africa and Africans in Antiquity*, which I edited, several contributors note such interpretations. For example, scholars from Zimbabwe attribute the great stone structures in that country to either Solomon[5] or Indians but not to the indigenous Bantu population. George Reisner of Harvard University, the great archaeologist of Nubia, was also disposed to ascribe innovations to newcomers and not natives. W. B. Emery posited a "dynastic race" for the flowering of Archaic Egypt.

David Hume (d. 1776) wrote in his *Essays and Treatises*: "I am apt to suspect the negroes . . . to be naturally inferior to the white. There never was a civilized nation of any other complexion than white, nor even any individual eminent either in action or speculation."[6] Basil Davidson notes the coincidence that in 1830, when the colonial partition of the African continent began, Georg Hegel, the famous German philosopher, dismissed Africans as insignificant to history.[7] Hegel wrote in his *Philosophy of History*:

2. Bosch, "Currents and Cross Currents," 1.
3. Douglas, *Black Christ*, 1.
4. For an interesting attempt to re-create an image of Jesus by a forensic scientist using Jewish skulls from Jerusalem, see Fillon, "Real Face of Jesus."
5. See chap. 3, above; and Carroll, "Solomonic Legend."
6. Cited in Harris, *Africans and Their History*, 19.
7. Davidson, *Africa in History*, xxii.

It is manifest that want of self-control distinguishes the character of the Negroes. This condition is capable of no development or culture, and as we have seen them at this day, such have they always been. . . . At this point we leave Africa, not to mention it again. For it is no historical part of the world; it has no movement or development to exhibit.[8]

A century later, C. G. Seligman, who applied social Darwinism to African ethnography, formulated the "Hamitic hypothesis," which held that Caucasian Hamites, including the Egyptians, created everything of value in Africa. In 1930 he wrote: "Apart from relatively late Semitic influence . . . the civilizations of Africa are the civilizations of the Hamites. . . . The incoming Hamites were pastoral 'Europeans'—arriving wave after wave—better armed as well as quicker witted than the dark agricultural Negroes."[9]

Afrocentrism

The cover of the September 23, 1991, issue of *Newsweek* featured the subject "Afrocentrism: Was Cleopatra Black?" In an understandable reaction to Eurocentric racist interpretations, many African Americans seek to reinterpret history and the Bible on an Afrocentric basis.

In growing numbers Afrocentric scholars have gained positions at major universities such as UCLA, Rutgers, Kent State, Temple, and City University of New York—not in mainstream departments, to be sure, but in separate African American studies departments with a small but committed clientele. Where their teachings have made a significant impact is at the level of public education (and in some private academies) in major cities. Arthur M. Schlesinger Jr. reports:

> Hilliard's African-American Baseline Essays were introduced into the school system of Portland, Oregon, in 1987. They have subsequently been the inspiration for Afrocentric curricula in Milwaukee, Indianapolis, Pittsburgh, Washington, D.C., Richmond, Atlanta, Philadelphia, Detroit, Baltimore, Camden, and other cities and continue at this writing to be urged on school boards and administrators anxious to do the right thing.[10]

How did Afrocentrism develop, and what are its major tenets?[11] There were earlier works such as Gerald Massey's *Ancient Egypt: The Light of the*

8. Cited by Harris, *Africans and Their History,* 19.
9. Cited by Sanders, "Hamitic Hypothesis," 521.
10. Schlesinger, *Disuniting of America,* 70.
11. Moses in Early et al., "Symposium," 46, asserts: "Afrocentrism is not a new movement. It makes one of its first appearances in an 1827 editorial in *Freedom's Journal,* the first black newspaper in the United States, which alleged a relationship between black Americans and the ancient Egyptians."

World (1907),[12] which anticipated the key claim that the cultural origins of humanity were to be traced to Africa, especially to what he called Old Kam (i.e., Egypt), and George G. M. James's *Stolen Legacy* (1954).[13] But the birth of the movement can be especially linked to the development, since 1965, of black studies programs at universities on the demand of African American students.

In the 1970s the works of a seminal scholar, Cheikh Anta Diop of Senegal, began appearing in English translations. Diop (1923–1986), who came from a Muslim background, was educated at the University of Paris. He was both a scientist, who became the director of a radiocarbon laboratory, and a prolific author, who in numerous publications set forth his thesis that the Egyptian civilization was a black African one.[14] When in 1967 the Congress of Africanness sponsored by the African Studies Association met in his home city of Dakar, Diop was not one of the participants. But his presentation in 1974 in Cairo became a chapter in UNESCO's *General History of Africa*.[15] Though Diop was and still is ignored by mainstream scholars, he has gathered a devoted following among current Afrocentric scholars.[16]

Molefi Kete Asante, who coined the word *Afrocentrism*, states: "I am most keenly a Diopian, believing essentially that Cheikh Anta Diop has said quite enough on the theories of culture and history to inform most of what I write."[17] The significance of Diop for Afrocentrism is highlighted in a preface to a collection of essays by Asante:

> Before the appearance of Cheikh Anta Diop's *African Origin of Civilization* (1971), African culture was typically examined by Western-trained scholars from a European perspective. Those scholars, often wrapped in the swaddling clothes of a fully emergent European ideology, were often incapable of understanding the unity of African culture. Diop's masterpiece, *African Origin of Civilization*, and its companion, *Cultural Unity of Black Africa*, turned historiography around and provided the basis for an Afrocentric transformation.[18]

12. See Bruce, "Ancient Africa."

13. Lefkowitz in her important critique, *Not out of Africa*, chap. 4, points out that Massey derived his view of Egyptian mysteries from classical sources, which do not accurately reflect Egyptian religion.

14. Among Diop's works translated from French into English are *African Origin of Civilization*, *Cultural Unity of Black Africa*, and *On Science, History, and Technology*.

15. Diop, "Origin of the Ancient Egyptians."

16. Matthews, "Proposal for an Afro-centric Curriculum," sets forth a proposal for seminaries and other schools.

17. Asante, *Kemet, Afrocentricity, and Knowledge*, preface.

18. Asante and Asante, *African Culture*, 3.

Charles Finch even declares: "Posterity will undoubtedly place him [Diop] in the company of Herodotus, Manetho, and Ibn Khaldun as an historian whose work not only changed the way we look at history but made history itself."[19]

According to Cain Hope Felder, there are three major types of Afrocentrism:

1. "There is Afrocentrism that stresses corrective historiography. Accordingly, Africa and persons of African descent are centered on as proactive in written history and not as passive stereotypes and objects of history."[20]
2. "For years, various proponents of Afrocentrism have argued for a common cultural heritage, world view, and ethos, suggesting variously that there were unique unifying factors."[21]
3. There is a Black Nationalist version represented by Al Cleague and Leonard Jeffries: "Here skin color determined by percentages of melanin provides a reverse racialist mode of valorization."[22]

Felder himself maintains: "I remain skeptical about the second form of Afrocentrism and reject outright this third form as potentially damaging to the entire multiculturalist movement within America."[23]

With some variations, Afrocentrism in its most conventional form maintains the following theses:

1. A cultural and linguistic unity unites all Africans. Diop noted that ancient Egyptian had links with Wolof, a language spoken in Senegal. Indeed, Diop and Theophile Obenga, a scholar from the Congo, argue for the genetic relationship of all African languages.
2. Egypt is an integral part of Africa, and ancient Egyptians were black Africans. Diop declares: "The oneness of Egyptian and Black culture could not be stated more clearly. Because of this essential identity of genius, culture and race, today all Negroes can legitimately trace their culture to ancient Egypt and build a modern culture on that foundation."[24] Diop and his followers argue this from linguistics and the appearance of selected Egyptians. They also assume that the Egyptian word for their land—*Kemet* (black)—refers

---

19. Van Sertima and Williams, *Great African Thinkers*, 1.227. Diop is dubbed "the Pharaoh of African studies"; see Tolbert, "Africa and the Bible," 5.
20. Felder, "Afrocentrism," 51. See also idem, "Racial Motifs."
21. Felder, "Afrocentrism," 51.
22. Ibid., 52.
23. Ibid.
24. Diop, *African Origin of Civilization*, 140.

to the people and not to the land, as Egyptologists hold.[25] They also cite passages from classical writers such as Herodotus, who visited Egypt in the fifth century B.C.[26]

3. Egypt provided Greece with all of its major intellectual ideas. According to Diop: "The ancient Egyptians were Negroes. The moral fruit of their civilization is to be counted among the assets of the Black world. . . . Pythagorean mathematics, the theory of the four elements of Thales of Miletus, Epicurean materialism, Platonic idealism, Judaism, Islam, and modern science are rooted in Egyptian cosmogony and science."[27] Diop also claims that the ancient Egyptians developed metallurgy around 2700 B.C. and dispersed its knowledge through the continent, a claim that is not considered seriously by reputable scholars.[28]

4. Blacks were ultimately the originators of most of Western civilization. Jeffries, who was for a time removed from his post at the City University of New York for anti-Semitic remarks, declares: "The Greeks did not invent anything: they just inherited knowledge that was taught them by our African ancestors."[29]

5. Not only the Egyptians but also the ancient Sumerians were black. Some argue this from the designation "black-headed ones,"[30] though Sumerologists take this as simply a reference to hair color. Certainly depictions of Sumerians do not support such an assertion.

6. Diop claims that the Egyptian Akhenaten was the originator of monotheism: "Once again, Egypt is the beginning of everything. Akhenaten's monotheistic thinking precedes Moses, so it precedes all Judaism, if we put aside all legend. If we search written history proven by documents in chronological order, Egyptian monotheism precedes all the other monotheistic religions which have existed since, in this case, Judaism, Christianity, and Islam. The revealed religions borrowed from this Egyptian thought."[31] But the

25. See the comments of Sauneron, "Annex to Chapter 1," 51; cf. Kees, *Ancient Egypt*, 36: "The 'black' fertile soil which gave Egypt its name *Kemet* ('the Black')."

26. Cf. Hansberry, *Africa and Africans*.

27. Diop, *African Origin of Civilization*, xiv.

28. Miller and Van der Merwe, "Early Metal Working," 7: "Egypt does not appear to have had a direct formative influence on the advent of metallurgy elsewhere in Africa other than at Meroe." For ancient metallurgy, see Yamauchi, "Metal Sources and Metallurgy."

29. Jeffries, "Afrocentrism vs. Eurocentrism," 22. Cf. the full title of James's *Stolen Legacy: The Greeks Were Not the Authors of Greek Philosophy, but the People of North Africa, Commonly Called the Egyptians*.

30. For example, Copher, "Black Presence in the Old Testament," 54.

31. Finch, "Further Conversations with the Pharaoh [i.e., Diop]," 233.

view that Moses borrowed monotheism from Akhenaten, a thesis popularized by Freud and supported to a degree by W. F. Albright, is not really tenable.[32] Elsewhere Diop suggests: "One needs only to meditate on Osiris, the redeemer-god, who sacrifices himself, dies, and is resurrected to save mankind, a figure essentially identifiable with Christ."[33]

7. Some Afrocentrists maintain that all the biblical figures in both the Old Testament and the New Testament were blacks. Diop declares: "Even the Blacks of Palestine, these Biblical cousins of the Egyptians, the Canaanites of the Bible, descendants of the Natufians of the Mesolithic period, opposed a fierce resistance in their different cities, which were all conquered and annexed to the Egyptian Empire."[34]

Criticisms of Afrocentric Views

What shall we say about these differing points of view?

1. The history of interpretation warns us to be aware of biases, both our own and those of others, in interpreting history.
2. There is clear evidence of a Eurocentric racist bias in certain interpretations that exalt whites and denigrate blacks.
3. The recently spawned Afrocentric interpretations focus on some legitimate concerns. The Egyptian language, once classified as Hamito-Semitic, is now recognized by Joseph Greenberg as part of a broad range of Afroasiatic languages that include Berber, Chadic, and Omotic. Egyptian has links not so much with Wolof, as Diop claims, but with Hausa, a dialect spoken in Nigeria, as pointed out by linguist Carleton Hodge.[35]
4. According to Bruce Williams, the roots of pharaonic Egypt may go back to Qustul in Nubia.[36] Other Egyptologists, however, do not attach the same significance to the Qustul finds.[37]
5. As Afrocentric scholars push their thesis to extreme conclusions, they undermine their credibility by claiming one and all as black and therefore staking the claim of blacks to every imaginable cultural and intellectual achievement. For example, Walter McCray lists

32. See Yamauchi, "Akhenaten, Moses, and Monotheism."

33. Diop, *African Origin of Civilization*, xiv. For a critique of such comparisons, which were popularized by James Frazer, see Yamauchi, "Easter—Myth, Hallucination, or History?"

34. Diop, *Civilization or Barbarism*, 94.

35. Hodge, "Hausa-Egyptian Establishment"; idem, "Role of Egyptian"; idem, "Afroasiatic."

36. Williams, "Lost Pharaohs of Nubia"; cf. "Rescued Nubian Treasures Reflect Black Influence on Egypt," *New York Times* (Feb. 11, 1992): B5, B8. See chap. 2, above.

37. For example, Trigger et al., *Ancient Egypt*, 62.

as black peoples not only Cush, Ethiopia, and Egypt but also Canaanites, Elamites, and Hittites, and as black individuals not only Ebed-Melech the Cushite (Jer. 38–39) and Taharqa (2 Kings 19:9; Isa. 37:9) but also Melchizedek, Ephron the Hittite, Rahab the harlot, and the Queen of Sheba.[38] John Henrik Clarke's claim that Cleopatra was black is buttressed by citations from Shakespeare and from Ripley's *Believe It or Not* and is illustrated by a painting by Earl Sweeney.[39] But the Ptolemaic dynasty, which ruled Egypt after Alexander, was Macedonian and believed so strongly in preserving the purity of the royal line that they adopted the Egyptian practice of consanguineous marriages—that is, marriages between brothers and sisters.

6. As to the question of whether the Egyptians were black, the answer is not so simple as Afrocentrists assert. Frank Yurco points out that the ancient Egyptians would not have thought in terms of a simple dichotomy: "The ancient Egyptians, like their modern descendants, were of varying complexions of color, from the light Mediterranean type (like Nefertiti), to the light brown of Middle Egypt, to the darker brown of Upper Egypt, to the darkest shade around Aswan and the First Cataract region, where even today the population shifts to Nubian."[40] Frank Snowden Jr., a distinguished African American classics scholar who rejects the identification of Egyptians as blacks, points out that the Greeks and Romans were well acquainted in art and text with blacks from the area especially of Meroe: "This group possesses, among others, these characteristics: color varying from reddish-brown to deep brownish-black; tightly curled and wiry hair described as woolly, frizzly, or kinky; a broad, flattened nose; thick lips, usually puffy and everted; prognathism, often marked in the sub-nasal region."[41] Egyptians were in contact with the darker Nubians of the First and Second Cataracts already in the Old Kingdom.[42] An increasing number of individuals, including some introduced into royal harems, came from this region in the Middle Kingdom. Egyptians made

38. McCray, *Black Presence in the Bible*, 27–28.

39. Clarke, "African Warrior Queens," 127.

40. Yurco, "Were the Ancient Egyptians Black or White?" 24. Cf. Trigger, "Nubian, Negro, Black, Nilotic?" 27: "On an average, between the Delta in northern Egypt and the Sudd of the Upper Nile, skin color tends to darken from light brown to what appears to the eye as bluish black, hair changes from wavy-straight to curly or kinky, noses become flatter and broader, lips become thicker and more everted."

41. Snowden, *Blacks in Antiquity*, 8; see also idem, "Attitudes towards Blacks."

42. Bennett, "Africa and the Biblical Period," 492: "In terms of physical racial characteristics the Egyptians of the ancient Near East were a brown-skinned people with long hair, whose history is the story of their contact and intercourse with darker, curly-haired peoples up the Nile in Nubia."

contact with negroid tribes of central Africa in the New Kingdom.[43] These contacts are reflected in the clear depiction of black-complexioned and negroid types in Egyptian art. Snowden concludes: "Though not very numerous, the realistic portrayals of blacks in early Egyptian art are sufficient to illustrate the types of Kushites known prior to the New Kingdom and to show that *Nehesyu*, a word used of southerners as early as 2300 B.C., included peoples with Negroid features."[44] The Egyptians accurately depicted their enemies and their allies. They made a clear color distinction between themselves and the black Nubians, whom they rhetorically denounced with insulting epithets. Though the use of reddish-brown for men and yellow for women was conventional, one cannot simply dismiss this as a ceremonial color for blacks, as Diop and his followers urge.[45]

7. Cheikh Anta Diop, whom Afrocentrists adopt as their intellectual star, is not a trustworthy guide in either linguistics or history, as already indicated.[46] He simply makes too many unsupportable statements. For example, in answer to a question as to when the truth about the beginning of world civilization was falsified, he responded as follows: "It's around 1525 B.C. that Egypt was conquered by Cambyses, the Persian King. The command that Cambyses gave was to destroy everything that revealed the greatness of Egypt. The temples were torn down and the libraries were destroyed. ... Cambyses also destroyed all of the Egyptian intelligentsia. The Egyptian priests fled to western Asia."[47] Unfortunately, almost everything about this statement is a false conclusion or is unsupportable.[48]

8. Afrocentric scholars neglect the very real contributions of the black Cushites, Nubians, and Meroites to the biblical narrative and to African civilization, because these are not as universally known as those of the Egyptians.[49]

Despite these severe strictures, we can thank Afrocentric scholars for calling attention to the neglected evidence of significant passages that refer to blacks in both the Old Testament and the New Testament, such as Moses' Cushite wife, Pharaoh Taharqa of the (Cushite) 25th Dynasty, and the Ethiopian eunuch of Candace.

43. Junker, "First Appearance of the Negroes." Cf. LaSor, "Cush."
44. Snowden, *Before Color Prejudice*, 11–12.
45. Brunson, "Ancient Egyptians," 53–54.
46. See the review article by MacGaffey, "Who Owns Ancient Egypt?"
47. Van Sertima and Williams, *Great African Thinkers*, 1.348.
48. See Yamauchi, *Persia and the Bible*, chap. 3.
49. See Roth, "Building Bridges to Afrocentrism," 16.

Appendix

MARTIN BERNAL'S
BLACK ATHENA
REVIEWED

The views of Cyrus H. Gordon[1] and Michael C. Astour[2] with respect to the interaction between the Aegean and the Near East inspired a specialist in Chinese political history, Martin Bernal, to produce one of the most provocative and controversial studies to roil the study of ancient history in recent years: *Black Athena: The Afroasiatic Roots of Classical Civilization,*

An earlier version of this essay appeared in the *Journal of Ancient Civilizations* 14 (1999): 145–52. Used by permission.

1. See especially Gordon, *Common Background of Greek and Hebrew Civilizations.* Gordon's extraordinary scholarship is acknowledged by several Festschriften: *Orient and Occident* (ed. Hoffner), *Bible World* (ed. Rendsburg et al.), and *Boundaries of the Ancient Near Eastern World* (ed. Lubetski, Gottlieb, and Keller). See also the special issue of *Biblical Archaeologist* 59 (1996).

2. See Astour, *Hellenosemitica.* Astour's contributions are acknowledged in *Crossing Boundaries and Linking Horizons* (ed. Young, Chavalas, and Averbeck). I had the privilege of studying with Michael Astour under Professor Gordon at Brandeis University in the early 1960s.

volume 1: *The Fabrication of Ancient Greece, 1785–1985* (1987), and volume 2: *The Archaeological and Documentary Evidence* (1991).[3] These two volumes have called forth nearly a hundred reviews and numerous symposia, at which Bernal has tried to respond to his many critics. A volume of critical essays was edited by Mary R. Lefkowitz and Guy MacLean Rogers: *Black Athena Revisited* (1996).

Bernal, a specialist in Chinese political affairs at Cornell University, came to a midlife crisis in 1975. He relates, "At this stage, led by my friend David Owen,[4] I became heavily influenced by the works of Cyrus Gordon and Michael Astour on general contacts between Semitic and Greek civilizations."[5] He immersed himself in a very broad range of studies, including ancient languages. As the grandson of the most famous British authority on Egyptian grammar, Alan Gardiner, Bernal had long been interested in Egyptian.

Also as the son of a famous Marxist historian of science, John Desmond Bernal, Martin had been a liberal critic of the establishment. He makes explicit the motive of his project: "The political purpose of *Black Athena* is, of course, to lessen European cultural arrogance."[6] Despite some carping about statements taken out of context, many scholars, even among his critics, agree that the most valuable part of Bernal's first volume is his exposure of some of the racist ideology—especially of German and British scholars of the nineteenth century—in the fabrication of what he calls the Aryan Model of ancient history.[7] According to Bernal, this model created the image of a pure, northern race who created the Greek civilization, unsullied by contamination from external cultures. The Broad Aryan Model, established by the 1840s, denied Egyptian influence; the Extreme Aryan Model, which flourished in the 1920s and 1930s, denied even Phoenician influences.[8]

On the other hand, the Ancient Model as set forth in the Greek sources themselves, such as Herodotus (2.50), acknowledged indebtedness to the Phoenicians and Egyptians.[9] Bernal proposes what he calls the Revised

3. The first volume won the Socialist Review Book Award for 1987 and an American Book Award in 1990.

4. Owen, who was a student of Gordon, is the chair of the Department of Near Eastern Studies at Cornell. Another of Gordon's students in this department is Gary Rendsburg.

5. Bernal, *Black Athena*, 1.xiii. Elsewhere, in "Responses to Critical Reviews," 130, Bernal states that he has "accepted most—though not all—of the ideas of Gordon and Astour."

6. Bernal, *Black Athena*, 1.73.

7. Coleman, "Case against Martin Bernal's *Black Athena*," 77.

8. Bernal, "*Black Athena*: Hostilities to Egypt."

9. Herodotus learned by inquiry that "the names of almost all of the gods came from Egypt to Greece." Herodotus indeed gives us valuable information about the Scythians and about the Persian conflict with the Greeks, but he also provides some misinformation. See Yamauchi, *Foes from the Northern Frontier*; idem, *Persia and the Bible*; idem, "Herodotus—Historian or Liar?"; idem, "Herodotus" (1992); idem, "Herodotus" (1999).

Ancient Model, which would derive much of the roots of Greek civilization from Egyptian colonists on Crete and Greece in the Middle Bronze
and Late Bronze Ages (2000–1200 B.C.). His Revised Ancient Model "ac-
cepts that there were Egyptian and Phoenician settlements and that there
were massive and fundamental cultural influences on the Aegean from
the near East."[10] The consequences of Bernal's revisionism is expressed as
follows: "If I am right in urging the overthrow of the Aryan Model and its
replacement by the Revised Ancient one, it will be necessary not only to
rethink the fundamental bases of 'Western Civilization' but also to recognize the penetration of racism and 'continental chauvinism' into all our
historiography, the philosophy of writing history."[11]

Archaeological Evidence

Bernal interprets massive drainage works and grain-storage facilities
in Boiotia (the area north of Athens) in the third millennium B.C. as evidence of Egyptian presence in Greece.[12] Heracles may have been a reflection of a Boiotian pharaoh.[13] He believes that Egyptians settled Crete late
in the third millennium and early second millennium B.C. Following the
lead of Frank Stubbings in the *Cambridge Ancient History,* he views the famous shaft graves of Grave Circle A, found by Heinrich Schliemann at
Mycenae in 1876, as the products of the Hyksos dynasty, who had been
expelled from Egypt in the sixteenth century B.C.[14] He cites the evidence
of Hyksos Pharaoh Khyan, whose objects have been found in Crete, Anatolia, and Baghdad.

Textual Evidence

Basing his reconstruction on references to Senusret in Herodotus 2.102–
11, Bernal envisions an extensive Egyptian campaign through Anatolia
and perhaps into the Cyclades islands of the Aegean, across the straits at

10. Bernal, "Image of Ancient Greece," 125.
11. Bernal, "First by Land."
12. Bernal, *Black Athena*, 2.3.
13. Ibid., 2.109–20.
14. Ibid., 2.380. Bernal believes that the biblical account of the Israelites' sojourn in
Egypt is based on a garbled memory of the Hyksos conquest of Egypt and suggests that the
Israelite Yahweh was the same as the Hyksos god Seth (ibid., 1.66). Cf. Allen, "*Black Athena*:
An Interview," 20. On the credibility of the biblical account, see Hoffmeier, *Israel in Egypt.*
In the same interview Bernal contends that Israelite monotheism was derived from that of
Pharaoh Akhenaten (fourteenth century B.C.) and that the tradition of Christ's resurrection
is patterned after the Osiris tradition. On the former issue, see Yamauchi, "Akhenaten,
Moses and Monotheism"; on the latter issue, see Yamauchi, "Easter—Myth, Hallucination,
or History?"

Troy, and back around the northern coast of the Black Sea. The remnants of pharaoh's army that he left in Colchis, on the eastern shore of the Black Sea, Herodotus characterized as "dark-skinned and woolly-haired."

Bernal writes that Herodotus's "portrayal of the Egyptians as black . . . inspired the title of this series."[15] Bernal takes this reference to suggest that "many of the most powerful Egyptian dynasties . . . were made up of pharaohs whom one can usefully call black."[16] This was especially true of the 11th Dynasty.

Linguistic Evidence

Bernal claims that he can propose plausible Egyptian and Semitic etymologies for Greek words that do not have Indo-European roots. He suggests that of the non-Indo-European words some 25% are Semitic and some 20%–25% may be derived from Egyptian,[17] a thesis he promises to develop more fully in a projected third volume. He believes that the name of the Greek goddess Athena was derived from the Egyptian goddess Neith, hence the title of his series: *Black Athena*.[18] Specifically he derives Athena from Egyptian *Ḥt Nt* (house of Neith). He also derives the name *Aphrodite* from *pr wȝdyt*, the name for Buto, the city of Hathor, the Egyptian goddess of love.

In contrast to the traditional view that the Greeks borrowed the Phoenician alphabet in the eighth century B.C., when we first have such texts after the Greek dark age, Bernal proposes that the alphabet was borrowed as early as the fifteenth century.[19]

Reception by Afrocentric Scholars

Bernal expresses a certain degree of empathy with the thinking of African American scholars. For example, he quotes with approval the view of African American scholar G. G. M. James, "whose fascinating little book *Stolen Legacy* also makes a plausible case for Greek science and philosophy having borrowed massively from Egypt."[20] Afrocentric scholars, however, do not think that he has gone far enough.[21]

When asked about the uses made of *Black Athena* by black racists, Bernal responds: "I am infinitely less concerned by black racism than I am by

15. Bernal, *Black Athena*, 1.53.
16. Ibid., 1.242.
17. Ibid., 1.xiv.
18. Ibid., 1.21.
19. Ibid., 1.39. Cf. Bernal, *Cadmean Letters*.
20. Bernal, *Black Athena*, 1.38.
21. Carruthers, "Outside of Academia," 471: "Although this is an advance over the pure White Supremacist position, it is somewhat less than some of us will accept."

white racism, and white racists, directly or indirectly, make constant use of orthodox views of the classical world and the Aryan model."[22] But critics of Afrocentrism believe that Bernal's work is "dangerous." Lefkowitz concludes: "To the extent that Bernal has contributed to the provision of an apparently respectable underpinning for Afrocentric fantasies, he must be held culpable, even if his intentions are honorable and his motives are sincere."[23]

Though Bernal says nothing about the role of women, his challenge to the establishment is also welcomed by feminist scholars. A special issue of the *Journal of Women's History* (4.3 [1993]) was devoted to *Black Athena*.[24]

Critical Responses

The vast majority of classical and Near Eastern scholars are skeptical or critical.[25] Stubbings's linkage of Grave Circle A to the Hyksos, upon which Bernal builds, was undermined some years ago by the discovery of Grave Circle B, which indicates that the Shaft Grave culture antedated the date of the expulsion of the Hyksos. Moreover, leading art historian Emily Vermeule asserts: "There is nothing truly Egyptian in the Shaft Graves."[26]

James Muhly, who was earlier critical of the views of Gordon and Astour, also takes strong exception to Bernal's interpretation of the archaeological data. He does not believe that the Phoenicians advanced westward into the Mediterranean prior to the eighth century.[27] Muhly's student, Eric Cline, compiled a comprehensive list of about eight hundred objects of Egyptian and Near Eastern origins in the Aegean area from the Late Bronze Age period. He is sympathetic to Bernal's view that "there was prolonged, sustained, and probably continuous contact and trade between Egypt and the Aegean throughout the Late Bronze Age, and transfers of ideas and innovations no doubt occurred." However, Cline, whose work Bernal frequently cites, disagrees with Bernal's "contention that the Aegean was under Egyptian hegemony during this time."[28] Cline believes that these objects and Egyptian texts are evidence

22. Bernal, *Black Athena*, 2.xxii.
23. Lefkowitz, "Ancient History, Modern Myths," 20.
24. Cf. Bach, "Whitewashing Athena."
25. Poliakoff, "Roll Over, Aristotle," gives a good survey of reviews. For a thorough and balanced assessment, see Berlinerblau, *Heresy in the University.*
26. Vermeule, *Art of the Shaft Graves at Mycenae*, 18.
27. Muhly, "Black Athena versus Traditional Scholarship."
28. Cline, "Content and Trade or Colonization?" 36. See also idem, *Sailing the Wine-Dark Sea.*

of a possible diplomatic relationship between these two areas in the reign of Amenhotep III.[29]

Bernal's interpretation of Herodotus to support the notion that Egyptians were black is disputed by the leading authority on blacks in antiquity, Frank Snowden Jr., an African American scholar himself. Snowden concludes: "In short, this Herodotean passage comparing Egyptians to Colchians is not useful as evidence for the identification of Egyptians with Ethiopians, i.e., Negroes or blacks—the purpose which Professor Bernal would have it serve."[30]

Bernal's heavy reliance on, and interpretation of, Herodotus is questioned. Lefkowitz, for example, says: "Bernal relies too much on Herodotus' treatment of Egypt."[31] Bernal's treatment of the Egyptian evidence is strenuously disputed by Egyptologists. Especially harsh is James Weinstein's conclusion: "It is not inconceivable that pieces of Bernal's thesis may someday prove correct, but this volume is so littered with factual errors, misstatements, citations of outdated and inappropriate sources, flimsy toponomy identifications, and a host of methodological difficulties that it is impossible to accept his 'Revised Ancient Model.'"[32]

Despite these criticisms, there is no doubt that Bernal's works arouse enormous interest and are works that cannot be ignored. One benefit of the controversy is that it calls attention to the fact that many other scholars (Walter Burkert, Sarah Morris, Martin West) have identified quite valid Near Eastern parallels and influences on Greek civilization.[33] Thanks to Bernal, no one studying the classical world can any longer afford to ignore the wider Mediterranean and Near Eastern horizons of that world, including Egypt.

29. Cline, "Amenhotpe III and the Aegean." Cf. Kitchen, "Theban Topographical Lists." See also O'Connor and Cline, *Amenhotep III*. The subject of such relations was the theme of a conference organized by Eric Cline and Diane Harris at the University of Cincinnati. See Cline and Harris-Cline, *Aegean and the Orient*.

30. Snowden, "Bernal's 'Blacks,'" 89. See also idem, "Attitudes towards Blacks."

31. Lefkowitz, *Black Athena Revisited*, 14.

32. Weinstein, review of Bernal's *Black Athena*, 381. Bernal attempts to vigorously rebut all such criticisms at great length (550 pages) in *Black Athena Writes Back*, a book dedicated to "Cyrus Gordon and Michael Astour who have led the way."

33. Burstein, "Challenge of *Black Athena*," 13.

BIBLIOGRAPHY

This lengthy bibliography is included to enable readers to benefit more fully from the extensive research behind this book. Interspersed among familiar works are books and articles known only to scholars working in specialized fields of study. Because of the wide range of subject areas touched on in this book, resources that are well known to one reader may be completely unfamiliar to another. It is hoped that all readers will find items of interest that will provoke further study.

Aaron, D. H. "Early Rabbinic Exegesis on Noah's Son, Ham, and the So-Called 'Hamitic Myth.'" *Journal of the American Academy of Religion* 63 (1995): 721–59.

Abbot, N. "Pre-Islamic Arab Queens." *American Journal of Semitic Languages* 58 (1941): 1–22.

Abdelaim, M. K. "Libyan Nationalism and Foreign Rule in Graeco-Roman Times." In *Libya Antiqua: Report and Papers of the Symposium Organized by UNESCO in Paris, 16 to 18 January 1984*, 153–63. Paris: UNESCO, 1986.

Abou-Assaf, A. *Der Tempel von ʿAin Dara*. Mainz: Zabern, 1990.

Abou-Assaf, A., P. Bordreuil, and A. R. Millard. *La statue de Tell Fekherye et son inscription bilingue assyro-araméenne*. Paris: Éditions recherche sur les civilisations, 1982.

Ackerman, S. "Why Is Miriam Also among the Prophets? (And Is Zipporah among the Priests?)" *Journal of Biblical Literature* 121 (2002): 47–80.

Adamo, D. T. *Africa and Africans in the Old Testament*. San Francisco: International Scholars Publications, 1998.

———. "The African Wife of Moses: An Examination of Numbers 12:1–9." *Africa Theological Journal* 18 (1989): 230–37.

———. "Ancient Africa and Genesis 2:10–14." *Journal of Religious Thought* 49 (1992): 33–43.

———. *Explorations in African Biblical Studies*. Eugene, Ore.: Wipf & Stock, 2001.

———. "The Images of Cush in the Old Testament: Reflections on African Herme-neutics." In *Interpreting the Old Testament in Africa*, ed. M. Getui, K. Holter, and V. Zinkuratire, 65–74. New York: Lang, 2001.

Adams, W. Y. "The Ballaña Kingdom and Culture: Twilight of Classical Nubia." In *Africa and Africans in Antiquity*, ed. E. M. Yamauchi, 159–79. East Lansing: Mich-igan State University Press, 2001.

———. "The Coming of Nubian Speakers to the Nile Valley." In *The Archaeological and Linguistic Reconstruction of African History*, ed. C. Ehret and M. Posnansky, 11–38. Berkeley: University of California Press, 1982.

———. "Doubts about the Lost Pharaohs." *Journal of Near Eastern Studies* 44 (1985): 185–92.

———. "Kush and the Peoples of Northeast Africa." In *Africa in Antiquity: The Arts of Ancient Nubia and the Sudan*, ed. F. Hintze, 9–13. Meroitica 5. Berlin: Akade-mie-Verlag, 1979.

———. *Nubia: Corridor to Africa*. Princeton: Princeton University Press, 1977.

———. "Post-Pharaonic Nubia: Archaeology, I." *Journal of Egyptian Archaeology* 50 (1964): 7–14, 117–20; 51 (1965): 160–78.

———. "Reflections on the Archaeology of Kerma." In *Ägypten und Kusch*, ed. E. Endesfelder et al., 41–52. Berlin: Akademie-Verlag, 1977.

Adams, W. Y., J. A. Alexander, and R. Allen. "Qaṣr Ibrîm 1980 and 1982." *Journal of Egyptian Archaeology* 69 (1983): 43–60.

Adamson, P. B. "Human Diseases and Deaths in the Ancient Near East." *Welt des Orients* 13 (1982): 5–14.

Adler, M. N., trans. *The Itinerary of Benjamin of Tudela*. 1907. Reprinted New York: Feldheim, 1967.

Afshar, A., W. Dutz, and M. Taylor. "Giraffes at Persepolis." *Archaeology* 27 (1974): 114–17.

Aharoni, Y. "Beersheba." In *Encyclopedia of Archaeological Excavations in the Holy Land*, ed. M. Avi-Yonah, 1.164–65. London: Oxford University Press, 1975.

———. "The Solomonic Districts." *Tel Aviv* 3 (1976): 5–15.

———. "The Solomonic Temple, the Tabernacle, and the Arad Sanctuary." In *Ori-ent and Occident: Essays Presented to Cyrus H. Gordon on the Occasion of His Sixty-fifth Birthday*, ed. H. A. Hoffner Jr., 1–8. Alter Orient und Altes Testament 24.1. Kevelaer: Butzon & Bercker/Neukirchen-Vluyn: Neukirchener Verlag, 1973.

Ahlström, G. W. "Pharaoh Shoshenq's Campaign to Palestine." In *History and Tra-ditions of Early Israel*, ed. A. Lemaire and B. Otzen, 1–15. Leiden: Brill, 1993.

Albenda, P. "Observations on Egyptians in Assyrian Reliefs." *Bulletin of the Egypto-logical Seminar* 4 (1982): 5–23.

Albers, F. J. "The Pyramid Tomb of Tanutamen, Last Nubian Pharaoh, and His Mother, Queen Qalhata." *KMT: A Modern Journal of Ancient Egypt* 14.2 (2003): 52–63.

Albright, F. P. "The Excavation of the Temple of the Moon at Mârib (Yemen)." *Bul-letin of the American Schools of Oriental Research* 128 (1952): 28–38.

Albright, W. F. *Archaeology and the Religion of Israel*. 3d ed. Baltimore: Johns Hop-kins University Press, 1953.

——. "Egypt and the Early History of the Negeb." *Journal of the Palestine Oriental Society* 4 (1924): 131–61.

——. *From the Stone Age to Christianity.* 2d ed. Garden City, N.Y.: Doubleday, 1957.

——. "Ivory and Apes of Ophir." *American Journal of Semitic Languages* 37 (1921): 144–45.

——. "The Location of the Garden of Eden." *American Journal of Semitic Languages* 39 (1922–23): 15–19.

——. "The Mouth of the Rivers." *American Journal of Semitic Languages* 35 (1919): 161–93.

——. "The Role of the Canaanites in the History of Civilization." In *The Bible and the Ancient Near East*, ed. G. E. Wright, 328–62. Garden City, N.Y.: Doubleday, 1961.

——. *Yahweh and the Gods of Canaan.* Garden City, N.Y.: Doubleday, 1968.

Aldred, C. *The Temple of Dendur.* New York: Metropolitan Museum of Art, 1978.

Ali Al-Khalifa, S. H., and M. Rice. *Bahrain through the Ages: The Archaeology.* London: KPI, 1986.

Allen, D. C. *The Legend of Noah: Renaissance Rationalism in Art, Science, and Letters.* Urbana: University of Illinois Press, 1949.

Allen, N. "*Black Athena*: An Interview with Martin Bernal." *Free Inquiry* 10 (1990): 18–22.

Altenmüller, H., and A. Moussa. "Die Inschriften der Taharkastele von der Dahschurstrasse." *Studien zur altägyptischen Kultur* 9 (1981): 57–84.

Andersen, K. T. "The Queen of the Habasha in Ethiopian History, Tradition, and Chronology." *Bulletin of the School of Oriental and African Studies* 63 (2000): 31–63.

Anderson, J. G. C. "Augustan Edicts from Cyrene." *Journal of Roman Studies* 17 (1927): 39–48.

Anderson, R. W., Jr. "Zephaniah Ben Cushi and Cush of Benjamin: Traces of Cushite Presence in Syria-Palestine." In *The Pitcher Is Broken*, ed. S. W. Holloway and L. K. Handy, 45–70. Sheffield: Sheffield Academic Press, 1995.

ANET = Ancient Near Eastern Texts Relating to the Old Testament, ed. J. B. Pritchard. Princeton: Princeton University Press, 1955.

Anonymous. "A Message from the Gods? Axum Stela Struck by Lightning." *Archaeology Odyssey* 5.5 (2002): 12.

Applebaum, S. "The Jewish Revolt in Cyrene in 115–117, and the Subsequent Recolonisation." *Journal of Jewish Studies* 2 (1951): 177–86.

——. "Jewish Status at Cyrene in the Roman Period." *La Parola del Passato* 19 (1964): 291–303.

——. *Jews and Greeks in Ancient Cyrene.* Leiden: Brill, 1979.

——. "A Lamp and Other Remains of the Jewish Community of Cyrene." *Israel Exploration Journal* 7 (1957): 154–62.

——. "A Note on the Work of Hadrian at Cyrene." *Journal of Roman Studies* 40 (1950): 87–90.

Asante, M. K. *Kemet: Afrocentricity and Knowledge.* Trenton: Africa World, 1990.

Asante, M. K., and K. W. Asante. *African Culture: The Rhythms of Unity.* Westport, Conn.: Greenwood, 1985.

Ash, P. S. *David, Solomon, and Egypt: A Reassessment.* Sheffield: Sheffield Academic Press, 1999.

Ashley, T. R. *The Book of Numbers.* New International Commentary on the Old Testament. Grand Rapids: Eerdmans, 1993.

Astour, M. *Hellenosemitica.* Leiden: Brill, 1965.

Atiya, A. S. *History of Eastern Christianity.* Notre Dame: University of Notre Dame Press, 1968.

Atiya, A. S., and H. G. Fischer. "The Facsimile Found: The Recovery of Joseph Smith's Papyrus Manuscripts." *Dialogue* 2 (1967): 50–64.

Aubin, H. T. *The Rescue of Jerusalem: The Alliance between Hebrews and Africans in 701 B.C.* New York: Soho, 2002.

Avigad, N. "Baruch the Scribe and Jerahmeel the King's Son." *Biblical Archaeologist* 42 (1979): 114–18.

———. "A Depository of Inscribed Ossuaries in the Kidron Valley." *Israel Exploration Journal* 12 (1962): 1–12.

Bacchielli, L., et al. *L'Agorà di Cirene.* Monografie di archeologia libica 7. Rome: "L'Erma" di Bretschneider, 1965.

Bach, A. "Whitewashing Athena: Gaining Perspective on Bernal and the Bible." *Journal for the Study of the Old Testament* 77 (1998): 3–19.

Badawy, A. "Askut: A Middle Kingdom Fortress in Nubia." *Archaeology* 18.2 (1965): 124–31.

Baer, K. "The Breathing Permit of Hôr: A Translation of the Apparent Source of the Book of Abraham." *Dialogue* 3 (1968): 109–31.

Bailey, R. C. "Beyond Identification: The Use of Africans in Old Testament Poetry and Narratives." In *Stony the Road We Trod: African American Biblical Interpretation,* ed. C. H. Felder, 165–84. Minneapolis: Fortress, 1991.

Baines, J., and J. Málek. *Atlas of Ancient Egypt.* New York: Facts on File, 1980.

Baker, D. W. "Cushan." In *The Anchor Bible Dictionary,* ed. D. N. Freedman et al., 1.1219–20. New York: Doubleday, 1992.

———. "Lud." In *The Anchor Bible Dictionary,* ed. D. N. Freedman et al., 4.397. New York: Doubleday, 1992.

———. "Ophir." In *The Anchor Bible Dictionary,* ed. D. N. Freedman et al., 5.26–27. New York: Doubleday, 1992.

Ballard, R. D., et al. "Iron Age Shipwrecks in Deep Water off Ashkelon, Israel." *American Journal of Archaeology* 106 (2000): 151–68.

Bamberger, B. "Solomon and Sheba." *Jewish Quarterly Review* 66 (1976): 245–46.

Bamberger, H. "Aaron: Changing Perspectives." *Judaism* 42 (1993): 201–13.

Bard, K. A., and R. Fattovich. "Some Remarks on the Processes of State Formation in Egypt and Ethiopia." In *Africa and Africans in Antiquity,* ed. E. M. Yamauchi, 276–90. East Lansing: Michigan State University Press, 2001.

Barker, G., J. Lloyd, and J. Reynolds, eds. *Cyrenaica in Antiquity.* Oxford: British Archaeological Reports, 1985.

Barnett, R. D. *Illustrations of Old Testament History.* London: British Museum, 1966.

Bassett, F. W. "Noah's Nakedness and the Curse of Canaan: A Case of Incest?" *Vetus Testamentum* 21 (1971): 232–37.

Bates, O. *The Eastern Libyans.* London: Macmillan, 1914.

Bates, R. D. "Could Taharqa Have Been Called to the Battle of Eltekeh? A Response to William H. Shea." *Near East Archaeological Society Bulletin* 46 (2001): 43–63.

Beardsley, G. H. *The Negro in Greek and Roman Civilization.* Baltimore: Johns Hopkins University Press, 1929.

Becking, B. *The Fall of Samaria: An Historical and Archaeological Study.* Leiden: Brill, 1992.

Bellis, A. O. "The Queen of Sheba: A Gender-Sensitive Reading." *Journal of Religious Thought* 51 (1994–95): 17–28.

Beltrami, V. "Population of Cyrenaica and Eastern Sahara before the Greek Period." In *Cyrenaica in Antiquity,* ed. G. Barker, J. Lloyd, and J. Reynolds, 135–44. Oxford: British Archaeological Reports, 1985.

Ben-Jochanan, Y. *Africa: Mother of Western Civilization.* Baltimore: Black Classic, 1988.

Bennett, R. A. "Africa and the Biblical Period." *Harvard Theological Review* 64 (1971): 483–500.

Ben Zvi, E. "Who Wrote the Speech of Rabshakeh and When?" *Journal of Biblical Literature* 109 (1990): 79–92.

Berkowitz, L. "Has the U.S. Geological Survey Found King Solomon's Gold Mines?" *Biblical Archaeology Review* 3 (1977): 1, 28–33.

Berlinerblau, J. *Heresy in the University.* New Brunswick: Rutgers University Press, 1999.

Bernal, M. *Black Athena: The Afroasiatic Roots of Classical Civilization,* vol. 1: *The Fabrication of Ancient Greece, 1785–1985.* New Brunswick: Rutgers University Press, 1987.

———. *Black Athena: The Afroasiatic Roots of Classical Civilization,* vol. 2: *The Archaeological and Documentary Evidence.* New Brunswick: Rutgers University Press, 1991.

———. "*Black Athena*: Hostilities to Egypt in the Eighteenth Century." In *The "Racial" Economy of Science,* ed. S. Harding, 47–63. Bloomington: Indiana University Press, 1993.

———. *Black Athena Writes Back.* Durham: Duke University Press, 2001.

———. *Cadmean Letters: The Transmission of the Alphabet to the Aegean and Further West before 1400 B.C.* Winona Lake, Ind.: Eisenbrauns, 1990.

———. "First by Land, Then by Sea: Thoughts about the Social Formation of the Mediterranean and Greece." In *Geography in Historical Perspective,* ed. E. Genovese and L. Hochberg, 3–33. Oxford: Blackwell, 1989.

———. "The Image of Ancient Greece as a Tool for Colonialism and European Hegemony." In *Social Reconstruction of the Past: Representation as Power,* ed. G. C. Bond and A. Gilliam, 119–28. London: Routledge, 1994.

———. "Responses to Critical Reviews of *Black Athena,* Volume I." *Journal of Mediterranean Archaeology* 3 (1990): 111–37.

Betto, F. *Fidel and Religion.* Sydney: Pathfinder, 1986.

Bietak, M. "Avaris and Piramesse: Archaeological Exploration in the Eastern Nile Delta." *Proceedings of the British Academy* 65 (1979): 225–90.

Blackburn, R. *The Making of New World Slavery: From the Baroque to the Modern, 1492–1800.* London: Verso, 1997.

Bimson, J. "King Solomon's Mines: A Reassessment of Finds in the Arabah." *Tyndale Bulletin* 32 (1981): 123–49.

Blaiklock, E. M., and R. K. Harrison, eds. *The New International Dictionary of Biblical Archaeology.* Grand Rapids: Zondervan, 1983.

Blakely, J. A., and J. A. Sauer. "The Road to Wadi al-Jubah: Archaeology on the Ancient Spice Route in Yemen." *Expedition* 27 (1985): 2–9.

Boardman, J. *The Greeks Overseas: Their Early Colonies and Trade.* 2d ed. London: Thames & Hudson, 1973.

Boardman, J., and J. Hayes. *Excavations at Tocra, 1963–1965.* 2 vols. London: British School of Archaeology at Athens, 1966–73.

Boardman, J., et al., eds. *The Assyrian and Babylonian Empires.* 2d ed. The Cambridge Ancient History, vol. 3.2. Cambridge: Cambridge University Press, 1991.

Bonnet, C. *Édifices et rites funéraires à Kerma.* Paris: Errance, 2000.

———. "Excavations at the Nubian Royal Town of Kerma, 1975–91." *Antiquity* 66 (1992): 611–25.

———. "Les fouilles archéologiques de Kerma (Soudan)." *Genava* 26 (1978): 107–27; 28 (1979–80): 31–62; 30 (1982): 1–42.

———. "Kerma: An African Kingdom of the Second and Third Millennia B.C." *Archaeology* 36 (1983): 38–445.

———. "Kerma: Rapport préliminaire sur les campagnes de 1995–1996 et 1996–1997." *Genava* 45 (1997): 96–123.

———. "Kerma: Rapport préliminaire sur les campagnes de 1997–1998 et 1998–1999." *Genava* 47 (1999): 55–86.

———. "Kerma: Rapport préliminaire sur les campagnes de 1999–2000 et 2000–2001." *Genava* 49 (2001): 199–218.

———. *Kerma: Royaume de Nubie.* Geneva: Mission archéologique de l'Université de Genève au Soudan, 1990.

———. *Kerma: Territoire et métropole.* Cairo: Institut français d'archéologie du Caire, 1986.

Bordreuil, P. "The South-Arabian Abecedary." *Near Eastern Archaeology* 63.4 (2000): 197.

Borger, R. *Die Inschriften Asarhaddons Königs von Assyrien.* Graz: Seelbstverlage des herausgebers, 1956.

Borowski, O. *Every Living Thing: Daily Use of Animals in Ancient Israel.* Walnut Creek, Calif.: Altamira, 1998.

———. "The Table of Nations (Genesis 10)—A Socio-Cultural Approach." *Zeitschrift für die alttestamentliche Wissenschaft* 98 (1986): 14–31.

Bosch, D. J. "Currents and Cross Currents in South African Black Theology." *Journal of Religion in Africa* 6 (1974): 1–22.

Bourriau, J. "Relations between Egypt and Kerma during the Middle and New Kingdoms." In *Egypt and Africa: Nubia from Prehistory to Islam,* ed. W. V. Davies, 129–44. London: British Museum, 1991.

Bowen, R. L., and F. P. Albright. *Archaeological Discoveries in South Arabia.* Baltimore: Johns Hopkins University Press, 1958.

Bradbury, L. "Following Thutmose I on His Campaign to Kush." *KMT: A Modern Journal of Ancient Egypt* 3.3 (1992): 51–59.

———. "*Kpn*-boats, Punt Trade, and a Lost Emporium." *Journal of the American Research Center in Egypt* 33 (1998): 37–60.

Bradley, L. R. "The Curse of Canaan and the American Negro." *Concordia Theological Monthly* 42.2 (1971): 100–110.

Braund, D. "The Social and Economic Context of the Roman Annexation of Cyrenaica." In *Cyrenaica in Antiquity,* ed. G. Barker, J. Lloyd, and J. Reynolds, 319–23. Oxford: British Archaeological Reports, 1985.

Breasted, J. H., ed. and trans. *Ancient Records of Egypt: Historical Documents from the Earliest Times to the Persian Conquest.* Chicago: University of Chicago Press, 1906–7. Reprinted New York: Russell & Russell, 1962.

Bregman, J. *Synesius of Cyrene: Philosopher-Bishop.* Berkeley: University of California Press, 1982.

Breton, J.-F. *Arabia Felix from the Time of the Queen of Sheba.* Notre Dame: University of Notre Dame Press, 2001.

Brier, B. "The Other Pyramids." *Archaeology* 55.5 (2002): 54–58.

Bright, J. *A History of Israel.* 3d ed. Philadelphia: Westminster, 1981.

Bringhurst, N. G. *Saints, Slaves, and Blacks: The Changing Place of Black People within Mormonism.* Westwood, Conn.: Greenwood, 1981.

Briquel-Chattonet, F. *Les relations entre les cités de la côte phénicienne et les royaumes d'Israël et de Juda.* Louvain: Peeters, 1992.

Brock, S. P. "Some Syriac Legends concerning Moses." *Journal of Jewish Studies* 33 (1982): 237–58.

Browne, G. M. *Literary Texts in Old Nubian.* Vienna: Institut für Afrikanistik der Universität, 1989.

Browne, S. G. *Leprosy in the Bible.* London: Christian Medical Fellowship, 1979.

Bruce, D. D. "Ancient Africa and the Early Black American Historians, 1883–1915." *American Quarterly* 36 (1984): 684–99.

Bruce, F. F. *Commentary on the Book of the Acts.* Grand Rapids: Eerdmans, 1983.

———. "Philip and the Ethiopian." *Journal of Semitic Studies* 34 (1989): 377–86.

Brunner, U. *Die Erforschung der antiken Oase von Mārib mit Hilfe geomorphologischer Untersuchungsmethoden.* Mainz: Zabern, 1987.

Brunson, J. "Ancient Egyptians: 'The Dark Red Race Myth.'" In *Egypt Revisited,* ed. I. Van Sertima, 53–54. New Brunswick: Transaction, 1989.

Brunt, P. A., and J. M. Moore, eds. *Res Gestae Divi Augusti.* London: Oxford University Press, 1967.

Budd, P. J. *Numbers.* Word Biblical Commentary 5. Waco: Word, 1984.

Budge, E. A. W. *The Queen of Sheba and Her Only Son Menyelek.* London: Hopkinson, 1922.

Bugner, L., ed. *The Image of the Black in Western Art,* vol. 1: *From the Pharaohs to the Fall of the Roman Empire.* New York: Morrow, 1976.

Bullard, R. G. "The Berbers of the Maghreb and Ancient Carthage." In *Africa and Africans in Antiquity*, ed. E. M. Yamauchi, 180–209. East Lansing: Michigan State University Press, 2001.

Bulliet, R. W. *The Camel and the Wheel.* Cambridge: Harvard University Press, 1975.

Burns, J. B. "Solomon's Egyptian Horses and Exotic Wives." *Forum* 7.1–2 (1991): 29–44.

Burns, R. J. *Has the Lord Indeed Spoken Only through Moses?* Atlanta: Scholars Press, 1987.

Burstein, S. M. "Axum and the Fall of Meroe." *Journal of the American Research Center in Egypt* 28 (1981): 47–50.

———. "The Axumite Inscription from Meroe and Late Meroitic Chronology." *Meroitica* 7 (1984): 220–21.

———. "The Challenge of *Black Athena*: An Interim Assessment." *Ancient History Bulletin* 8.1 (1994): 11–17.

———. "Cornelius Gallus and Aethiopia." *Ancient History Bulletin* 2.1 (1988): 16–20.

———. *Graeco-Africana: Studies in the History of Greek Relations with Egypt and Nubia.* New Rochelle: Caratzas, 1995.

———. "The Hellenistic Fringe: The Case of Meroe." In *Hellenistic History and Culture*, ed. P. Green, 38–54. Berkeley: University of California Press, 1993.

———. "Herodotus and the Emergence of Meroe." *Journal of the Society for the Study of Egyptian Antiquities* 11.1 (1981): 1–5.

———. "The Kingdom of Meroe." In *Africa and Africans in Antiquity*, ed. E. M. Yamauchi, 132–58. East Lansing: Michigan State University Press, 2001.

———. "The Nubian Campaign of C. Petronius and George Reisner's Second Meroitic Kingdom." *Zeitschrift für ägyptische Sprache und Altertumskunde* 106 (1979): 95–106.

———. "Psamtek I and the End of Nubian Domination in Egypt." *Journal of the Society for the Study of Egyptian Antiquities* 14.2 (1984): 31–34.

Burstein, S. M., ed. *Ancient African Civilizations: Kush and Axum.* Princeton: Wiener, 1998.

Burstein, S. M., trans. *Agatharchides of Cnidus: On the Erythraean Sea.* London: Hakluyt Society, 1989.

Buswell, J. *Slavery, Segregation and Scripture.* Grand Rapids: Eerdmans, 1964.

Buxton, D. *The Abyssinians.* London: Thames & Hudson, 1970.

Calhoon, R. H. "The African Heritage: Slavery, and Evangelical Christianity among American Blacks." *Fides et Historia* 21 (1989): 61–66.

Caminos, R. A. "The Nitocris Adoption Stela." *Journal of Egyptian Archaeology* 50 (1964): 71–100.

Canova, G. "La leggenda della regina di Saba." *Quaderni di Studi Arabi* 5–6 (1987–88): 105–19.

———. *Talʾabî Storia di Bilqîs regina di Saba.* Venice: Marsilio, 2000.

Cansdale, G. *All the Animals of the Bible Land.* Grand Rapids: Zondervan, 1970.

Caputo, G. "La sinagoga di Berenice in una iscrizione greca inedita." *La Parola del Passato* 12 (1957): 132–34.

Carroll, S. T. "Solomonic Legend: The Muslims and the Great Zimbabwe." *International Journal of African Historical Studies* 21 (1988): 233–47.

———. "Wrestling in Ancient Nubia." *Journal of Sport History* 15 (1988): 121–37.

Carruthers, J. "Outside of Academia: Bernal's Critique of the Black Champions of Ancient Egypt." *Journal of Black Studies* 22 (1992): 459–76.

Cary, M., and E. H. Warmington. *The Ancient Explorers.* Baltimore: Penguin, 1963.

Castiglioni, A., and A. J. Vercoutter. *Das Goldland der Pharaonen.* Mainz: Zabern, 1998.

Chamoux, F. "Du Silphion." In *Cyrenaica in Antiquity,* ed. G. Barker, J. Lloyd, and J. Reynolds, 165–82. Oxford: British Archaeological Reports, 1985.

Charles, P. "Les noirs, fils de Cham le maudit." *Nouvelle revue théologique* 55 (1978): 721–39.

Chastel, A. "La légende de la reine de Saba." *Revue de l'histoire des religions* (1939): 199–20.

Chevannes, B. *Rastafari: Roots and Ideology.* Syracuse: Syracuse University Press, 1994.

Childs, B. S. *Isaiah and the Assyrian Crisis.* London: SCM, 1967.

Christensen, D. L. "The Identity of 'King So' in Egypt (2 Kings xvii 4)." *Vetus Testamentum* 39.2 (1989): 140–53.

Christidès, J. "L'enigme d'Ophir." *Revue biblique* 77 (1970): 240–47.

Clancy, F. "Shishak/Shoshenq's Travels." *Journal for the Study of the Old Testament* 86 (1999): 3–23.

Clapp, N. *Sheba: Through the Desert in Search of the Legendary Queen.* Boston: Houghton Mifflin, 2001.

Clark, J. D., ed. *The Cambridge History of Africa,* vol. 1: *From the Earliest Times to c. 500 B.C.* New York: Cambridge University Press, 1982.

Clarke, J. H. "African Warrior Queens." In *Black Women in Antiquity,* ed. I. Van Sertima, 123–34. New Brunswick: Transaction, 1988.

Clements, R. E. *Isaiah and the Deliverance of Jerusalem.* Sheffield: University of Sheffield Press, 1980.

Cline, E. H. "Amenhotpe III and the Aegean: A Reassessment of Egypto-Aegean Relations in the 14th Century B.C." *Orientalia* 56 (1987): 1–36.

———. "Content and Trade or Colonization? Egypt and the Aegean in the 14th–13th Centuries B.C." *Minos* 25–26 (1990–91): 7–36.

———. *Sailing the Wine-Dark Sea: International Trade and the Late Bronze Age Aegean.* Oxford: Tempus Reparatum, 1994.

Cline, E. H., and D. Harris-Cline, eds. *The Aegean and the Orient in the Second Millennium.* Liège: Université de Liège, 1998.

Clouse, R. G., R. V. Pierard, and E. M. Yamauchi. *Two Kingdoms: The Church and Culture through the Ages.* Chicago: Moody, 1993.

Coats, G. W. "Humility and Honor: A Moses Legend in Numbers 12." In *Art and Meaning: Rhetoric in Biblical Literature,* ed. D. J. A. Clines et al., 87–107. Sheffield: JSOT Press, 1982.

———. *Moses—Heroic Man, Man of God.* Sheffield: JSOT Press, 1988.

Cogan, M. *1 Kings.* Anchor Bible 10. Garden City, N.Y.: Doubleday, 2001.

———. "Sennacherib's Siege of Jerusalem." *Biblical Archaeology Review* 27.1 (2001): 40–45, 69.

Cogan, M., and H. Tadmor. *II Kings*. Anchor Bible 11. Garden City, N.Y.: Doubleday, 1988.

Cohen, H. H. *The Drunkenness of Noah*. University, Ala.: University of Alabama Press, 1974.

Cohen, M. "Ham." In *The Encyclopaedia of Islam*, ed. B. Lewis et al., 3.104–5. Leiden: Brill, 1971.

Cohen, S. J. D. "Solomon and the Daughter of Pharaoh: Inter-marriage, Conversion, and the Impurity of Women." *Journal of the Ancient Near Eastern Society* 16–17 (1984–85): 23–38.

Coleman, J. E. "The Case Against Martin Bernal's *Black Athena*." *Archaeology* 45.5 (1992): 48–52, 77–78, 80–81.

Conwell, D. "On Ostrich Eggs and Libyans." *Expedition* 29.3 (1987): 25–34.

Conzelmann, H. *The Acts of the Apostles*. Philadelphia: Fortress, 1987.

Copher, C. B. "The Black Presence in the Old Testament." In *Stony the Road We Trod: African American Biblical Interpretation*, ed. C. H. Felder, 146–64. Minneapolis: Fortress, 1991.

———. "Blacks and Jews in Historical Interaction: The Biblical/African Experience." *Journal of the Interdenominational Theological Center* 3 (1975): 9–16.

———. "Egypt and Ethiopia in the Old Testament." *Journal of African Civilizations* 6 (1984): 164–77.

Cornell, T., and J. Matthews. *Atlas of the Roman World*. Oxford: Phaidon, 1982.

Cozzolino, C. "The Land of Pwnt." In *Sesto congresso internazionale di egittologia*, ed. G. Zaccone and T. R. Di Netro, 2.391–98. Turin: Società Italiana, 1993.

Crocker, P. T. "The City of Meroe and the Ethiopian Eunuch." *Buried History* 22.3 (1986): 53–72.

———. "Cush and the Bible." *Buried History* 22.2 (1986): 27–38.

Cross, F. M. *Canaanite Myth and Hebrew Bible*. Cambridge: Harvard University Press, 1973.

———. "Early Alphabetic Scripts." In *Symposia Celebrating the Seventy-fifth Anniversary of the Founding of the American Schools of Oriental Research*, ed. F. M. Cross, 97–123. Cambridge, Mass.: American Schools of Oriental Research, 1979.

———. *From Epic to Canaan*. Baltimore: Johns Hopkins University Press, 1998.

Dafaʿlla, S. B. "The Origin of the Napatan State." *Meroitica* 15 (1999): 129–45.

Dalglish, E. R. "Cushi." In *The Anchor Bible Dictionary*, ed. D. N. Freedman et al., 1.1220. New York: Doubleday, 1992.

Dalley, S. "Foreign Chariotry and Cavalry in the Armies of Tiglath-pileser III and Sargon II." *Iraq* 47 (1985): 31–48.

Daum, W., ed. *Die Königin von Saba*. Zurich: Belser, 1988.

Davey, C. "Temples of the Levant and the Buildings of Solomon." *Tyndale Bulletin* 31 (1980): 107–46.

Davidson, B. *Africa in History*. New York: Macmillan, 1991.

Davies, M. L. "Levitical Leprosy: Uncleanness in the Psyche." *Expository Times* 99 (1988): 36–39.

Davies, W. V., ed. *Egypt and Africa*. London: British Museum, 1991.

Davis, D. B. *Slavery and Human Progress*. New York: Oxford University Press, 1984.

Day, J. "Molech: A God of Human Sacrifice in the Old Testament." *Journal of Biblical Literature* 111 (1992): 117–20.

———. *Molech: God of Human Sacrifice in the Old Testament*. Cambridge: Cambridge University Press, 1989.

———. "The Problem of 'So, King of Egypt' in 2 Kings xvii 4." *Vetus Testamentum* 42 (1992): 289–301.

Decock, P. B. "The Understanding of Isaiah 53:7–8 in Acts 8:32–33." *Neotestamentica* 14 (1981): 111–33.

DeFelice, J. "Tin and Trade: An Archaeometallurgical Approach to Dating the Exodus." M.A. thesis, Miami University, Oxford, Ohio, 1994.

Delcor, M. "La reine de Saba et Salomon." In *Tradicio i Traduccio de la Paraula*, 307–24. Montserrat: Asociación Biblica et Catalunya, 1993.

Depuydt, L. "The Date of Piye's Egyptian Campaign and the Chronology of the Twenty-Fifth Dynasty." *Journal of Egyptian Archaeology* 79 (1993): 269–74.

Derchain, P. "Les plus ancient témoignages de sacrifices d'enfants chez les Sémites occidentaux." *Vetus Testamentum* 20 (1970): 351–55.

Desanges, J. "Les relations de l'empire romain avec l'Afrique nilotique et érythéenne, d'Auguste à Probus." In *Aufstieg und Niedergang der römischen Welt*, ed. H. Temporini and W. Hasse, 2.10.1.3–43. Berlin: de Gruyter, 1988.

———. "Le statue et les limites de la Nubie romaine." *Chronique d'égypte* 86 (1969): 139–47.

Deutsches archäologisches Institut, Sanʿa. *Archäologische Berichte aus dem Yemen*. Mainz: Zabern, 1982.

Dever, W. "Palaces and Temples in Canaan and Ancient Israel." In *Civilizations of the Ancient Near East*, ed. J. Sasson, 1.605–14. Peabody, Mass.: Hendrickson, 2000.

Dever, W., et al. "Further Excavations at Gezer, 1967–71." *Biblical Archaeologist* 34 (1971): 94–132.

Diebner, B. J. "For He Had Married a Cushite Woman." *Nubica* 1–2 (1990): 499–504.

Dillard, R. B. *2 Chronicles*. Word Biblical Commentary 15. Waco: Word, 1987.

Dinkler, E. "König Ezana von Aksum und das Christentum." In *Ägypten und Kusch*, ed. E. Endesfelder et al., 121–32. Berlin: Akademie-Verlag, 1977.

———. "Philippus und der ἀνὴρ αἰθίοψ (Apg 8,26–40)." In *Jesus und Paulus: Festschrift für Werner Georg Kümmel zum 70. Geburtstag*, ed. E. E. Ellis and E. Grässer, 85–95. Göttingen: Vandenhoeck & Ruprecht, 1975.

Dion, P. E. "Sennacherib's Expedition to Palestine." *Église et théologie* 20 (1989): 5–25.

Diop, C. A. *The African Origin of Civilization: Myth or Reality?* New York: Hill, 1974.

———. *Civilization or Barbarism*. Brooklyn: Hill, 1991.

———. *The Cultural Unity of Black Africa*. London: Karnak, 1989.

———. *On Science, History, and Technology*. New York: ECA, 1990.

———. "Origin of the Ancient Egyptians." In *General History of Africa*, vol. 2: *Ancient Civilizations of Africa*, ed. G. Mokhtar, 15–32. London: Currey/Berkeley: University of California Press, 1990.

Dixon, D. M. "The Origin of the Kingdom of Kush (Napata-Meroë)." *Journal of Egyptian Archaeology* 50 (1964): 121–32.

———. "The Transplantation of Punt Incense Trees in Egypt." *Journal of Egyptian Archaeology* 55 (1969): 55–65.

Dixon, J. "The Land of Yam." *Journal of Egyptian Archaeology* 44 (1958): 49–55.

Doll, S. K. "The Day Hour Texts on the Sarcophagi of Anlamani and Aspelta." In *Studies in Ancient Egypt, the Aegean, and the Sudan*, ed. W. K. Simpson and W. M. Davis, 43–54. Boston: Museum of Fine Arts, 1981.

———. "Identification and Significance of the Texts and Decorations on the Sarcophagi of Anlamani and Aspelta." In *Meroitic Studies*, ed. N. B. Millet and A. L. Kelley, 276–80. Berlin: Akademie-Verlag, 1982.

———. "Texts and Decoration on the Napatan Sarcophagi of Anlamani and Aspelta." Ph.D. diss., Brandeis University, 1978.

Dombrowski, B., and F. Dombrowski. "Frumentius/Abba Salama." *Oriens christianus* 68 (1984): 114–69.

Dompere, K. K. *Africentricity and African Nationalism: Philosophy and Ideology for Africa's Complete Emancipation.* Langley Park, Md.: IAAS, 1992.

Dothan, T. "Ekron's Identity Confirmed." *Archaeology* 51.1 (1998): 30–31.

Dothan, T., S. Gitin, and J. Naveh. "A Royal Dedicatory Inscription from Ekron." *Israel Exploration Journal* 47 (1997): 1–16.

Douglas, K. B. *The Black Christ.* Maryknoll, N.Y.: Orbis, 1994.

Drake, St. C. *Black Folk Here and There: An Essay in History and Anthropology.* Los Angeles: Center for Afro-American Studies, University of California, 1987.

Duling, D. "Solomon, Exorcism, and the Son of David." *Harvard Theological Review* 68 (1975): 235–52.

Duling, D., trans. "Testament of Solomon." In *The Old Testament Pseudepigrapha*, ed. J. H. Charlesworth, 1.982–83. Garden City, N.Y.: Doubleday, 1983.

Dunham, D. *Excavations at Kerma*, part 6. Boston: Museum of Fine Arts, 1982.

———. *The Royal Cemeteries of Kush.* 5 vols. Cambridge: Harvard University Press, 1950–63.

———. *The Second Cataract Forts*, vol. 2: *Uronarti, Shalfak, Mirgissa.* Boston: Museum of Fine Arts, 1967.

———. *Two Royal Ladies of Meroë.* Boston: Museum of Fine Arts, 1924.

Dunham, D., and J. M. A. Janssen. *The Second Cataract Forts*, vol. 1: *Semna, Kumma.* Boston: Museum of Fine Arts, 1960.

Early, G., W. J. Moses, L. Wilson, and M. R. Lefkowitz. "Symposium: Historical Roots of Afrocentrism." *Academic Questions* 7.2 (1994): 44–54.

Edel, E. "Die Ländernamen Unternubiens und die Ausbreitung der C-Gruppe nach den Reiseberichten des Ḥrw-ḫwjf." *Orientalia* 36 (1967): 132–58.

Eden, C., and G. Bawden. "History of Taymaʾ and Hejazi Trade during the First Millennium B.C." *Journal of the Economic and Social History of the Orient* 32 (1989): 48–103.

Edwards, D. N. *The Archaeology of the Meroitic State.* Oxford: Tempus Reparatum, 1996.

Edwards, I. E. S. *The Pyramids of Egypt.* Harmondsworth/Baltimore: Penguin, 1975.

Eide, T., et al., eds. *Fontes Historiae Nubiorum*. Bergen: University of Bergen Press, 1994.

El-Athram, R. "The Silphium Plant in Cyrenaica." In *Libya antiqua: Report and Papers of the Symposium Organized by UNESCO in Paris, 16 to 18 January 1984*, 23–27. Paris: UNESCO, 1986.

Elrashedy, F. "Attic Imported Pottery in Classical Cyrenaica." In *Cyrenaica in Antiquity*, ed. G. Barker, J. Lloyd, and J. Reynolds, 205–18. Oxford: British Archaeological Reports, 1985.

Embry, J. L. *Black Saints in a White Church: Contemporary African American Mormons*. Salt Lake City: Signature, 1994.

Emery, W. B. *Archaic Egypt*. Baltimore: Penguin, 1961.

———. *Egypt in Nubia*. London: Hutchinson, 1965.

———. *Lost Land Emerging*. New York: Scribner, 1967.

———. *Nubian Treasure*. London: Methuen, 1948.

Emery, W. B., H. S. Smith, and A. R. Millard. *The Fortress at Buhen: The Archaeological Report*. London: Egypt Exploration Society, 1979.

Endesfelder, E., et al., eds. *Ägypten und Kusch*. Berlin: Akademie-Verlag, 1977.

Eph'al, I. *The Ancient Arabs*. Jerusalem: Magnes, 1982.

Epstein, I., ed. *Hebrew-English Edition of the Babylonian Talmud*. London: Soncino, 1969.

Evans, C. A. "Jesus and the Ossuaries." *Bulletin for Biblical Research* 13 (2003): 21–46.

———. *Jesus and the Ossuaries*. Waco: Baylor University Press, forthcoming.

Evans, W. M. "'From the Land of Canaan to the Land of Guinea': The Strange Odyssey of the Sons of Ham." *American Historical Review* 85 (1980): 15–43.

Evans-Pritchard, E. *The Sanusi of Cyrenaica*. Oxford: Clarendon, 1949.

Faber, E. *Jews, Slaves, and the Slave Trade: Setting the Record Straight*. New York: New York University Press, 1998.

Fairservis, W. A. *The Ancient Kingdoms of the Nile*. New York: New American Library, 1962.

Farrar, F. W. *The Life of Christ*. London: Cassell, 1894.

Fattovich, R. "The Problem of Punt in the Light of Recent Fieldwork in the Eastern Sudan." In *Akten des vierten Internationalen Ägyptologen Kongresses*, ed. S. Schoske, 4.257–72. Hamburg: Buske, 1991.

———. "Punt, The Archaeological Perspective." In *Sesto congresso internazionale di egittologia*, ed. G. Zaccone and T. R. Di Netro, 2.399–403. Turin: Società Italiana, 1993.

Faulkner, R. O. *A Concise Dictionary of Middle Egyptian*. Oxford: Oxford University Press, 1962.

Fazzini, R. A. *Egypt: Dynasty XXII–XXV*. Leiden: Brill, 1988.

Felder, C. H. "Afrocentricity and Biblical Authority." *Theology Today* 49 (1992): 357–66.

———. "Afrocentrism, the Bible, and the Politics of Difference." *Journal of Religious Thought* 50 (1993–94): 45–56.

———. "The Presence of Blacks in Antiquity." In *Holy Bible: African American Jubilee Edition*, 109–26. New York: American Bible Society, 1999.

————. *Race, Racism, and the Biblical Narratives.* Minneapolis: Fortress, 2002.

————. "Racial Motifs in the Biblical Narratives." In *Voices from the Margin: Interpreting the Bible in the Third World*, ed. R. S. Sugirtharajah, 172–88. Maryknoll, N.Y.: Orbis, 1991.

————. *Troubling Biblical Waters.* Maryknoll, N.Y.: Orbis, 1989.

Felder, C. H., ed. *Stony the Road We Trod.* Minneapolis: Fortress, 1991.

————, ed. *The Original African Heritage Study Bible.* Nashville: Winston, 1993.

Feldman, L. H. *Josephus's Interpretation of the Bible.* Berkeley: University of California Press, 1998.

Fillon, M. "The Real Face of Jesus." *Popular Mechanics* 100 (Dec. 2002): 68–71.

Finch, C. S. "Further Conversations with the Pharaoh [i.e., Diop]." In *Great African Thinkers*, vol. 1: *Cheikh Anta Diop*, ed. I. Van Sertima and L. Williams, 227–37. New Brunswick: Transaction, 1986.

Fisher, M. C. "Some Contributions of Ethiopic Studies to the Understanding of the Old Testament." In *The Law and the Prophets: Old Testament Studies Prepared in Honor of Oswald Thompson Allis*, ed. J. H. Skilton, 71–86. Nutley, N.J.: Presbyterian & Reformed, 1974.

Flinder, A. "Is This Solomon's Seaport?" *Biblical Archaeology Review* 15.4 (1989): 30–43.

Fontaine, C. F. "More Queenly Proverb Performance: The Queen of Sheba in Targum Esther Sheni." In *Wisdom You Are My Sister*, ed. M. L. Barré, 216–33. Washington, D.C.: Catholic Biblical Association, 1997.

Fouchet, M.-P. *Rescued Treasures of Egypt.* New York: McGraw-Hill, 1965.

Fouts, D. M. "A Defense of the Hyperbolic Interpretation of Large Numbers in the Old Testament." *Journal of the Evangelical Theological Society* 40 (1997): 377–87.

Fox-Genovese, E., and E. D. Genovese. "The Divine Sanction of Social Order: Religious Foundations of the Southern Slaveholders' World View." *Journal of the American Academy of Religion* 55 (1987): 211–33.

Frame, G. "The Inscription of Sargon II at Tang-i Var." *Orientalia* 68 (1999): 31–57.

Franklin, N. "The Room V Reliefs at Dur-Sharrukin and Sargon II's Western Campaigns." *Tel Aviv* 21 (1994): 255–75.

Franz, G. "Is Mount Sinai in Saudi Arabia?" *Bible and Spade* 13.4 (2000): 101–14.

Fredrickson, G. M. *White Supremacy: A Comparative Study in American and South African History.* New York: Oxford University Press, 1981.

Freedman, D. N., et al., eds. *The Anchor Bible Dictionary.* 6 vols. New York: Doubleday, 1992.

Freedman, H., and M. Simon, eds. *Midrash Rabbah: Genesis.* London: Soncino, 1939.

Frend, W. H. C. "Coptic, Greek and Nubian at Qasr Ibrim." *Byzantinoslavica* 33 (1972): 224–29.

Gadallah, F. F. "Meroitic Problems and a Comprehensive Meroitic Bibliography." *Kush* 11 (1963): 196–216.

Gage, W. A., and J. R. Beck. "The Gospel, Zion's Barren Woman, and the Ethiopian Eunuch." *Crux* 30.2 (1994): 35–43.

Gaines, J. H. "Seductress, Heroine, or Murderer?" *Bible Review* 17.5 (2001): 12–20, 43–44.

Galand, L. "Le libyque et les études sémitiques." *Semitica* 38 (1990): 122–24.

Gallagher, W. R. *Sennacherib's Campaign to Judah: New Studies.* Leiden: Brill, 1999.

García Martínez, F. *The Dead Sea Scrolls Translated: The Qumran Texts in English.* 2d ed. Leiden: Brill/Grand Rapids: Eerdmans, 1996.

Gardiner, A. H. "An Ancient List of the Fortresses of Nubia." *Journal of Egyptian Archaeology* 3 (1916): 184–92.

———. *Egypt of the Pharaohs.* Oxford: Clarendon, 1961.

———. *Egyptian Grammar: Being an Introduction to the Study of Hieroglyphs.* 3d ed. London: Oxford University Press, 1957.

Garlake, P. *Great Zimbabwe.* London: Thames & Hudson, 1973.

Garstang, J. *Meroë, the City of the Ethiopians.* Oxford: Clarendon, 1911.

Gaster, T. *Myth, Legend, and Custom in the Old Testament.* New York: Harper & Row, 1969.

Gaventa, B. R. "Ethiopian Eunuch." In *The Anchor Bible Dictionary,* ed. D. N. Freedman et al., 2.667. New York: Doubleday, 1992.

———. *From Darkness to Light: Aspects of Conversion in the New Testament.* Philadelphia: Fortress, 1986.

Gelb, I. J. "Makkan and Meluḫḫa in Early Mesopotamian Sources." *Revue d'assyriologie* 64 (1970): 1–8.

Getui, M., K. Holter, and V. Zinkuratire, eds. *Interpreting the Old Testament in Africa.* New York: Lang, 2001.

Ginzberg, L. *The Legends of the Jews.* 7 vols. Philadelphia: Jewish Publication Society, 1909–38.

Gitton, M., and J. Leclant. "Gottesgemahlin." In *Lexikon der Ägyptologie,* ed. W. Helck, E. Otto, and W. Westendorf, 2.792–812. Wiesbaden: Harrassowitz, 1972.

Giveon, R. *Les bédouins shosou des documents égyptiens.* Leiden: Brill, 1971.

———. *The Impact of Egypt on Canaan.* Göttingen: Vandenhoeck & Ruprecht, 1978.

Glanzman, W. "Digging Deeper: The Results of the First Season of the Activities of the AFSM on the Mahram Bilqis." *Proceedings of the Seminar for Arabian Studies* 28 (1998): 89–104.

Glueck, N. *Rivers in the Desert: The Story of the Negev.* New York: Grove, 1960.

Godlewski, W. "Christian Nubia—After the Nubian Campaign." *Actes de la VIIIe conférence internationale des études nubiennes,* 267–77. Lille: Université Charles-de-Gaulle, 1998.

Goedicke, H. "Harkhuf's Travels." *Journal of Near Eastern Studies* 40 (1981): 1–20.

Goldenberg, D. M. "The Curse of Ham: A Case of Rabbinic Racism?" In *Struggles in the Promised Land,* ed. J. Salzman and C. West, 21–51. New York: Oxford University Press, 1997.

———. *The Curse of Ham: Race and Slavery in Early Judaism, Christianity, and Islam.* Princeton: Princeton University Press, forthcoming.

———. "The Image of the Black in Jewish Culture." *Jewish Quarterly Review* 93 (2003): 557–79.

———. "Rabbinic Knowledge of Black Africa." *Jewish Studies Quarterly* 5 (1998): 318–28.

———. "Scythian-Barbarian: The Permutations of a Classical Topos in Jewish and Christian Texts of Late Antiquity." *Journal of Jewish Studies* 49 (1998): 87–102.

Goldstein, J. *II Maccabees.* Anchor Bible 41A. Garden City, N.Y.: Doubleday, 1983.

Gonçalves, F. J. *L'expédition de Sennachérib en Palestine dans la littérature hébraïque ancienne*. Paris: n.p., 1986.
Goodchild, R. G. *Cyrene and Apollonia: An Historical Guide*. 3d ed. Tripoli: Libyan Department of Antiquities, 1970.
———. *Kyrene und Apollonia*. Zurich: Raggi, 1971.
———. *Libyan Studies: Select Papers of the Late R. G. Goodchild*, ed. J. Reynolds. London: Elek, 1976.
———. "The Temple of Zeus at Cyrene." *Papers of the British School at Rome* 26 (1958): 30–62.
Goodchild, R. G., J. Pedley, and D. White. *Apollonia: The Port of Cyrene*. Tripoli: Libyan Department of Antiquities, 1977.
Goodchild, R. G., and J. Reynolds. "The Temple of Zeus at Cyrene." *Papers of the British School at Rome* 26 (1958): 30–62.
Goodkind, H. W. "Lord Kingsborough Lost His Fortune Trying to Prove the Maya Were Descendants of the Ten Lost Tribes." *Biblical Archaeology Review* 11.5 (1985): 54–65.
Gordon, C. H. *The Common Background of Greek and Hebrew Civilizations*. New York: Norton, 1965.
———. "The Wine-Dark Sea." *Journal of Near Eastern Studies* 37 (1978): 51–52.
Gordon, M. *Slavery in the Arab World*. New York: New Amsterdam, 1992.
Görg, M. "Ofir und Punt." *Biblische Nötizen* 82 (1996): 5–8.
———. "Ophir, Tarschisch und Atlantis." *Biblische Nötizen* 15 (1981): 76–86.
———. "Wo Lag das Paradies?" *Biblische Nötizen* 2 (1977): 23–32.
———. "Zur Identität des Pishon." *Biblische Nötizen* 40 (1987): 11–13.
Gratien, B. *Les cultures Kerma: Essai de classification*. Lille: Université de Lille, 1978.
Graves, R., and R. Patai. *Hebrew Myths*. Garden City, N.Y.: Doubleday, 1964.
Gray, J. *I and II Kings*. 2d ed. Old Testament Library. London: SCM, 1970.
Grayson, A. K. "Sennacherib and Esarhaddon." In *The Cambridge Ancient History*, ed. J. Boardman et al., 2.2.103–41. Cambridge: Cambridge University Press, 1991.
Green, A. R. W. "The Identity of King So of Egypt—An Alternative Interpretation." *Journal of Near Eastern Studies* 52 (1993): 99–108.
———. *The Role of Human Sacrifice in the Ancient Near East*. Missoula, Mont.: Scholars Press, 1975.
———. "Solomon and Siamun." *Journal of Biblical Literature* 97 (1978): 353–67.
Greene, L. J. *The Negro in Colonial New England, 1620–1776*. Port Washington: Kennikat, 1966.
Greener, L. *High Dam over Nubia*. London: Cassell, 1962.
Greenfield, J. C. "The Small Caves of Qumran." *Journal of the American Oriental Society* 89 (1969):128–40.
Greenfield, J. C., and M. Mayerhofer. "The ʾalgummīm/ʾalmuggīm-Problem Reexamined." In *Hebräische Wortforschung: Festschrift zum 80. Geburtstag von Walter Baumgartner*, 83–89. Vetus Testamentum Supplement 16. Leiden: Brill, 1967.
Griffith, F. L. *Meroitic Inscriptions: Napata to Philae and Miscellaneous*. Warminster: Aris & Phillips, 1976.

Grimal, N. *A History of Ancient Egypt*. Oxford: Blackwell, 1992.

——. *La stèle triomphale de Pi(ʿank)y au Musée du Caire*. Cairo: L'institut français d'archéologie orientale, 1981.

Grohmann, E. "Kandake." In *Paulys Realencyclopädie der classischen Altertumswissenschaft* 20 Halbband. Stuttgart: Druckenmüller, 1858. Reprinted 1919.

Groom, N. *Frankincense and Myrrh: A Study of the Arabian Incense Trade*. London: Longman, 1981.

Grossfeld, B. *The Two Targums of Esther*. Collegeville, Minn.: Liturgical Press, 1986.

Gruchy, J. W. de. *The Church Struggle in South Africa*. Grand Rapids: Eerdmans, 1979.

Gundry, R. H. *Mark*. Grand Rapids: Eerdmans, 1993.

Haak, R. D. "'Cush' in Zephaniah." In *"The Pitcher Is Broken,"* ed. L. K. Handy and S. W. Holloway, 238–51. Sheffield: Sheffield Academic Press, 1995.

Habachi, L. "Mentuhotpe, the Vizier and Son-in-Law of Taharqa." In *Ägypten und Kusch*, ed. E. Endesfelder et al., 165–70. Berlin: Akademie-Verlag, 1977.

Habsburg, M. von. "Egyptian Influence in Cyrenaica during the Ptolemaic Period." In *Cyrenaica in Antiquity*, ed. G. Barker, J. Lloyd, and J. Reynolds, 357–64. Oxford: British Archaeological Reports, 1985.

Haggard, H. R. *King Solomon's Mines*. London: Cassell, 1886.

Haile, G. "Ethiopian Orthodox Church." In *Encyclopedia of Africa South of the Sahara*, ed. J. Middleton, 2.76–83. New York: Scribner, 1997.

Hallo, W. W. *Origins: The Ancient Near Eastern Background of Some Modern Western Institutions*. Leiden: Brill, 1996.

Hamilton, V. P. *The Book of Genesis: Chapters 1–17*. New International Commentary on the Old Testament. Grand Rapids: Eerdmans, 1990.

Hancock, G. *The Sign and the Seal: The Quest for the Lost Ark of the Covenant*. New York: Crown, 1992.

Hansberry, W. L. *Africa and Africans as Seen by Classical Writers*, ed. J. E. Harris. Washington, D.C.: Howard University Press, 1981.

Harden, D. *The Phoenicians*. 2d ed. N.Y.: Praeger, 1963.

Hardie, F. *The Abyssinian Crisis*. London: Batsford, 1974.

Haring, B. "Libyans in the Theban Region, 20th Dynasty." In *Sesto congresso internazionale di egittologia*, ed. G. Zaccone and T. R. Di Netro, 2.159–65. Turin: Società Italiana, 1993.

Harris, J. "Ethiopia Demands Its Ancient Stela . . . Italy Demurs." *Archaeology Odyssey* 5.4 (2002): 13.

Harris, J. E. *Africans and Their History*. New York: New American Library, 1987.

Harris, J. R., ed. *The Legacy of Egypt*. 2d ed. 2 vols. Oxford: Clarendon, 1971.

Harris, R. L., G. L. Archer, and B. K. Waltke. *Theological Wordbook of the Old Testament*. 2 vols. Chicago: Moody, 1980.

Hausman, G., ed. *The Kebra Nagast*. New York: St. Martin's, 1997.

Haycock, B. G. "Landmarks in Cushite History." *Journal of Egyptian Archaeology* 58 (1972): 225–45.

——. *The Sudan in Africa*. Khartoum: Khartoum University Press, 1974.

Haynes, J. L. *Nubia: Ancient Kingdoms of Africa*. Boston: Museum of Fine Arts, 1992.

Haynes, S. R. *Noah's Curse: The Biblical Justification of American Slavery.* Oxford: Oxford University Press, 2002.

Hays, J. D. "The Cushites: A Black Nation in Ancient History." *Bibliotheca Sacra* 153 (1996): 270–80.

———. *From Every People and Nation.* Downers Grove, Ill.: InterVarsity, 2003.

———. "From the Land of the Bow: Black Soldiers." *Bible Review* 14.4 (1998): 28–51, 55.

———. "Moses: The Private Man behind the Public Leader." *Bible Review* 16 (2000): 17–26, 60–62.

Heidorn, L. A. "The Horses of Kush." *Journal of Near Eastern Studies* 56 (1997): 105–14.

———. "The Saite and Persian Period Forts at Dorginarti." In *Egypt and Africa: Nubia from Prehistory to Islam,* ed. W. V. Davies, 205–19. London: British Museum, 1991.

Heimerdinger, J. "La foi de l'eunuque éthiopien." *Études théologiques et religieuses* 63.4 (1988): 521–28.

Henning, R. *Terrae incognitae.* 4 vols. Leiden: Brill, 1936–40.

Henze, P. *Layers of Time: A History of Ethiopia.* New York: St. Martin's, 2000.

Herzog, R. *Punt.* Glückstadt: Augustin, 1968.

Hess, R. L. "The Itinerary of Benjamin of Tudela: A Twelfth-Century Jewish Description of North-east Africa." *Journal of African History* 6.1 (1965): 15–24.

Hestrin, R., et al., eds., *Inscriptions Reveal.* 2d ed. Jerusalem: Israel Museum, 1973.

Hidal, S. "The Land of Cush in the Old Testament." *Svensk exegetisk årsbok* 41–42 (1976–77): 97–106.

Hill, C. A. "The Garden of Eden: A Modern Landscape." *Perspectives on Science and the Christian Faith* 52 (2000): 31–46.

Hinkel, F. "Meroitic Architecture." In *Sudan: Ancient Kingdoms of the Nile,* ed. D. Wildung, 391–417. Paris: Flammarion, 1997.

Hintze, F. "The Kingdom of Kush: The Meroitic Period." In *Africa in Antiquity,* ed. S. Hochfield and E. Riefstahl, 1.89–105. New York: Brooklyn Museum, 1978.

———. "Meroitic Chronology: Problems and Prospects." *Meroitica* 1 (1973): 127–44.

———. *Studien zur meroitischen Chronologie und zu den Opfertafeln aus den Pyramideen von Meroe.* Berlin: Akademie Verlag, 1959.

Hintze, F., and U. Hintze. *Civilizations of the Old Sudan: Kerma, Kush, Christian Nubia.* Leipzig: Kunst & Wissenschaft, 1968.

Hirth, V. "Die Königin von Saba und der Kammerer aus dem Morgenland." *Biblische Notizen* 83 (1996): 13–15.

Hoberman, B. "The Ethiopian Legend of the Ark." *Biblical Archaeologist* 46 (1983): 113–14.

Hochfield, S., and E. Riefstahl. *Africa in Antiquity,* vol. 1: *The Arts of Ancient Nubia and the Sudan.* Brooklyn: Brooklyn Museum, 1978.

Hodge, C. T. "Afroasiatic." In *Africa and Africans in Antiquity,* ed. E. M. Yamauchi, 15–27. East Lansing: Michigan State University Press, 2001.

———. "Hausa-Egyptian Establishment." *Anthropological Linguistics* 8.1 (1966): 40–67.

———. "The Role of Egyptian within Afroasiatic(/Lislakh)." In *Linguistic Change and Reconstruction Methodology,* ed. P. Baldi, 639–59. Mouton: de Gruyter, 1990.

Hoerth, A. J., G. L. Mattingly, and E. M. Yamauchi, eds. *Peoples of the Old Testament World.* Grand Rapids: Baker, 1994.

Hoffmeier, J. K. "Egypt's Role in the Events of 701 B.C. in Jerusalem." In *Jerusalem in Bible and Archaeology: The First Temple Period,* ed. A. G. Vaughn and A. E. Killebrew, 219–34. Society of Biblical Literature Symposium Series 18. Atlanta: Society of Biblical Literature, 2003.

———. *Israel in Egypt.* New York: Oxford University Press, 1997.

Hoffner, H. A., Jr., ed. *Orient and Occident: Essays Presented to Cyrus H. Gordon on the Occasion of His Sixty-fifth Birthday.* Alter Orient und Altes Testament 24.1. Kevelaer: Butzon & Bercker/Neukirchen-Vluyn: Neukirchener Verlag, 1973.

Hofmann, I. *Beiträge zur meroitischen Chronologie.* St. Augustin bei Bonn: Anthropos-Instituts, 1978.

———. "Der Wein- und Ölimport im meroitischen Reich." In *Egypt and Africa: Nubia from Prehistory to Islam,* ed. W. V. Davies, 234–45. London: British Museum, 1991.

———. "Kleopatra-Kandake." *Göttinger Miszellen* 52 (1981): 33–35.

———. "Kuschiten in Palästina." *Göttinger Miszellen* 46 (1981): 9–10.

———. "Notizen zu den Kampfszenen am sogenannten Sonnentempel von Meroe." *Anthropos* 70 (1975): 513–36.

Hofmann, I., and A. Vorbichler. *Der Äthiopenlogos der Herodot.* Vienna: Institut für Afrikanistik und Ägyptologie, 1979.

Hoftijzer, J. "Some Remarks to the Tale of Noah's Drunkenness." In *Studies on the Book of Genesis,* by B. Gemser et al., 22–27. Oudtestamentische Stüdien 12. Leiden: Brill, 1958.

Hölscher, W. *Libyer und Ägypter.* Glückstadt: Augustin, 1955.

Holy Bible: African American Jubilee Edition. New York: American Bible Society, 1999.

Horn, S. H. "Did Sennacherib Campaign Once or Twice against Hezekiah?" *Andrews University Seminary Studies* 4 (1966): 1–28.

———. "Who Was Solomon's Egyptian Father-in-Law?" *Bible Review* 12 (1967): 3–17.

Horsley, G. H. R. *New Documents Illustrating Early Christianity.* 2 vols. North Ryde, N.S.W.: Macquarie University Press, 1981–82.

Horton, F. L., Jr., and J. A. Blakely. "'Behold, Water!' Tell el-Hesi and the Baptism of the Ethiopian Eunuch (Acts 8:26–40)." *Revue biblique* 107 (2000): 56–71.

Hoskins, L. A., ed. *Afrocentrism vs. Eurocentrism: The National Debate.* Kent, Ohio: Institute for African American Affairs, Kent State University, 1991.

Howard, G. S., and J. Tanner. "The Source of the Book of Abraham Identified." *Dialogue* 3.2 (1968): 92–98.

Howard, R. P. "The Book of Abraham in the Light of History and Egyptology." *Courage* 1 (1970): 33–47.

Hoyland, R. G. *Arabia and the Arabs.* London: Routledge, 2001.

Hubbard, D. A. "The Literary Sources of the Kebra Nagast." Ph.D. diss., St. Andrews University, 1957.

Huddleston, J. R. "Nahum, Nineveh, and the Nile." *Journal of Near Eastern Studies* 62 (2003): 97–110.

Huffman, T. N. *Symbols in Stone: Unraveling the Mystery of Great Zimbabwe.* Johannesburg: Witwatersrand University Press, 1987.

Hulse, E. V. "The Nature of Biblical 'Leprosy.'" *Palestine Exploration Quarterly* 197 (1975): 87–105.

Huntingford, G. W. B., trans. *The Periplus of the Erythraean Sea.* London: Hakluyt Society, 1980.

Hutton, R. R. "Cush the Benjaminite and Psalm Midrash." *Hebrew Annual Review* 10 (1986): 123–37.

Huzar, E. G. "Augustus, Heir of the Ptolemies." In *Aufstieg und Niedergang der römischen Welt*, ed. H. Temporini and W. Hasse, 2.10.1.343–82. Berlin: de Gruyter, 1988.

Ikeda, Y. "King Solomon and His Red Sea Trade." In *Near Eastern Studies Dedicated to H.I.H. Prince Takahito Mikasa*, ed. M. Mori, H. Ogawa, and M. Yoshikawa, 13–32. Wiesbaden: Harrassowitz, 1991.

———. "King Solomon's Trade in Horses and Chariots in Its International Setting." In *Studies in the Period of David and Solomon and Other Essays*, ed. T. Ishida, 215–38. Winona Lake, Ind.: Eisenbrauns, 1982.

Isaac, E. "Concept biblique et rabbinique de la malédiction de Noé." *Service international de documentation judéo-chrétienne* 11.2 (1978): 16–21.

———. *The Ethiopian Church.* Boston: Sawyer, 1968.

———. "Genesis, Judaism, and the 'Sons of Ham.'" *Slavery and Abolition* 1.1 (May 1980): 3–17. Reprinted in *Slaves and Slavery in Muslim Africa*, ed. J. R. Willis, 75–79. London: Cass, 1985.

———. "Ham." In *The Anchor Bible Dictionary*, ed. D. N. Freedman et al., 3.31–32. New York: Doubleday, 1992.

———. "Is the Ark of the Covenant in Ethiopia?" *Biblical Archaeology Review* 19.4 (1993): 60–63.

———. "The Legend of Solomon and Sheba." *Biblical Archaeology Review* 19.4 (1993): 62–63.

———. "Relations between the Hebrew Bible and Africa." *Journal of Semitic Studies* 26 (1964): 87–98.

Ishida, T. *Studies in the Period of David and Solomon and Other Essays.* Winona Lake, Ind.: Eisenbrauns, 1982.

Isichei, E. *A History of Christianity in Africa.* Grand Rapids: Eerdmans, 1995.

Isserlin, B. S. J. *The Israelites.* London: Thames & Hudson, 1998.

James, G. G. M. *Stolen Legacy.* Trenton: Africa World, 1954. Reprinted 1992.

James, P., ed. *Centuries of Darkness.* New Brunswick: Rutgers University Press, 1993.

James, P., et al. "Centuries of Darkness: Context, Methodology and Implications." *Cambridge Archaeological Journal* 1.2 (1991): 228–35.

James, T. G. H. *Excavating in Egypt: The Egypt Exploration Society, 1882–1982.* London: British Museum, 1982.

Jameson, S. "Chronology of the Campaign of Aelius Gallus and C. Petronius." *Journal of Roman Studies* 58 (1968): 71–84.

Janssen, J. M. A. "Que sait-on actuellement du Pharaon Taharqa?" *Biblica* 34 (1953): 23–43.

Jaritz, K. "Tilmun-Makan-Meluḫḫa." *Journal of Near Eastern Studies* 27 (1968): 209–13.

Jeffries, L. "Afrocentrism vs. Eurocentrism: The National Debate." In *Afrocentrism vs. Eurocentrism: The National Debate*, ed. L. A. Hoskins, 20–24. Kent, Ohio: Kent State University Institute for African American Affairs, 1991.

Jensen, R. M. "The Two Faces of Jesus." *Bible Review* 18.5 (2002): 42–50, 59.

Jesi, F. "Rapport sur les recherches relative quelques figurations du sacrifice humain dans l'égypte pharaonique." *Journal of Near Eastern Studies* 17 (1958): 194–203.

Johns, A. H. "Solomon and the Queen of Sheba." *Abr-Nahrain* 24 (1986): 58–82.

Jordan, W. D. *The White Man's Burden: Historical Origins of Racism in the United States*. New York: Oxford University Press, 1974.

———. *White over Black: American Attitudes toward the Negro, 1550–1812*. New York: Oxford University Press, 1974.

Junker, H. "The First Appearance of the Negroes in History." *Journal of Egyptian Archaeology* 7 (1921): 121–32.

Kadish, G. E. "Old Kingdom Egyptian Activity in Nubia." *Journal of Egyptian Archaeology* 52 (1966): 22–33.

———. Review of R. Herzog's *Punt*. *Bibliotheca orientalis* 28 (1971): 53–56.

Kahn, D. "The Inscription of Sargon II at Tang-i Var and the Chronology of Dynasty 25." *Orientalia* 70 (2001): 1–18.

Kaiser, W. C. *A History of Israel*. Nashville: Broadman & Holman, 1998.

Kane, S. "Sculpture from the Cyrene Demeter Sanctuary in Its Mediterranean Context." In *Cyrenaica in Antiquity*, ed. G. Barker, J. Lloyd, and J. Reynolds, 237–48. Oxford: British Archaeological Reports, 1985.

Kaplan, S. "Ezana's Conversion Reconsidered." *Journal of Religion in Africa* 13 (1982): 100–109.

Kass, L. R. "Seeing the Nakedness of His Father." *Commentary* 93 (June 1992): 41–47.

Keating, R. *Nubian Rescue*. London: Hale, 1975.

———. *Nubian Twilight*. New York: Harcourt, Brace & World, 1963.

Keener, C. S., and G. Usry. *Defending Black Faith*. Downers Grove, Ill.: InterVarsity, 1997.

Kees, H. *Ancient Egypt*. Chicago: University of Chicago Press, 1961.

Kemp, B. "Explaining Ancient Crises." *Cambridge Archaeological Journal* 1.2 (1991): 239–44.

———. "Old Kingdom, Middle Kingdom, and 2d Intermediate Period in Egypt." In *The Cambridge History of Africa*, vol. 1: *From the Earliest Times to c. 500 B.C.*, ed. J. D. Clark, 658–769. Cambridge: Cambridge University Press, 1982.

Kendall, T. "Ethnoarchaeology in Meroitic Studies." In *Studia Meroitica, 1984*, ed. S. Donadoni and S. Wenig, 625–745. Berlin: Akademie-Verlag, 1989.

———. *Gebel Barkal Epigraphic Survey: 1986, Preliminary Report of First Season's Activity*. Boston: Museum of Fine Arts, 1986.

———. *Kerma and the Kingdom of Kush, 2500–1500 B.C.* Washington, D.C.: National Museum of African Art, 1997.

———. "Kingdom of Kush." *National Geographic* 178.5 (1990): 96–125.

———. *Kush: Lost Kingdom of the Nile.* Brockton, Mass.: Brockton Art Museum, 1982.

———. "The Origin of the Napatan State: El Kurru and the Evidence for the Royal Ancestors." *Meroitica* 15 (1999): 3–101.

———. *A Proposal to Excavate the "Sun Temple" Meroë, Sudan.* Boston: Museum of Fine Arts, 1983.

———. "A Response to László Török's 'Long Chronology' of Nuri." *Meroitica* 15 (1999): 164–76.

Kent, R. G. *Old Persian: Grammar, Texts, Lexicon.* 2d ed. American Oriental Studies 33. New Haven: American Oriental Society, 1953.

Kenyon, K. M. *Jerusalem.* New York: McGraw-Hill, 1967.

———. "New Evidence on Solomon's Temple." *Mélanges de l'Université Saint-Josephe* 45–46 (1969–70): 137–49.

———. *Royal Cities of the Old Testament.* New York: Schocken, 1971.

Kessler, D. "Zu den Feldzügen des Tefnachte, Namlot und Pije in Mittelägypten." *Studien zur altägyptischen Kultur* 9 (1981): 227–51.

Kirwan, L. P. *Rome beyond the Southern Egyptian Frontier.* London: British Academy, 1978.

Kitchen, K. A. "Ancient Arabia and the Bible." *Archaeology in the Biblical World* 3 (1995): 26–34.

———. *The Bible in Its World.* Downers Grove, Ill.: InterVarsity, 1977.

———. "The Controlling Role of External Evidence in Assessing the Historical Status of the Israelite United Monarchy." In *Windows into Old Testament History,* ed. V. P. Long, D. W. Baker, and G. J. Wenham, 111–30. Grand Rapids: Eerdmans, 2002.

———. *Documentation for Ancient Arabia,* vol. 1: *Chronological Framework and Historical Sources.* Liverpool: Liverpool University Press, 1994.

———. *Documentation for Ancient Arabia,* vol. 2: *Bibliographical Catalogue of Texts.* Liverpool: Liverpool University Press, 2000.

———. "Egypt and East Africa." In *The Age of Solomon,* ed. L. K. Handy, 106–25. Leiden: Brill, 1997.

———. "Egypt and Israel during the First Millennium B.C." In *Congress Volume: Jerusalem, 1986,* ed. J. A. Emerton, 107–23. Vetus Testamentum Supplement 40. Leiden: Brill, 1988.

———. "Egypt, the Levant and Assyria in 701 B.C." In *Fontes atque pontes: Eine Festgabe für Hellmut Brunner,* ed. Manfred Görg, 243–53. Ägypten und altes Testament 5. Wiesbaden: Harrassowitz, 1983.

———. "Egyptian Chronology: Problem or Solution?" *Cambridge Archaeological Journal* 1.2 (1991): 235–39.

———. "Further Thoughts on Egyptian Chronology in the Third Intermediate Period." *Revue d'égyptologie* 34 (1982–83): 59–69.

―――. "Further Thoughts on Punt and Its Neighbours." In *Studies on Ancient Egypt in Honour of H. S. Smith*, ed. A. Leahy and J. Tait, 173–78. London: Egypt Exploration Society, 1999.

―――. "The Great Biographical Stela of Setau, Viceroy of Nubia." *Orientalia lovanensia periodica* 6 (1975): 295–302.

―――. "The Historical Chronology of Ancient Egypt: A Current Assessment." *Acta archaeologica* 67 (1996): 1–13.

―――. "Historical Observations on Ramesside Nubia." In *Ägypten und Kush*, ed. E. Endesfelder et al., 213–26. Berlin: Akademie-Verlag, 1977.

―――. "How We Know When Solomon Ruled." *Biblical Archaeology Review* 27.5 (2001): 32–37, 58.

―――. "The Land of Punt." In *The Archaeology of Africa*, ed. T. Shaw et al., 587–608. London: Routledge, 1993.

―――. "Late-Egyptian Chronology and the Hebrew Monarchy." *Journal of the Ancient Near Eastern Society* 5 (1973): 225–33.

―――. *Pharaoh Triumphant: The Life and Times of Ramesses II*. Mississauga, Ont.: Benben, 1982.

―――. "Punt and How to Get There." *Orientalia* 40 (1971): 184–207.

―――. "Regnal and Genealogical Data of Ancient Egypt (Absolute Chronology I): The Historical Chronology of Egypt, a Current Assessment." In *The Synchronisation of Civilisations in the Eastern Mediterranean in the Second Millennium B.C.*, ed. M. Bietak, 39–52. Vienna: Österreichischen Akademie der Wissenschaften, 2000.

―――. "Sheba and Arabia." In *The Age of Solomon*, ed. L. K. Handy, 126–53. Leiden: Brill, 1997.

―――. "Shishak's Military Campaign in Israel Confirmed." *Biblical Archaeology Review* 15.3 (1989): 32–33.

―――. "The Shoshenqs of Egypt and Palestine." *Journal for the Study of the Old Testament* 93 (2001): 3–12.

―――. "Theban Topographical Lists, Old and New." *Orientalia* 34 (1965): 1–9.

―――. *The Third Intermediate Period in Egypt (1100–650 B.C.)*. Rev. ed. Warminster: Aris & Phillips, 1999.

―――. "Where Did Solomon's Gold Go?" *Biblical Archaeology Review* 15.3 (1989): 30–31.

―――. "Zerah." In *Illustrated Bible Dictionary*, ed. J. D. Douglas, 3.1682. Leicester: InterVarsity/Wheaton: Tyndale, 1980.

―――. "Zerah." In *New Bible Dictionary*, ed. J. D. Douglas et al., 1280. 2d ed. Leicester: Inter-Varsity, 1982.

Kiuchi, N. "A Paradox of Skin Disease." *Zeitschrift für die alttestamentliche Wissenschaft* 113 (2001): 505–14.

Klengel, H. "Das Land Kusch in den Keilschrifttexten von Amarna." In *Ägypten und Kusch*, ed. E. Endesfelder et al., 227–32. Berlin: Akademie-Verlag, 1977.

Klerk, W. A. de. *The Puritans in Africa: A Story of Afrikanerdom*. London: Collins, 1975.

Knauf, E. A. *Midian*. Wiesbaden: Harrassowitz, 1988.

———. "Midianites and Ishmaelites." In *Midian, Edom, and Moab*, ed. J. F. A. Sawyer and D. J. A. Clines, 147–72. Sheffield: JSOT Press, 1983.

———. "Zerah." In *The Anchor Bible Dictionary*, ed. D. N. Freedman et al., 6.1080–
81. New York: Doubleday, 1992.

Knoppers, G. N. "The Vanishing Solomon: The Disappearance of the United Monarchy from Recent Histories of Ancient Israel." *Journal of Biblical Literature* 116
(1997): 19–44.

Kohl, P. L. Review of *Centuries of Darkness*, edited by P. James. *Journal of Interdisci-
plinary History* 21 (1995): 274–75.

Kraeling, C. H. *Ptolemais: City of the Libyan Pentapolis*. Chicago: University of Chicago Press, 1963.

Kramer, S. N. *The Sumerians: Their History, Culture, and Character*. Chicago: University of Chicago Press, 1971.

Kuhrt, A. *The Ancient Near East, c. 3000–330 B.C.*, vol. 2. London: Routledge, 1995.

Lambdin, T. O. "Ethiopia." In *Interpreter's Dictionary of the Bible*, ed. G. A. Buttrick
et al., 2.176–77. Nashville: Abingdon, 1962.

———. *Introduction to Classical Ethiopic (Ge'ez)*. Missoula, Mont.: Scholars Press,
1978.

Lance, H. D. "Solomon, Siamun, and the Double Ax." In *Magnalia Dei, the Mighty
Acts of God: Essays on the Bible and Archaeology in Memory of G. Ernest Wright*, ed.
F. M. Cross, W. E. Lemke, and P. D. Miller Jr., 209–23. Garden City, N.Y.: Dou-
bleday, 1976.

LaRonde, A. "La cyrènaïque romaine, des origines à la fin des Sèvéres (96 av. J.-C.–
235 ap. J.-C.)." In *Aufstieg und Niedergang der römischen Welt*, ed. H. Temporini
and W. Hasse, 2.10.1.1006–64. Berlin: de Gruyter, 1988.

LaSor, W. S. "Cush." In *The International Standard Bible Encyclopedia*, ed. G. W. Bromiley, 1.839. Grand Rapids: Eerdmans, 1986.

Lassner, J. *Demonizing the Queen of Sheba*. Chicago: University of Chicago Press,
1993.

———. "Ritual Purity and Political Exile: Solomon, the Queen of Sheba, and the
Events of 586 B.C.E. in a Yemenite Folktale." In *Solving Riddles and Untying
Knots: Biblical, Epigraphic, and Semitic Studies in Honor of Jonas C. Greenfield*, ed.
Z. Zevit, S. Gitin, and M. Sokoloff, 117–36. Winona Lake, Ind.: Eisenbrauns,
1995.

Lawrence, J. M. "Publius Sulpicius Quirinius and the Syrian Census." *Restoration
Quarterly* 34 (1992): 193–205.

Leahy, A. "The Adoption of Ankhnesneferibre at Karnak." *Journal of Egyptian Archaeology* 82 (1996): 145–65.

———. "The Libyan Period in Egypt: An Essay in Interpretation." *Libyan Studies*
16 (1985): 51–65.

———. "Tantuamon, Son of Shabako?" *Göttinger Miszellen* 83 (1984): 43–45.

Leahy, A., ed. *Libya and Egypt c. 1300–750 B.C.* London: School of Oriental and African Studies, 1990.

Leclant, J. "The Empire of Kush: Napata and Meroe." In *General History of Africa*,
vol. 2: *Ancient Civilizations of Africa*, ed. G. Mokhtar, 161–71. London: Currey/
Berkeley: University of California Press, 1990.

———. *Enquêtes sur les sacerdoces et les sanctuaires égyptiens à l'époque dite "Éthiopienne."* Cairo: L'institut français d'archéologie orientale, 1954.

———. "An Introduction to the Civilization of Nubia: From the Earliest Times to the New Kingdom." In *Africa in Antiquity: The Arts of Ancient Nubia and the Sudan,* ed. F. Hintze, 15–18. Meroitica 5. Berlin: Akademie-Verlag, 1979.

———. *Montouemhat, Quatrième prophète d'Amon, Prince de la Ville.* Cairo: L'institut français d'archéologie orientale, 1961.

———. *Recherches sur les monuments thébains de la XXVe dynastie dite éthiopienne.* Cairo: L'institut français d'archéologie orientale, 1965.

———. "Taharqa." In *Lexikon der Ägyptologie,* ed. W. Helck and E. Otto, 6.156–84. Wiesbaden: Harrassowitz, 1972.

Lefkowitz, M. R. "Ancient History, Modern Myths." In *Black Athena Revisited,* ed. M. R. Lefkowitz and G. M. Rogers, 3–23. Chapel Hill: North Carolina University Press, 1996.

———. *Not out of Africa.* New York: Basic, 1996.

Lefkowitz, M. R., and G. M. Rogers, eds. *Black Athena Revisited.* Chapel Hill: University of North Carolina Press, 1996.

Lehner, M. *The Complete Pyramids.* New York: Thames & Hudson, 1997.

Lemonick, M. D., and A. Dorfman. "Searching for Sheba." *Time* (Sept. 10, 2001): 58–61.

Leroy, J. "Les 'éthiopiens' de Persepolis." *Annales de l'éthiopia* 3 (1963): 293–97.

Lévy, J. "Moïse en éthiope." *Revue des études juives* 53 (1907): 201–14.

Lewis, B. *Race and Slavery in the Middle East.* New York: Oxford University Press, 1990.

Lewis, J. P. "John Lewis (Johann Ludwig) Burckhardt: Explorer in Disguise." *Near East Archaeological Society Bulletin* 45 (2000): 13–22.

———. *A Study of the Interpretation of Noah and the Flood in Jewish and Christian Literature.* Leiden: Brill, 1968.

Lewis, N., and M. Reinhold, eds. *Roman Civilization,* vol. 2: *The Empire.* New York: Harper & Row, 1966.

Lichtheim, M. *Ancient Egyptian Literature,* vol. 1: *The Old and Middle Kingdoms.* Berkeley: University of California Press, 1975.

———. *Ancient Egyptian Literature,* vol. 2: *The New Kingdom.* Berkeley: University of California Press, 1976.

———. *Ancient Egyptian Literature,* vol. 3: *The Late Period.* Berkeley: University of California Press, 1980.

Lipiński, E. "Nimrod et Assur." *Revue biblique* 73 (1966): 77–99.

Little, T. *High Dam at Aswan.* New York: Day, 1965.

Littmann, E. *The Legend of the Queen of Sheba in the Tradition of Axum.* Leiden: Brill, 1904.

Liverani, M. "Early Caravan Trade between South-Arabia and Mesopotamia." *Yemen* 1 (1992): 111–15.

———. "The Libyan Caravan Road in Herodotus iv.181–185." *Journal of the Economic and Social History of the Orient* 43.4 (2000): 496–519.

Livingston, D. "Tirhaka: King of Ethiopia, Successor to Piankhy." In *The Law and the Prophets: Old Testament Studies Prepared in Honor of Oswald Thompson Allis*, ed. J. H. Skilton, 402–12. Nutley, N.J.: Presbyterian & Reformed, 1974.

Lloyd, A. B. "Herodotus on Egyptians and Libyans." In *Hérodote et les peuples non Grecs*, ed. G. Nenci, 215–53. Geneva: Hardt, 1990.

———. "Necho and the Red Sea." *Journal of Egyptian Archaeology* 63 (1977): 148–55.

Lloyd, J. "Some Aspects of Urban Development at Eusperides/Berenice." In *Cyrenaica in Antiquity*, ed. G. Barker, J. Lloyd, and J. Reynolds, 49–66. Oxford: British Archaeological Reports, 1985.

Lösch, S. "Der Kämmerer der Königin Kandake (Apg. 8,27)." *Theologische Quartalschrift* 111 (1930): 477–519.

Lubetski, L., C. Gottlieb, and S. Keller, eds. *Boundaries of the Ancient Near Eastern World*. Sheffield: Sheffield Academic Press, 1998.

Lucas, A., and J. R. Harris. *Ancient Egyptian Materials and Industries*. 1962. Reprinted Mineola, N.Y.: Dover, 1999.

Lüddeckens, E. "*Nhsj* und *kš* in ägyptischen Personennamen." In *Ägypten und Kusch*, ed. E. Endesfelder et al., 182–91. Berlin: Akademie-Verlag, 1977.

Lüderitz, G. *Corpus jüdischer Zeugnisse aus der Cyrenaika*. Wiesbaden: Reichert, 1983.

Luz, H., and O. Luz. "Proud Primitives: The Nuba People." *National Geographic* 130.5 (1966): 673–99.

MacGaffey, W. "Who Owns Ancient Egypt?" *Journal of African History* 32 (1991): 515–19.

Machinist, P. "The *Rab Šâqêh* at the Wall of Jerusalem: Israelite Identity in the Face of the Assyrian 'Other.'" *Hebrew Studies* 41 (2000): 151–68.

Maisler, B. "Two Hebrew Ostraca from Tell Qasile." *Journal of Near Eastern Studies* 10 (1951): 265–67.

Malamat, A. "Aspects of the Foreign Policies of David and Solomon." *Journal of Near Eastern Studies* 22 (1963): 1–17.

———. "The Kingdom of David and Solomon in Its Contact with Egypt and Aram Naharaim." *Biblical Archaeologist* 21 (1958): 96–102.

———. "A Political Look at the Kingdom of David and Solomon and Its Relations with Egypt." In *Studies in the Period of David and Solomon and Other Essays*, ed. T. Ishida, 189–204. Winona Lake, Ind.: Eisenbrauns, 1982.

Malloch, T. R. "Rastafarianism: A Radical Caribbean Movement or Religion." *Center Journal* 4.4 (1985): 67–87.

Manuelian, P. D. *Living in the Past: Studies in Archaism of the Egyptian Twenty-sixth Dynasty*. London: Kegan Paul, 1994.

Marcus, H. G. *The Life and Times of Menelik II*. Oxford: Clarendon, 1975.

Margalit, B. "Why King Mesha of Moab Sacrificed His Oldest Son." *Biblical Archaeology Review* 12.6 (1986): 62–64, 76.

Marinatos, S. "The 'Libya Fresco' from Thera." *Athens Annals of Archaeology* 7 (1974): 87–94.

Markoe, G. E. *Phoenicians*. Berkeley: University of California Press, 2000.

Martin, C. J. "A Chamberlain's Journey and the Challenges of Interpretation for Liberation." *Semeia* 47 (1989): 105–35.

———. "The Function of Acts 8:26–40 within the Narrative Structure of the Book of Acts: The Significance of the Eunuch's Provenance for Acts 1:8c." Ph.D. diss., Duke University, 1985.

Martin, T. *The Jewish Onslaught: Despatches from the Wellesley Battlefront.* Dover, Mass.: Majority, 1993.

Massey, G. *Ancient Egypt: The Light of the World.* 1907. Reprinted Baltimore: Black Classics, 1992.

Master, D. M. "The Origin of Jewish Elements in Early Ethiopian Christianity." M.A. thesis, Miami University, Oxford, Ohio, 1995.

Matthews, D. "Proposal for an Afro-centric Curriculum." *Journal of the American Academy of Religion* 62 (1995): 885–92.

Mauss, A. L. "Mormonism and the Negro: Faith, Folklore, and Civil Rights." *Dialogue* 2.4 (1967): 18–39.

Mayerson, P. "A Confusion of Indias: Asian India and African India in the Byzantine Sources." *Journal of the American Oriental Society* 113 (1993): 169–74.

McCray, W. A. *The Black Presence in the Bible.* 2 vols. Chicago: Black Light Fellowship, 1990.

McIntosh, R. J. "Riddle of Great Zimbabwe." *Archaeology* 51.4 (1998): 44–49.

McKenzie, S. L. "Ham/Canaan, Cursing of." In *The Oxford Companion to the Bible,* ed. B. M. Metzger and M. D. Coogan, 268. New York: Oxford University Press, 1993.

———. "Response: The Curse of Ham and David H. Aaron." *Journal of the American Academy of Religion* 65 (1997): 183–86.

McKissic, W. *Beyond Roots: In Search of Blacks in the Bible.* Wenonah, N.J.: Renaissance, 1990.

Meek, T. "Moses and the Levites." *American Journal of Semitic Languages* 56 (1939): 113–20.

Meester, P. de. "Le pèlerin d'ethiopie." *Telema* 18 (1979): 3–18.

———. "'Philippe et l'eunuque éthiopien' ou 'le baptême d'un pèlerin de Nubie'?" *Nouvelle revue théologique* 103 (1981): 360–74.

Mendenhall, G. A. "Midian." In *The Anchor Bible Dictionary,* ed. D. N. Freedman et al., 4.815–18. New York: Doubleday, 1992.

Merrill, E. H. *Kingdom of Priests: A History of Old Testament Israel.* Grand Rapids: Baker, 1996.

———. "The Peoples of the Old Testament according to Genesis 10." *Bibliotheca Sacra* 154 (1997): 3–22.

Mettinger, T. *Solomonic State Officials.* Lund: Gleerup, 1971.

Metzger, B. M. *An Introduction to the Apocrypha.* New York: Oxford University Press, 1957.

Mikre-Sellassie, G. A. "The Bible and Its Canon in the Ethiopian Orthodox Church." *Bible Translator* 44.1 (1993): 111–23.

Millard, A. R. "Does the Bible Exaggerate King Solomon's Golden Wealth?" *Biblical Archaeology Review* 15.3 (1989): 20–29, 31, 34.

———. "The Etymology of Eden." *Vetus Testamentum* 34 (1984): 103–6.

———. "King Solomon in His Ancient Context." In *The Age of Solomon,* ed. L. K. Handy, 30–53. Leiden: Brill, 1997.

———. "King Solomon's Gold: Biblical Records in the Light of Antiquity." *Bulletin of the Society for Mesopotamian Studies* 15 (1988): 5–11.

———. "King Solomon's Shields." In *Scripture and Other Artifacts: Bible and Archaeology in Honor of Philip J. King*, ed. M. D. Coogan, J. C. Exum, and L. E. Stager, 286–95. Louisville: Westminster John Knox, 1994.

———. "Large Numbers in the Assyrian Royal Inscriptions." In *Ah, Assyria . . . : Studies in Assyrian History and Ancient Near Eastern Historiography Presented to Hayim Tadmor*, ed. M. Cogan and I. Eph'al, 213–22. Jerusalem: Magnes, 1991.

———. "On Giving the Bible a Fair Go." *Buried History* 35.4 (1999): 5–12.

———. "Sennacherib's Attack on Hezekiah." *Tyndale Bulletin* 36 (1985): 61–77.

———. "Solomon in All His Glory." *Vox evangelica* 12 (1981): 5–18.

———. "Texts and Archaeology: Weigh the Evidence: The Case for King Solomon." *Palestine Exploration Quarterly* 123 (1991): 19–27.

Miller, D. E., and N. J. Van der Merwe. "Early Metal Working in Sub-Saharan Africa: A Review of Recent Research." *Journal of African History* 35 (1994): 1–36.

Miller, J. M. "Separating the Solomon of History from the Solomon of Legend." In *The Age of Solomon*, ed. L. K. Handy, 1–29. Leiden: Brill, 1997.

———. "Solomon: International Potentate or Local King?" *Palestine Exploration Quarterly* 123 (1991): 28–31.

Millet, B. "Meroitic Nubia." Ph.D. diss., Yale University, 1968.

Mingazzini, P. *L'insula di Giasone Magno a Cirene.* Monografie di archeologia libica 8. Rome: "L'Erma" di Bretschneider, 1966.

Minter, W. *King Solomon's Mines Revisited.* New York: Basic, 1986.

Mitchell, B. M. "Cyrene and Persia." *Journal of Hellenic Studies* 86 (1966): 99–113.

Mitchell, T. C. "Where Was Putu-Iaman?" *Proceedings of the Seminar for Arabian Studies* 22 (1992): 69–80.

Mokhtar, R. G., ed. *Ancient Civilizations of Africa.* London: Currey, 1990.

Molin, G. "'Ebed-Melek, der Kuschit." In *Al-Hudhud: Festschrift Maria Höfner zum 80. Geburtstag*, ed. R. G. Stiegner, 219–23. Graz: Karl-Franzens-Universität, 1981.

Monson, J. M. "The New 'Ain Dara Temple." *Biblical Archaeology Review* 26.3 (2000): 20–35, 67.

———. "The Temple of Solomon: Heart of Jerusalem." In *Zion, City of Our God*, ed. R. S. Hess and G. Wenham, 1–22. Grand Rapids: Eerdmans, 1999.

Montgomery, J. A. *Arabia and the Bible.* Philadelphia: University of Pennsylvania Press, 1934. Reprinted New York: Ktav, 1969.

Montgomery, J. A., and H. S. Gehman. *The Book of Kings.* International Critical Commentary. Edinburgh: Clark, 1951.

Moorehead, A. *The Blue Nile.* New York: Harper & Row, 1962.

———. *The White Nile.* New York: Harper & Row, 1960.

Moran, W. L., ed. and trans. *The Amarna Letters.* Baltimore: Johns Hopkins University Press, 1992.

Morkot, R. G. *The Black Pharaohs: Egypt's Nubian Rulers.* London: Rubicon, 2000.

———. "The Empty Years of Nubian History." In *Centuries of Darkness*, ed. P. James, 204–19. New Brunswick: Rutgers University Press, 1993.

———. "Kingship and Kinship." *Meroitica* 15 (1999): 180–98.

———. "Nubia in the New Kingdom: The Limits of Egyptian Control." In *Egypt and Africa: Nubia from Prehistory to Islam*, ed. W. V. Davies, 294–301. London: British Museum, 1991.

———. "'There Are No Elephants in Dóngola': Notes on Nubian Ivory." In *Actes de la VIIIe conférence internationale des études nubiennes*, 3.147–53. Lille: Université Charles-de-Gaulle, 1998.

Morris, C. A. "The Queen of Sheba and African Matriarchal Precedence." *Journal of the Interdenominational Theological Center* 19 (1991–92): 72–87.

Morris, W. W. "The Queen of Sheba." *Daughters of Sarah* 21 (winter 1995): 15–18.

Morrison, J. D., ed. *Masterpieces of Religious Verse*. New York: Harper, 1948.

Mosala, I. *Biblical Hermeneutics and Black Theology in South Africa*. Grand Rapids: Eerdmans, 1987.

Moussa, A. M. "A Stela of Taharqa from the Desert Road at Dahshur." *Mitteilungen des deutschen archäologischen Instituts, Abteilung Kairo* 37 (1981): 331–38.

Muhly, J. D. "Black Athena versus Traditional Scholarship." *Journal of Mediterranean Archaeology* 3.1 (1990): 83–110.

———. "Solomon, the Copper King." *Expedition* 29.2 (1987): 38–47.

———. "Timna and King Solomon." *Bibliotheca orientalis* 41 (1984): 275–92.

Müller, G. "Simon von Kyrene—Kreuzträger, Pilger, Bauer, Augenzeuge und Typos der nachfolge." *Herbergen der Christenheit: Jahrbuch für deutsche Kirchengeschichte* (1985–86): 53–71.

Munro-Hay, S. *Aksum: An African Civilisation of Late Antiquity.* Edinburgh: Edinburgh University Press, 1991.

———. *Excavations at Aksum*. London: British Institute in Eastern Africa, 1989.

Myers, J. M. *II Chronicles*. Anchor Bible 13. Garden City, N.Y.: Doubleday, 1965.

Myśliwiec, K. *The Twilight of Ancient Egypt: First Millennium B.C.E.* Ithaca: Cornell University Press, 2000.

Na'aman, N. "The Brook of Egypt and Assyrian Policy on the Border of Egypt." *Tel Aviv* 6 (1979): 68–90.

———. "The Debated Historicity of Hezekiah's Reform in the Light of Historical and Archaeological Research." *Zeitschrift für die alttestamentliche Wissenschaft* 107 (1995): 183–95.

———. "Hezekiah and the Kings of Assyria." *Tel Aviv* 21 (1994): 235–54.

———. "The Historical Background to the Conquest of Samaria (720 B.C.)." *Biblica* 71 (1990): 206–25.

Nasgowitz, D. *Ptolemais Cyrenaica*. Chicago: University of Chicago Press, 1980.

Naveh, J. "Achish-Ikausu in the Light of the Ekron Dedication." *Bulletin of the American Schools of Oriental Research* 310 (1998): 35–37.

Ndoro, W. "Great Zimbabwe." *Scientific American* 277.5 (1997): 94–99.

Neiman, D. "The Date and Circumstances of the Cursing of Canaan." In *Biblical Motifs: Origins and Transformations*, ed. D. Neiman, 113–34. Cambridge: Harvard University Press, 1966.

———. "Eden: The Garden of God." *Acta antiqua* 17 (1969): 109–24.

———. "Mythological Antecedents of the Two Enigmatic Rivers of Eden." In *Proceedings of the World Congress of Jewish Studies*, ed. A. Shina, 1.321–28. Jerusalem: World Union of Jewish Studies, 1973.

Nielsen, K. *Incense in Ancient Israel*. Leiden: Brill, 1986.

North, R. "Ophir/Parvaim and Petra/Jotheel." *Proceedings of the Fourth World Congress of Jewish Studies*, 1.197–202. Jerusalem: World Union of Jewish Studies, 1967.

Ntintili, P. V. "The Presence and Role of Africans in the Bible." In *Holy Bible: African American Jubilee Edition*, 97–108. New York: American Bible Society, 1999.

O'Connor, D. "Ancient Egypt and Black Africa—Early Contacts." *Expedition* 14 (1971): 2–9.

———. *Ancient Nubia: Egypt's Rival in Africa*. Philadelphia: University Museum, 1993.

———. "Chiefs or Kings? Rethinking Early Nubian Politics." *Expedition* 35.2 (1993): 4–14.

———. "Egyptians and Libyans in the New Kingdom." *Expedition* 29.3 (1987): 35–37.

———. "Kerma and Egypt: The Significance of the Monumental Buildings Kerma I, II, and XI." *Journal of the American Research Center in Egypt* 21 (1984): 65–108.

———. "The Locations of Yam and Kush and Their Historical Implications." *Journal of the American Research Center in Egypt* 23 (1986): 27–50.

———. Review of B. Gratien's *Les cultures Kerma*. *Bibliotheca orientalis* 37 (1980): 326–29.

O'Connor, D., and E. H. Cline, *Amenhotep III: Perspectives on His Reign*. Ann Arbor: University of Michigan Press, 1998.

O'Neill, J. P. *Egyptian Art in the Age of the Pyramids*. New York: Metropolitan Museum of Art, 1999.

Onolemhemhen, D. N., and K. Gessesse. *The Black Jews of Ethiopia: The Last Exodus*. Lanham, Md.: Scarecrow, 1998.

O'Toole, R. F. "Philip and the Ethiopian Eunuch (Acts viii 25–40)." *Journal for the Study of the New Testament* 17 (1983): 25–34.

Oulette, J. "The Basic Structure of Solomon's Temple and Archaeological Research." In *The Temple of Solomon: Archaeological Fact and Medieval Tradition in Christian, Islamic, and Jewish Art*, ed. J. Gutmann, 1–20. Missoula, Mont.: Scholars Press, 1976.

Pankhurst, R. *The Ethiopians*. Oxford: Blackwell, 1998.

Parker, H. M. "Solomon and the Queen of Sheba." *Iliff Review* 24 (fall 1967): 17–23.

Parker, R. A. "The Joseph Smith Papyri: A Preliminary Report." *Dialogue* 3.2 (1968): 86–92.

Parker, R. A., J. Leclant, and J.-C. Goyon. *The Edifice of Taharqa by the Sacred Lake of Karnak*. Providence: Brown University Press, 1979.

Parr, P. J. "Pottery of the Late Second Millennium B.C." In *Araby the Blest: Studies in Arabian Archaeology*, ed. D. T. Potts, 72–89. Copenhagen: Carsten Niebuhr Institute of Ancient Near Eastern Studies, University of Copenhagen, 1988.

Peebles, M. S. "African Edenic Women and the Scriptures." In *The Original African Heritage Study Bible: King James Version, with Special Annotations Relative to the African/Edenic Perspective*, ed. C. H. Felder, 1808–11. Nashville: Winston, 1993.

Pennacchietti, F. A. "The Queen of Sheba, the Glass Floor and the Floating Tree-Trunk." *Henoch* 22.2–3 (2000): 223–46.

Perbal, A. "La race nègre et la malédiction de Cham." *Revue de l'Université d'Ottawa* 10 (1940): 156–77.

Perowne, S. *The Later Herods*. London: Hodder & Stoughton, 1958.

Peterson, T. *Ham and Japheth: The Mythic World of Whites in the Antebellum South*. Metuchen: Scarecrow, 1978.

Pfeiffer, H. "Der Baum in der Mitte des Gartens." *Zeitschrift für die alttestamentliche Wissenschaft* 113 (2001): 2–16.

Phillips, W. *Qatabân and Sheba*. London: Gollancz, 1955.

Phillipson, D. "Excavations at Aksum, Ethiopia, 1993–4." *Antiquaries Journal* 75 (1995): 1–44.

Pickthall, M. M., trans. *The Meaning of the Glorious Koran*. New York: New American Library, 1953.

Pirenne, J. *La Grèce et Saba*. Paris: Académie des inscriptions et belles lettres, 1955.

———. *Le royaume sud-arabe de Qatabân et sa datations*. Louvain: Leuven University Press, 1961.

———. *Les témoins écrits de la région de Shabwa et l'histoire*. Paris: Geuthner, 1990.

Poliakoff, M. "Roll Over, Aristotle: Martin Bernal and His Critics." *Academic Questions* 4.3 (1991): 12–28.

Porten, B. *Archives from Elephantine*. Berkeley: University of California Press, 1968.

Porter, R. J. "What Did Philip Say to the Eunuch?" *Expository Times* 100.2 (1988): 54–55.

Posener, G. *Cinq figurines d'envoûtement*. Cairo: Institut français d'archéologie orientale du Caire, 1987.

———. "L'or de Pount." In *Ägypten und Kusch*, ed. E. Endesfelder et al., 337–42. Berlin: Akademie-Verlag, 1977.

———. "Pour une localisation du pays Kousch au Moyen Empire." *Kush* 6 (1958): 39–65.

———. *Princes et pays d'Asie et de Nubie*. Brussels: Fondations égyptologique Reine Élisabeth, 1940.

Potts, D. T., ed. *Araby the Blest: Studies in Arabian Archaeology*. Copenhagen: Carsten Niebuhr Institute of Ancient Near Eastern Studies, University of Copenhagen, 1988.

Powers, T. "Treasures in the Storeroom: Family Tomb of Simon of Cyrene." *Biblical Archaeology Review* 29.4 (2003): 46–51.

Pratico, G. D. "Where Is Ezion-geber?" *Biblical Archaeology Review* 12.5 (1986): 24–35.

Previn, D. "Sheba and Solomon." *Union Seminary Quarterly Review* 43.1–4 (1989): 59–66.

Priese, K.-H. *The Gold of Meroe*. New York: Metropolitan Museum of Art, 1993.

———. "Meroitic Writing and Languages." In *Sudan: Ancient Kingdoms of the Nile*, ed. D. Wildung, 253–64. Paris: Flammarion, 1997.

Pritchard, J. B. "The Megiddo Stables: A Reassessment." In *Near Eastern Archaeology in the Twentieth Century*, ed. J. A. Sanders, 268–76. Garden City, N.Y.: Doubleday, 1970.

Pritchard, J. B., ed. *Ancient Near Eastern Texts Relating to the Old Testament* [*ANET*]. Princeton: Princeton University Press, 1955.

────. *Solomon and Sheba*. London: Phaidon, 1974.

Quinn, J. A. *The Evolution of the Ethiopian Jews*. Philadelphia: University of Pennsylvania Press, 1992.

Radday, Y. T. "The Four Rivers of Paradise." *Hebrew Studies* 23 (1982): 23–31.

Rainey, A. F. "Stones for Bread: Archaeology versus History." *Near Eastern Archaeology* 64.3 (2001): 140–49.

Rajak, T. "Moses in Ethiopia: Legend and Literature." *Journal of Jewish Studies* 29 (1978): 111–22.

Rapuano, Y. "Did Philip Baptize the Eunuch at Ein Yael?" *Biblical Archaeology Review* 16.6 (1990): 44–49.

Raven, S. *Rome in Africa*. 3d ed. London: Routledge, 1993.

Reade, J. E. "Sargon's Campaigns of 720, 716, and 715 B.C.: Evidence from the Sculptures." *Journal of Near Eastern Studies* 35 (1976): 95–104.

Redford, D. B. *Egypt, Canaan, and Israel in Ancient Times*. Princeton: Princeton University Press, 1992.

────. "Kush." In *The Anchor Bible Dictionary*, ed. D. N. Freedman et al., 4.109–11. New York: Doubleday, 1992.

────. "A Note on the Chronology of Dynasty 25 and the Inscription of Sargon II at Tang-i Var." *Orientalia* 68 (1999): 58–60.

────. "The Pyramids of Meroe and the Candaces of Ethiopia." *Museum of Fine Arts Bulletin* 21 (April 1923): 12–27.

────. "Sais and the Kushite Invasions of the Eight Century B.C." *Journal of the American Research Center in Egypt* 22 (1985): 5–15.

────. "Studies in Relations between Palestine and Egypt: The Taxation System of Solomon." In *Studies in the Ancient Palestinian World*, ed. J. W. Wevers and D. B. Redford, 141–56. Toronto: University of Toronto Press, 1972.

────. "Taharqa in Western Asia and Libya." *Eretz-Israel* 24 (1993): 188–91.

Reisner, G. A. *Excavations at Kerma*. 3 vols. Cambridge: Peabody Museum, 1923.

────. "The Meroitic Kingdom of Ethiopia: A Chronological Outline." *Journal of Egyptian Archaeology* 9 (1923): 34–75.

────. "Preliminary Report on the Harvard-Boston Excavations at Nûri: The Kings of Ethiopia after Tirhaqa." *Harvard African Studies* 2 (1918): 1–64.

Rendsburg, G., et al., eds. *The Bible World: Essays in Honor of Cyrus H. Gordon*. New York: Ktav: 1980.

Reynolds, J. "The Christian Inscriptions of Cyrenaica." *Journal of Theological Studies* n.s. 11 (1960): 284–94.

────. "Cyrenaica, Pompey, and Cn. Cornelius Lentulus Marcellinus." *Journal of Roman Studies* 53 (1962): 97–103.

────. "Hadrian, Antoninus Pius, and the Cyrenaican Cities." *Journal of Roman Studies* 68 (1978): 111–21.

────. "The Jewish Revolt of A.D. 115 in Cyrenaica." *Proceedings of the Cambridge Philological Society* 3 (1958–59): 24–28.

────. "Libyans and Greeks in Rural Cyrenaica." *Quaderni di archeologia della Libya* 12 (1987): 379–83.

Rice, G. "The African Roots of the Prophet Zephaniah." *Journal of Religious Thought* 36 (1979): 21–31.

———. "Two Black Contemporaries of Jeremiah." *Journal of Religious Thought* 32 (1975): 95–109.

———. "The Curse That Never Was, Genesis 9:18–27." *Journal of Religious Thought* 29 (1972): 5–27.

Ricks, S. D. "Sheba, Queen of." In *The Anchor Bible Dictionary,* ed. D. N. Freedman et al., 5.1170–71. New York: Doubleday, 1992.

Riefenstahl, L. *The Last of the Nuba.* New York: Harper & Row, 1974.

Ripinsky, M. M. "The Camel in Ancient Arabia." *Antiquity* 49 (1975): 295–98.

Ritner, R. K. "'The Breathing Permit of Hôr' among the Joseph Smith Papyri." *Journal of Near Eastern Studies* 62 (2003): 161–80.

Roberts, D. "On the Frankincense Trail." *Smithsonian Magazine* 29.7 (1998): 120–35.

Roberts, R. J. *A Passion for Gold.* Reno/Las Vegas: University of Nevada Press, 2002.

Robinson, B. P. "The Jealousy of Miriam: A Note on Num 12." *Zeitschrift für die alttestamentliche Wissenschaft* 101 (1989): 428–32.

Ross, A. P. "Studies in the Book of Genesis, part 1: The Curse of Canaan." *Bibliotheca Sacra* 137 (1980): 223–40.

Roth, A. M. "Building Bridges to Afrocentrism: A Letter to My Egyptological Colleagues." *American Research Center in Egypt Newsletter* 167 (Sept. 1995): 1, 14–17.

Rothenberg, B. "Ancient Copper Industries in the Western Arabah." *Palestine Exploration Quarterly* 94 (1962): 5–72.

———. *Timna.* London: Thames & Hudson, 1972.

Rowley-Conwy, P. "The Camel in the Nile Valley." *Journal of Egyptian Archaeology* 74 (1988): 245–48.

Runnalls, D. "Moses' Ethiopian Campaign." *Journal for the Study of Judaism* 14 (1983): 135–56.

Russmann, E. R. "Egypt and the Kushites: Dynasty XXV." In *Africa and Africans in Antiquity,* ed. E. M. Yamauchi, 113–31. East Lansing: Michigan State University Press, 2001.

———. "Mentuemhat's Kushite Wife (Further Remarks on the Decoration of the Tomb of Mentuemhat, 2)." *Journal of the American Research Center in Egypt* 34 (1997): 21–39.

———. "Relief Decoration in the Tomb of Mentuemhat (TT 34)." *Journal of the American Research Center in Egypt* 31 (1994): 1–19.

———. *The Representation of the King in the XXVth Dynasty.* Brussels: Fondations égyptologique Reine Élisabeth, 1974.

Ryckmans, J. *L'institution monarchique en Arabie mérfidionale avant l'Islam.* Louvain: Leuven University Press, 1951.

Saggs, H. W. F. "The Nimrud Letters, 1952—Part III." *Iraq* 18 (1956): 40–56.

Saleh, M., and H. Sourouzian. *Official Catalogue of the Egyptian Museum, Cairo.* Munich: Prestel, 1987.

Sales, R. H. "Human Sacrifice in Biblical Thought." *Journal of Bible and Religion* 25 (1957): 112–17.

Sanders, E. "Hamitic Hypothesis." *Journal of African History* 10 (1969): 521–32.

Sass, B. *The Genesis of the Alphabet and Its Development in the Second Millennium* B.C. Wiesbaden: Harrassowitz, 1988.

Sauer, J. A., and J. A. Blakely. "Archaeology along the Spice Route of Yemen." In *Araby the Blest: Studies in Arabian Archaeology*, ed. D. T. Potts, 90–111. Copenhagen: Carsten Niebuhr Institute of Ancient Near Eastern Studies, University of Copenhagen, 1988.

Sauneron, S. "Annex to Chapter 1." In *Ancient Civilizations of Africa*, ed. G. Mokhtar, 51. General History of Africa 2. London: Currey/Berkeley: University of California Press, 1990.

Säve-Söderbergh, T. "Kusch." In *Lexikon der Ägyptologie*, ed. W. Helck and E. Otto, 3.888–93. Wiesbaden: Harrassowitz, 1972.

———. *Temples and Tombs of Ancient Nubia*. London: Thames & Hudson, 1987.

Sawyer, J., and D. J. A. Clines. *Midian, Moab, and Edom*. Sheffield: JSOT Press, 1983.

Schaus, G. "The Evidence for Laconians in Cyrenaica in the Archaic Period." In *Cyrenaica in Antiquity*, ed. G. Barker, J. Lloyd, and J. Reynolds, 395–403. Oxford: British Archaeological Reports, 1985.

Schedl, C. "Sulaiman und die Königin von Saba." In *Al-Hudhud: Festschrift Maria Höfner zum 80. Geburtstag*, ed. R. G. Stiegner, 305–24. Graz: Karl-Franzens-Universität, 1981.

Schlesinger, A. M., Jr., *The Disuniting of America: Reflections on a Multicultural Society*. New York: Norton, 1998.

Schmid, H. "Der Tempelbau Salomos in religiongeschichtlicher Sicht." In *Archäologie und Altes Testament*, ed. A. Kuschke, 241–50. Tübingen: Mohr, 1970.

Schneider, S. "Semitic Influences and the Biblical Text." *Dor le-Dor* 10 (1981): 90–95.

Schreiber, S. "Verstehst du denn, was du liest?" *Studien zum Neuen Testament Umwelt* 21 (1996): 42–72.

Schreiden, R. "Les enterprises navales du roi Salamon." *Annuaire de l'institut de philologie et d'histoire orientale slaves* 13 (1953): 587–90.

Schürer, E. *The History of the Jewish People in the Age of Jesus Christ (175 B.C.–A.D. 135)*. Revised by G. Vermes and F. Millar. 3 vols. Edinburgh: Clark, 1973–87.

Scott, R. B. Y. "Solomon and the Beginnings of Wisdom in Israel." In *Wisdom in Israel and the Ancient Near East: Presented to Professor Harold Henry Rowley*, ed. M. Noth and D. W. Thomas, 262–79. Vetus Testamentum Supplement 3. Leiden: Brill, 1955.

Seitz, C. R. "Account A and the Annals of Sennacherib: A Reassessment." *Journal for the Study of the Old Testament* 58 (1993): 47–57.

Seligman, C. G. *Egypt and Negro Africa*. London: Routledge, 1934. Reprinted New York: AMS, 1978.

———. *Races of Africa*. 4th ed. New York: Oxford University Press, 1966.

Selman, M. J. *2 Chronicles*. Leicester: Inter-Varsity, 1994.

Sethe, K. *Die Ächtung feindlicher Fürsten, Völker und Dinge auf altägyptischen Tongefässscherben des mittleren Reiches*. Berlin: de Gruyter, 1926.

Shanks, H. "A 'Centrist' at the Center of Controversy: *BAR* Interviews Israel Finkelstein." *Biblical Archaeology Review* 28.6 (2002): 38–49, 64–66, 68.

———. "Jeremiah's Scribe and Confidant Speaks from a Hoard of Clay Bullae." *Biblical Archaeology Review* 13.5 (1987): 58–65.

Shaw, M. *The Kingdom of God in Africa*. Grand Rapids: Baker, 1996.

Shaw, T., et al., eds. *The Archaeology of Africa*. London: Routledge, 1993.

Shea, W. H. "Jerusalem under Siege: Did Sennacherib Attack Twice?" *Biblical Archaeology Review* 25.6 (1999): 36–44, 64.

———. "The Murder of Sennacherib and Related Issues." *Near East Archaeological Society Bulletin* 46 (2001): 25–42.

———. "The New Tirhakah Text and Sennacherib's Second Palestinian Campaign." *Andrews University Seminary Studies* 35 (1997): 181–87.

———. "Sennacherib's Second Palestinian Campaign." *Journal of Biblical Literature* 104 (1985): 401–18.

———. "'So,' Ruler of Egypt." *Andrews University Seminary Studies* 30 (1992): 201–15.

Shenk, C. E. "The Demise of the Church in North Africa and Nubia and Its Survival in Egypt and Ethiopia: A Question of Contextualization?" *Missiology* 21.2 (1993): 131–54.

Shinnie, P. L. *Ancient Nubia*. London: Kegan Paul, 1996.

———. "The Fall of Meroe." *Kush* 2 (1955): 82–85.

———. *Meroe*. London: Thames & Hudson, 1967.

———. "The Murals from the Augustus Temple, Meroe." In *Studies in Ancient Egypt, the Aegean, and the Sudan*, ed. W. K. Simpson and W. M. Davis, 167–72. Boston: Museum of Fine Arts, 1981.

Shinnie, P. L., and R. J. Bradley. *The Capital of Kush*, vol. 1: *Meroe Excavations, 1965–1972*. Berlin: Akademie-Verlag, 1980.

Silberman, L. H. "The Queen of Sheba in Judaic Tradition." In *Solomon and Sheba*, ed. J. B. Pritchard, 65–84. London: Phaidon, 1974.

Silver, D. J. "Moses and Hungry Birds." *Jewish Quarterly Review* 64 (1973): 123–53.

Silverman, D. "Pygmies and Dwarves in the Old Kingdom." *Serapis* 1 (1969): 53–62.

Silverman, R. A. "Ethiopia: Art and Architecture." In *Encyclopedia of Africa South of the Sahara*, ed. J. Middleton, 1.74–76. New York: Scribner, 1997.

Simons, J. *The Geographical and Topographical Texts of the Old Testament*. Leiden: Brill, 1959.

Smith, A. "'Do You Understand What You Are Reading?'" *Journal of the Interdenominational Theological Center* 22 (1994): 48–70.

Smith, C. B., II. "Mark the Evangelist and His Relationship to Alexandrian Christianity in Biblical, Historical and Traditional Literature." M.A. thesis, Miami University, Oxford, Ohio, 1992.

———. *No Longer Jews: The Search for Gnostic Origins*. Peabody, Mass.: Hendrickson, forthcoming.

Smith, H. S. *The Fortress of Buhen: The Inscriptions*. London: Egypt Exploration Society, 1976.

———. "Nubia." In *Excavating in Egypt: The Egypt Exploration Society, 1882–1982*, ed. T. G. H. James, 123–40. London: British Museum/Chicago: University of Chicago Press, 1982.

Smith, R. H. "Ethiopia." In *The Anchor Bible Dictionary*, ed. D. N. Freedman et al., 2.665–67. New York: Doubleday, 1992.

Smith, R. L. *Micah–Malachi*. Word Biblical Commentary 32. Waco: Word, 1984.

Smith, S. T. "Askut and the Role of the Second Cataract Forts." *Journal of the American Research Center in Egypt* 28 (1991): 107–32.

———. *Askut in Nubia*. London: Kegan Paul, 1995.

Smith, W. S. "The Land of Punt." *Journal of the American Research Center in Egypt* 1 (1962): 59–62.

Snowden, F. J., Jr. "Attitudes towards Blacks in the Greek and Roman World: Misinterpretations of the Evidence." In *Africa and Africans in Antiquity*, ed. E. M. Yamauchi, 246–75. East Lansing: Michigan State University Press, 2001.

———. *Before Color Prejudice: The Ancient View of Blacks*. Cambridge: Harvard University Press, 1983.

———. "Bernal's 'Blacks,' Herodotus, and Other Classical Evidence." *Arethusa* 22 (1989): 83–95.

———. *Blacks in Antiquity*. Cambridge: Harvard University Press, 1970.

———. "Ethiopians and the Graeco-Roman World." In *The African Diaspora: Interpretive Essays*, ed. M. L. Kilson and R. I. Rotberg, 11–36. Cambridge: Harvard University Press, 1976.

———. "Images and Attitudes: Ancient Views of Nubia and the Nubians." *Expedition* 35.2 (1993): 40–50.

Spalinger, A. "Assurbanipal and Egypt: A Source Study." *Journal of the American Oriental Society* 94 (1974): 316–28.

———. "The Date of the Death of Gyges and Its Historical Implications." *Journal of the American Oriental Society* 98 (1978): 400–409.

———. "Esarhaddon and Egypt: An Analysis of the First Invasion of Egypt." *Orientalia* 43 (1974): 295–321.

———. "The Foreign Policy of Egypt Preceding the Assyrian Conquest." *Chronique d'égypte* 53 (1978): 22–47.

———. "The Military Background of the Campaign of Piye (Piankhy)." *Studien zur altägyptischen Kultur* 7 (1979): 273–302.

———. "Psammetichus, King of Egypt: I." *Journal of the American Research Center in Egypt* 13 (1976): 133–47.

———. "Psammetichus, King of Egypt: II." *Journal of the American Research Center in Egypt* 15 (1978): 49–57.

———. "Some Notes on the Libyans of the Old Kingdom and Later Historical Reflexes." *Journal of the Society for the Study of Egyptian Antiquities* 9 (1979): 125–60.

———. "The Year 712 B.C. and Its Implications for Egyptian History." *Journal of the American Research Center in Egypt* 10 (1973): 95–101.

Speidel, M. P. "Nubia's Roman Garrison." In *Aufstieg und Niedergang der römischen Welt*, ed. H. Temporini and W. Hasse, 2.10.1.768–98. Berlin: de Gruyter, 1988.

Speiser, E. A. *Genesis*. Anchor Bible 1. Garden City, N.Y.: Doubleday, 1964.

———. "The Rivers of Paradise." In *Oriental and Biblical Studies*, ed. J. J. Finkelstein and M. Greenberg, 22–34. Philadelphia: University of Pennsylvania Press, 1967.

Spencer, F. S. "The Ethiopian Eunuch and His Bible: A Social-Science Analysis." *Biblical Theology Bulletin* 22.4 (1992): 155–65.

———. *The Portrait of Philip in Acts*. Sheffield: JSOT Press, 1992.

Spencer, W. D. *Dread Jesus*. London: SPCK, 1999.

Stager, L. E., and S. R. Wolff. "Child Sacrifice at Carthage." *Biblical Archaeology Review* 10.1 (1984): 31–51.

Stannish, S. M. "Evidence for the ʿAmarna Period from the Memphite Tombs of ʿAper-El, Horemheb, and Maʾya." Ph.D. diss., Miami University, Oxford, Ohio, 2001.

Stassen, S. L. "Die rol van Egipte, Kus en Seba in Jesaja 43:3 en 45:14." *Journal for Semitics* 4 (1992): 160–80.

Stern, E. *Archaeology of the Land of the Bible*, vol. 2: *The Assyrian, Babylonian, and Persian Periods (732–332 B.C.E.)*. New York: Doubleday, 2001.

Stieglitz, R. R. "Long-Distance Seafaring in the Ancient Near East." *Biblical Archaeologist* 47 (1984): 134–42.

Stiegner, R. G. "Die Königin von Sabaʾ in ihren Namen." Ph.D. diss., Universität Graz, 1979.

Stohlmann, S. "The Judaean Exile after 701 B.C.E." In *Scripture in Context: More Essays on the Comparative Method*, ed. W. W. Hallo, J. C. Moyer, and L. G. Perdue, 147–75. Winona Lake, Ind.: Eisenbrauns, 1983.

Stoneman, R. *Palmyra and Its Empire: Zenobia's Revolt against Rome*. Ann Arbor: University of Michigan Press, 1994.

Stordalen, T. *Echoes of Eden*. Louvain: Peeters, 2000.

Strouhal, E. "Evidence of the Early Penetration of Negroes into Prehistoric Egypt." *Journal of African History* 12 (1971): 1–9.

Swanson, M. W. "Colonizing the Past: Origin Myths of the Great Zimbabwe Ruins." In *Africa and Africans in Antiquity*, ed. E. M. Yamauchi, 291–320. East Lansing: Michigan State University Press, 2001.

Swete, H. B. *The Gospel according to St. Mark*. Grand Rapids: Eerdmans, 1952.

Tadmor, H. "Was the Biblical *Sarîs* a Eunuch?" In *Solving Riddles and Untying Knots: Biblical, Epigraphic, and Semitic Studies in Honor of Jonas C. Greenfield*, ed. Z. Zevit, S. Gitin, and M. Sokoloff, 317–25. Winona Lake, Ind.: Eisenbrauns, 1995.

Taylor, J. H. *Egypt and Nubia*. Cambridge: Harvard University Press, 1991.

Tetley, M. C. "The Date of Samaria's Fall as a Reason for Rejecting the Hypothesis of Two Conquests." *Catholic Biblical Quarterly* 64 (2002): 59–77.

Thomas, D. W., ed. *Documents from Old Testament Times*. New York: Harper, 1958.

Thompson, L. A. *Romans and Blacks*. Norman: University of Oklahoma Press, 1989.

Thompson, L. A., and J. Ferguson, eds. *Africa in Classical Antiquity*. Ibadan: Ibadan University Press, 1969.

Thornton, T. C. G. "To the End of the Earth: Acts 1.8." *Expository Times* 89 (1977–78): 374–75.

Tindel, R. D. "Zafar: Archaeology in the Land of Frankincense and Myrrh." *Archaeology* 37.2 (1984): 40–45.

Toit, A. du. "No Chosen People: The Myth of the Calvinist Origins of Afrikaner Nationalism and Racial Ideology." *American Historical Review* 88 (1983): 920–52.

Tolbert, R. "Africa and the Bible." M.A. thesis, Colgate Rochester Divinity School, 1985.

Tomasino, A. J. "History Repeats Itself: The 'Fall' and Noah's Drunkenness." *Vetus Testamentum* 42 (1992): 128–30.

Török, L. *The Birth of an Ancient African Kingdom: Kush and Her Myth of the State in the First Millennium* B.C. Lille: Université Charles-de-Gaulle, 1995.

———. *Economic Offices and Officials in Meroitic Nubia.* Budapest: L'Université Laránd Lötwös, 1979.

———. "The Emergence of the Kingdom of Kush and Her Myth of the State in the First Millennium B.C." In *Actes de la VIIIe conférence internationale des études nubiennes,* 1.203–28. Lille: Université Charles-de-Gaulle, 1998.

———. "Geschichte Meroes." In *Aufstieg und Niedergang der römischen Welt,* ed. H. Temporini and W. Hasse, 2.10.1.107–341. Berlin: de Gruyter, 1988.

———. "Inquiries into the Administration of Meroitic Nubia." *Orientalia* 46 (1977): 34–46.

———. *The Kingdom of Kush: Handbook of the Napatan-Meroitic Civilization.* Leiden: Brill, 1997.

———. *Meroe City, An African Capital: John Garstang's Excavations in the Sudan.* London: Egypt Exploration Society, 1997.

———. "The Origin of the Napatan State: The Long Chronology of the El Kurru Cemetery." *Meroitica* 15 (1999): 149–59.

———. *The Royal Crowns of Kush.* Oxford: British Archaeological Reports, 1987.

Trible, P. "Bringing Miriam out of the Shadows." *Bible Review* 5.1 (1989): 14–25, 34.

———. "Eve and Miriam: From the Margins to the Center." In *Feminist Approaches to the Bible,* ed. H. Shanks, 5–24. Washington, D.C.: Biblical Archaeology Society, 1995.

Trigger, B. "La Candace, personnage mysterieux." *Archeologia* 77 (Dec. 1974): 10–17.

———. *Nubia under the Pharaohs.* Boulder, Colo.: Westview, 1976.

———. "Nubian, Negro, Black, Nilotic?" In *Africa in Antiquity,* ed. S. Hochfield and E. Riefstahl, 26–35. Brooklyn: Brooklyn Museum, 1978.

Trigger, B., B. J. Kemp, D. O'Connor, and A. B. Lloyd. *Ancient Egypt: A Social History.* Cambridge: Cambridge University Press, 1983.

Troy, L. *Patterns of Queenship in Ancient Egyptian Myth and History.* Uppsala: Almquist & Wiksell, 1986.

Trumpf, J. "Alexander und die Königin von Saba.'" *Athenaeum* 44 (1966): 307–8.

Tsoukalas, S. *The Nation of Islam.* Phillipsburg, N.J.: Presbyterian & Reformed, 2001.

Twitchell, K. S. *Saudi Arabia.* 3d ed. New York: Greenwood, 1969.

Uhlenbrock, J. P. "History, Trade, and the Terracottas." *Expedition* 34.1–2 (1982): 16–23.

Ullendorff, E. "Candace (Acts 8.27) and the Queen of Sheba." *New Testament Studies* 2 (1955): 53–56.

———. *Ethiopia and the Bible.* London: Oxford University Press, 1968.

———. *The Ethiopians.* Oxford: Oxford University Press, 1973.

———. "The Queen of Sheba." *Bulletin of the John Rylands Library* (1962–63): 486–504.

———. "The Queen of Sheba in Ethiopian Tradition." In *Solomon and Sheba,* ed. J. B. Pritchard, 104–14. London: Phaidon, 1974.

Updegraff, R. T. "The Blemmyes, I." In *Aufstieg und Niedergang der römischen Welt*, ed. H. Temporini and W. Hasse, 2.10.1.44–106. Berlin: de Gruyter, 1988.

Usry, G., and C. S. Keener. *Black Man's Religion: Can Christianity Be Afrocentric?* Downers Grove, Ill.: InterVarsity, 1996.

Ussishkin, D. "Answers at Lachish." *Biblical Archaeology Review* 5.6 (1979): 16–39.

———. "The Assyrian Attack on Lachish: The Archaeological Evidence from the Southwest Corner of the Site." *Tel Aviv* 17 (1990): 53–86.

———. "Building IV in Hamath and the Temples of Solomon and Tell Tayanat." *Israel Exploration Journal* 16 (1966): 104–10.

———. *The Conquest of Lachish by Sennacherib*. Tel Aviv: Tel Aviv University Press, 1982.

———. "King Solomon's Palace and Building 1723 in Megiddo." *Israel Exploration Journal* 16 (1966): 174–86.

———. "King Solomon's Palaces." *Biblical Archaeologist* 36 (1973): 78–105.

———. "Was the Solomonic City Gate at Megiddo Built by King Solomon?" *Bulletin of the American Schools of Oriental Research* 239 (1980): 1–18.

Valbelle, D. "Kerma: Les inscriptions." *Genava* 49 (2001): 229–33.

Van Beek, G. W. "Frankincense and Myrrh." *Biblical Archaeologist* 23 (1960): 70–95.

———. "The Land of Sheba." In *Solomon and Sheba*, ed. J. B. Pritchard, 40–63. London: Phaidon, 1974.

———. "Recovering the Ancient Civilization of Arabia." *Biblical Archaeologist* 15 (1952): 2–18.

———. "The Rise and Fall of Arabia Felix." *Scientific American* 221.6 (1969): 36–46.

Van Beek, G. W., and A. Jamme. "An Inscribed South Arabian Clay Stamp from Bethel." *Bulletin of the American Schools of Oriental Research* 151 (1958): 15–16.

Van Beek, G. W., A. Jamme, and J. L. Kelso. "The Authenticity of the Bethel Stamp Seal." *Bulletin of the American Schools of Oriental Research* 199 (1970): 59–65.

Van der Horst, P. "Jewish Funerary Inscriptions." *Biblical Archaeology Review* 18.5 (1992): 46–57.

Van Sertima, I., ed. *Black Women in Antiquity*. New Brunswick: Transaction, 1984.

———. *Egypt Revisited*. New Brunswick: Transaction, 1989.

Van Sertima, I., and L. Williams, eds. *Great African Thinkers*, vol. 1: *Cheikh Anta Diop*. New Brunswick: Transaction, 1986.

Vandersleyen, C. "Des obstacles que constituent les cataractes du Nil." *Bulletin de l'institut français d'archéologie orientale* 69 (1969): 253–66.

Vantini, G. *Christianity in the Sudan*. Bologna: EMI, 1981.

———. "The Remotest Places Reached by Nubian Christianity in Sudan." In *Actes de la VIIIe conférence internationale des études nubiennes*, 239–43. Lille: Université Charles-de-Gaulle, 1998.

Ventris, M., and J. Chadwick. *Documents in Mycenaean Greek*. Cambridge: Cambridge University Press, 1959.

Vercoutter, J. "Das Gold Nubiens, Äthiopien im Altertum." In *Das Goldland der Pharaonen*, ed. A. Castiglioni, A. Castiglioni, and J. Vercoutter, 11–21. Mainz: Zabern, 1998.

———. "The Gold of Kush." *Kush* 7 (1959): 120–53.

―――. "The Iconography of the Black in Ancient Egypt: From the Beginnings to the Twenty-fifth Dynasty." In *The Image of the Black in Western Art*, ed. L. Bugner, 1.33–88. New York: Morrow, 1976.

―――. "L'image du noir dans l'égypte ancienne (dès origines à la XXVe dyn.)." In *Africa in Antiquity: The Arts of Ancient Nubia and the Sudan*, ed. F. Hintze, 19–22. Meroitica 5. Berlin: Akademie-Verlag, 1979.

―――. "Kushites and Meroites: Iconography of the African Rulers in Ancient Upper Nile." In *The Image of the Black in Western Art*, ed. L. Bugner, 1.89–132. New York: Morrow, 1976.

―――. *Mirgissa*. 2 vols. Paris: Direction générale des relations culturelles, scientifiques et techniques, 1970–75.

―――. "The Napatan Kings and Apis Worship." *Kush* 8 (1960): 62–76.

―――. "Un palais des 'Candace' contemporain d'Auguste." *Syria* 39 (1962): 263–99.

Vermes, G. "La figure de Moïse au tournant des deux testaments." In *Moïse: L'homme de l'alliance*, ed. H. Cazelles, 53–92. New York: Desclée, 1955.

Vermeule, E. *The Art of the Shaft Graves at Mycenae*. Cincinnati: University of Cincinnati Press, 1975.

Vernus, P. "Inscriptions de la troisième intermédiaire." *Bulletin de l'institut français d'archéologie orientale* 75 (1975): 13–66.

Vervenne, M. "What Shall We Do with the Drunken Sailor? A Critical Re-examination of Genesis 9.20–27." *Journal for the Study of the Old Testament* 68 (1995): 33–55.

Vogels, W. "Cham découvere les limites de son père Noé." *Nouvelle revue théologique* 109 (1987): 554–73.

Volkoff, O. V. *D'ou vient la rein de Saba²?* Cairo: L'institut français d'archéologie orientale, 1985.

Wachsmann, S. "Sailing into Egypt's Past." *Archaeology* 55.4 (2002): 36–39.

―――. *Seagoing Ships and Seamanship in the Bronze Age Levant*. College Station: Texas A&M University Press, 1998.

Wakely, R. "Ophir." In *New International Dictionary of Old Testament Theology and Exegesis*, ed. W. A. VanGemeren, 1.321–23. Grand Rapids: Zondervan, 1997.

Walker, S. "The Architecture of Cyrene and the Panhellenion." In *Cyrenaica in Antiquity*, ed. G. Barker, J. Lloyd, and J. Reynolds, 97–104. Oxford: British Archaeological Reports, 1985.

Wallace, H. N. *The Eden Narratives*. Atlanta: Scholars Press, 1985.

Walters, W. P. "Joseph Smith among the Egyptians." *Journal of the Evangelical Theological Society* 16 (1973): 25–45.

Wapnish, P. "Camel Caravans and Camel Pastoralists at Tell Jemmeh." *Journal of the Ancient Near Eastern Society* 13 (1981): 101–21.

Ward, P. *Touring Libya: The Eastern Provinces*. London: Faber & Faber, 1969.

Ward, W. A. "Phoenicians." In *Peoples of the Old Testament World*, ed. A. Hoerth, G. Mattingly, and E. M. Yamauchi, 183–206. Grand Rapids: Baker, 1994.

―――. Review of *Centuries of Darkness*, edited by P. James. *American Journal of Archaeology* 98 (1994): 362–63.

Watt, W. M. "The Queen of Sheba in Islamic Tradition." In *Solomon and Sheba*, ed. J. B. Pritchard, 85–103. London: Phaidon, 1974.

Wehr, H. *A Dictionary of Modern Written Arabic*. Ithaca: Cornell University Press, 1961.

Weinstein, J. M. Review of Bernal's *Black Athena*, vol. 2. *American Journal of Archaeology* 96 (1992): 381–83.

Welsby, D. A. *The Kingdom of Kush: The Napatan and Meroitic Empires*. Princeton: Wiener, 1998.

Wenham, G. J. *Genesis 1–15*. Word Biblical Commentary 1. Waco: Word, 1987.

Wenham, J. W. "Large Numbers in the Old Testament." *Tyndale Bulletin* 18 (1967): 19–53.

Wenig, S. "Bemerkungen zur Chronologie des Reiches von Meroe." *Mitteilungen des Instituts für Orientforschung* 13 (1967): 1–44.

West, D. C., and A. Kling. *The Libro de las profecías of Christopher Columbus*. Gainesville: University of Florida Press, 1991.

Westermann, C. *Genesis*, vol. 1. Neukirchen-Vluyn: Neukirchener Verlag, 1974.

White, D. "An Archaeological Survey of the Cyrenaican and Mamarican Regions of Northeast Africa." In *Africa and Africans in Antiquity*, ed. E. M. Yamauchi, 210–45. East Lansing: Michigan State University Press, 2001.

———. "Cyrene's Sanctuary of Demeter and Persephone: A Summary of a Decade of Excavation." *American Journal of Archaeology* 85 (1981): 13–30.

———. "Cyrene's Suburban Expansion South of Its Ramparts." *Cyrenaica in Antiquity*, ed. G. Barker, J. Lloyd, and J. Reynolds, 105–20. Oxford: British Archaeological Reports, 1985.

———. "Excavations at the Extramural Sanctuary of Demeter and Persephone at Cyrene, 1969–1981." *Expedition* 34.1–2 (1992): 3–5.

———. *The Extramural Sanctuary of Demeter and Persephone at Cyrene, Libya*. Philadelphia: University Museum, 1984.

———. "Illustrations by the Early Travelers." *Expedition* 34.1–2 (1992): 34–49.

———. "The Sanctuary's History and Architecture." *Expedition* 34.1–2 (1992): 6–10.

White, D., and J. Monge. "Statue Breakers and Spirit Exorcists." *Expedition* 34.1–2 (1982): 76–85.

White, D., et al. "Seven Recently Discovered Sculptures from Cyrene." *Expedition* 18 (1976): 14–32.

Wildung, D. "The Meroitic Pantheon." In *Sudan: Ancient Kingdoms of the Nile*, ed. D. Wildung, 265–300. Paris: Flammarion, 1997.

———. "Meroitic Treasure." In *Sudan: Ancient Kingdoms of the Nile*, ed. D. Wildung, 301–40. Paris: Flammarion, 1997.

Wildung, D., ed. *Sudan: Ancient Kingdoms of the Nile*. Paris: Flammarion, 1997.

Williams, B. "Forebears of Menes in Nubia: Myth or Reality?" *Journal of Near Eastern Studies* 46 (1987): 15–26.

———. "The Lost Pharaohs of Nubia." *Archaeology* 33.5 (1980): 12–21.

———. Review of T. Kendall's *Kerma and the Kingdom of Kush*. *Journal of Near Eastern Studies* 60 (2001): 197.

Williams, C. *The Destruction of Black Civilization*. Chicago: Third World, 1987.

Williams, D. J. *Acts: A Good News Commentary.* San Francisco: Harper & Row, 1985.

Willis, J. R., ed. *Slaves and Slavery in Muslim Africa*, vol. 1: *Islam and the Ideology of Enslavement.* London: Cass, 1985.

Wilson, J. A. "The Joseph Smith Egyptian Papyri." *Dialogue* 3.2 (1968): 67–86.

———. "The Libyans and the End of the Egyptian Empire." *American Journal of Semitic Languages* 51 (1934–35): 73–82.

Wimbush, V. L. *African Americans and the Bible.* New York: Continuum, 2000.

Wiseman, D. J. "Some Historical Problems in the Book of Daniel." In *Notes on Some Problems in the Book of Daniel*, by D. J. Wiseman et al., 9–18. London: Tyndale, 1965.

———. *The Vassal-Treaties of Esarhaddon.* London: British School of Archaeology in Iraq, 1958.

Wissmann, H. von. "Die Geschichte des Sabäerreiches und der Feldzug des Aelius Gallus." In *Aufstieg und Niedergang der römischen Welt*, ed. H. Temporini and W. Hasse, 2.10.1.308–544. Berlin: de Gruyter, 1988.

———. *Das Grossreich der Sabäer bis zu seinem Ende im frühen 4 Jh. v. Chr.* Vienna: Österreichischen Akademie der Wissenschaften, 1982.

Witherington, B., III. "Candace." In *The Anchor Bible Dictionary*, ed. D. N. Freedman et al., 1.837. New York: Doubleday, 1992.

Wittenberg, G. "'. . . Let Canaan Be His Slave' (Gen 9:26): Is Ham Also Cursed?" *Journal of Theology for Southern Africa* 74 (March 1991): 46–56.

Wood, B. *The Origins of American Slavery.* New York: Hill & Wang, 1997.

Woolley, C. L. *Ur of the Chaldees.* New York: Norton, 1965.

Yadin, Y. *The Art of Warfare in Biblical Lands.* 2 vols. London: Weidenfeld & Nicolson, 1963.

———. "In Defense of the Megiddo Stables." *Biblical Archaeology Review* 2 (1976): 18–22.

———. "An Inscribed South-Arabian Clay Stamp from Bethel?" *Bulletin of the American Schools of Oriental Research* 196 (1969): 37–45.

———. "Megiddo of the Kings of Israel." *Biblical Archaeologist* 33 (1970): 66–96.

———. "The Megiddo Stables." In *Magnalia Dei, the Mighty Acts of God: Essays on the Bible and Archaeology in Memory of G. Ernest Wright*, ed. F. M. Cross, W. E. Lemke, and P. D. Miller Jr., 249–52. Garden City, N.Y.: Doubleday, 1976.

———. "New Light on Solomon's Megiddo." *Biblical Archaeologist* 23 (1960): 62–68.

———. "Solomon's City Wall and Gate at Gezer." *Israel Exploration Journal* 8 (1958): 80–86.

Yafeh, H. L. *Intertwined Worlds: Medieval Islam and Bible Criticism.* Princeton: Princeton University Press, 1992.

Yamauchi, E. M. "Akhenaten, Moses, and Monotheism." In *Amarna in Retrospect: A Centennial Celebration*, ed. B. Beitzel and G. D. Young. Winona Lake, Ind.: Eisenbrauns, forthcoming.

———. "Aramaic." In *New International Dictionary of Biblical Archaeology*, ed. E. M. Blaiklock and R. K. Harrison, 38–41. Grand Rapids: Zondervan, 1983.

———. "Aramaic Magic Bowls." *Journal of the American Oriental Society* 85 (1965): 511–23.

————. "The Archaeological Background of Daniel." *Bibliotheca Sacra* 137 (1980): 3–16.

————. "The Archaeological Background of Ezra." *Bibliotheca Sacra* 137 (1980): 195–207.

————. *The Archaeology of New Testament Cities in Western Asia Minor*. Grand Rapids: Baker, 1980. Reprinted Eugene, Oreg.: Wipf & Stock, 2003.

————. "Athletics in the Ancient Near East." In *Daily Life in the Ancient Near East*, ed. R. E. Averbeck, M. W. Chavalas, and D. Weisberg, 491–500. Bethesda: CDL, 2002.

————. "Attitudes toward the Aged in Antiquity." *Near East Archaeological Society Bulletin* 45 (2000): 1–9.

————. "Babylon." In *Major Cities of the Biblical World*, ed. R. K. Harrison, 32–48. Nashville: Nelson, 1985.

————. "Chaldea, Chaldeans." In *New International Dictionary of Biblical Archaeology*, ed. E. M. Blaiklock and R. K. Harrison, 123–25. Grand Rapids: Zondervan, 1983.

————. "Critical Comments on the Search for Noah's Ark." *Near East Archaeological Society Bulletin* 10 (1977): 5–27.

————. "Cyrus H. Gordon and the Ubiquity of Magic in the Pre-Modern World." *Biblical Archaeologist* 59 (1996): 51–55.

————. "Easter—Myth, Hallucination, or History?" *Christianity Today* 18 (March 15, 1974): 4–7.

————. "The Eastern Jewish Diaspora under the Babylonians." In *Mesopotamia and the Bible*, ed. M. W. Chavalas and K. L. Younger Jr., 356–77. Grand Rapids: Baker, 2002.

————. "The Episode of the Magi." In *Chronos, Kairos, Christos: Nativity and Chronological Studies Presented to Jack Finegan*, ed. J. Vardaman and E. M. Yamauchi, 15–39. Winona Lake, Ind.: Eisenbrauns, 1989.

————. *Foes from the Northern Frontier*. Grand Rapids: Baker, 1982. Reprinted Eugene, Oreg.: Wipf & Stock, 2003.

————. *Greece and Babylon*. Grand Rapids: Baker, 1967.

————. "Havilah." In *Theological Wordbook of the Old Testament*, ed. R. L. Harris, G. L. Archer, and B. K. Waltke, 1.269–70. Chicago: Moody, 1980.

————. "Herodotus." In *The Anchor Bible Dictionary*, ed. D. N. Freedman et al., 3.180–81. New York: Doubleday, 1992.

————. "Herodotus." In *Encyclopedia of Historians and Historical Writing*, ed. K. Boyd, 528–29. London/Chicago: Dearborn, 1999.

————. "Herodotus—Historian or Liar?" In *Crossing Boundaries and Linking Horizons: Studies in Honor of Michael C. Astour*, ed. G. D. Young, M. W. Chavalas, and R. E. Averbeck, 599–614. Bethesda, Md.: CDL, 1997.

————. "Immanuel Velikovsky's Catastrophic History." *Journal of the American Scientific Affiliation* 25 (1973): 134–39.

————. "Josephus and the Scriptures." *Fides et Historia* 13 (1980): 42–63.

————. "Kassites." In *New International Dictionary of Biblical Archaeology*, ed. E. M. Blaiklock and R. K. Harrison, 276–78. Grand Rapids: Zondervan, 1983.

———. "Life, Death, and the Afterlife in the Ancient Near East." In *Life in the Face of Death: The Resurrection Message of the New Testament*, ed. R. N. Longenecker, 21–50. Grand Rapids: Eerdmans, 1998.

———. *Mandaic Incantation Texts*. New Haven: American Oriental Society, 1967.

———. "Meshech, Tubal, and Company." *Journal of the Evangelical Theological Society* 19 (1976): 239–47.

———. "Metal Sources and Metallurgy in the Biblical World." *Perspectives on Science and Christian Faith* 45 (1993): 252–59.

———. "Nineveh." In *Layman's Bible Dictionary*, ed. T. Butler, 1024–25. Nashville: Holman, 1991.

———. "Obelisk." In *The International Standard Bible Encyclopedia*, ed. G. W. Bromiley, 3.577–78. Grand Rapids: Eerdmans, 1986.

———. "Obelisks and Pyramids." *Near East Archaeological Society Bulletin* 24 (1985): 111–15.

———. *Persia and the Bible*. Grand Rapids: Baker, 1990.

———. Review of S. H. Ali Al-Khalifa and M. Rice's *Bahrain through the Ages. Near East Archaeological Society Bulletin* 28 (1987): 78–83.

———. "Shishak." In *New International Dictionary of Biblical Archaeology*, ed. E. M. Blaiklock and R. K. Harrison, 412–13. Grand Rapids: Zondervan, 1983.

———. "The Slaves of God." *Bulletin of the Evangelical Theological Society* 9 (1966): 31–49.

———. "Solomon." In *New International Dictionary of Biblical Archaeology*, ed. E. M. Blaiklock and R. K. Harrison, 419–22. Grand Rapids: Zondervan, 1983.

———. *The Stones and the Scriptures*. Philadelphia: Lippincott, 1972.

———. "Tiglath-pileser." In *New International Dictionary of Biblical Archaeology*, ed. E. M. Blaiklock and R. K. Harrison, 451–53. Grand Rapids: Zondervan, 1983.

Yamauchi, E. M., ed. *Africa and Africans in Antiquity*. East Lansing: Michigan State University Press, 2001.

Young, D. A. *The Biblical Flood: A Case Study of the Church's Response to Extrabiblical Evidence*. Grand Rapids: Eerdmans, 1995.

———. *Christianity and the Age of the Earth*. Grand Rapids: Zondervan, 1982.

———. *Creation and the Flood: An Alternative to Flood Geology and Theistic Evolution*. Grand Rapids: Baker, 1977.

Young, G. D., M. W. Chavalas, and R. E. Averbeck, eds. *Crossing Boundaries and Linking Horizons: Studies in Honor of Michael C. Astour*. Bethesda, Md.: CDL, 1997.

Younger, K. L., Jr. "The Deportations of the Israelites." *Journal of Biblical Literature* 117 (1998): 1–27.

———. "The Fall of Samaria in Light of Recent Research." *Catholic Biblical Quarterly* 61 (1999): 461–82.

———. "Recent Study on Sargon II, King of Assyria." In *Mesopotamia and the Bible*, ed. M. W. Chavalas and K. L. Younger Jr., 288–329. Grand Rapids: Baker, 2002.

Yoyotte, J. "Un porche doré." *Chronique d'égypte* 55 (1953): 28–38.

Yoyotte, J., and S. Sauneron. "La campagne nubienne de Psammétique II et sa signification historique." *Bulletin de l'institut français d'archéologie orientale* 30 (1952): 157–207.

Yurco, F. J. "Egypt and Nubia: Old, Middle, and New Kingdom Eras." In *Africa and Africans in Antiquity,* ed. E. M. Yamauchi, 28–112. East Lansing: Michigan State University Press, 2001.

———. "The Shabaka-Shebitku Coregency and the Supposed Second Campaign of Sennacherib against Judah: A Critical Assessment." *Journal of Biblical Literature* 110 (1991): 35–45.

———. "Were the Ancient Egyptians Black or White?" *Biblical Archaeology Review* 15.5 (1989): 24–31.

Zarins, J. "The Camel in Ancient Arabia." *Antiquity* 52 (1978): 44–46.

———. "On the Frankincense Trail." *Smithsonian Magazine* 29.7 (1998): 120–35.

———. "Persia and Dhofar." In *Crossing Boundaries and Linking Horizons: Studies in Honor of Michael C. Astour,* ed. G. D. Young, M. W. Chavalas, and R. E. Averbeck, 615–89. Bethesda, Md.: CDL, 1997.

Zevit, Z. "Three Debates about Biblical Archaeology." *Biblica* 83 (2002): 1–27.

Žabkar, L. *Apedemak, Lion God of Meroe.* Warminster: Aris & Phillips, 1975.

Zibelius, K. *Afrikanische Orts und Völkernamen in hieroglyphischen und hieratischen Texten.* Wiesbaden: Harrassowitz, 1972.

Zoghby, S. M. "Blacks and Arabs: Past and Present." *Current Bibliography on African Affairs* 3.5 (1970): 5–22.

CREDITS

2.20   Wadi es-Sebua temple, Nubia (reign of Ramesses II, year 44, 1235 B.C.) (Frank Joseph Yurco)
2.21   View of the excavations at Kerma, with the Western Deffufa in the background (C. Bonnet)
2.22   Grand Hut (2000–1500 B.C.) (C. Bonnet)
2.23   Bed with ivory inlays (reproduction; Nubian, 1700–1550 B.C.; by Joseph Gerte). Frame of rosewood, footboard of pine, inlays cast from originals. Rawhide lacing. Length: 183 cm. (72-1/16 in.) (Museum of Fine Arts, Boston; Director's Contingent Fund, 40.469) (©2002 Museum of Fine Arts, Boston)
2.24   Model of Kerma (C. Bonnet)
2.25   Funerary chapel K XI (C. Bonnet)
2.26   Tumulus K III, royal tomb of Kushite king, Kerma (Second Intermediate Period) (from Bruce Trigger, *Nubia under the Pharaohs* [London: Thames & Hudson, 1976])
2.27   Nubian prisoner, New Kingdom (1550–1307 B.C.) (courtesy, The Saint Louis Art Museum; purchase)
2.28   Nubian-Kushite prisoners from the Memphite tomb of Haremhab (limestone relief, reign of Tutankhamun, Dynasty 18, 1334–1325 B.C.) (courtesy of the Museo Civico Archeologico, Bologna [KS 1869 = 1887])
2.29   Stela of the Nubian soldier Nenu (painted limestone, Egyptian, Dynasty 9 to early Dynasty 11, 2100–2040 B.C.). Height: 37.12 cm. (14-5/8 in.); width: 45.03 cm. (17-3/4 in.) (Museum of Fine Arts, Boston; purchased by A. M. Lythgoe, 03.1848) (©2002 Museum of Fine Arts, Boston)
3.1   Hatshepsut (courtesy, The Metropolitan Museum of Art, Rogers Fund and Edward S. Harkness Gift, 1929 [29.3.2])
3.2   The courtyard of the Great Enclosure, Zimbabwe (Robert Harbison/1993 ©*The Christian Science Monitor*)
3.3   Ancient Arabia and environs (Kenneth A. Kitchen)
3.4   South Arabian stela with a camel and rider (©British Museum)
3.5   Left side of panel illustrating the *Kebra Negast* (C. Geyer)
3.6   Right side of panel illustrating the *Kebra Negast* (C. Geyer)
3.7   Detail of panel illustrating the *Kebra Negast*: Solomon accuses the Queen of Sheba of stealing his water (C. Geyer)
3.8   Detail of panel illustrating the *Kebra Negast*: Solomon seduces the Queen of Sheba (C. Geyer)
4.1   Temple of Amon, built by Thutmose III at the base of Gebel Barkal (Derek A. Welsby)
4.2   Offering table of King Piankhy (bronze, Nubian, reign of Piankhy, 747–716 B.C.). Height: 82 cm. (32-5/16 in.); diameter of foot: 45.5 cm. (17-15/16 in.) (courtesy, Museum of Fine Arts, Boston). Harvard University—Museum of Fine Arts Expedition, 21.3238 (©2002 Museum of Fine Arts, Boston)
4.3   Shebitku's tomb at el-Kurru (Derek A. Welsby)
4.4   Movements of Assyrian and Egyptian forces in 701 B.C. (Kenneth A. Kitchen)
4.5   Kneeling Taharqa from Kawa (©British Museum)
4.6   Gold ram-head earring (gold, Nubian, sixth century B.C.). Length: 3 cm. (1-3/16 in.) (courtesy, Museum of Fine Arts, Boston). Harvard University—Museum of Fine Arts Expedition, 23.333 (©2002 Museum of Fine Arts, Boston)
4.7   Taharqa as a sphinx, from Kawa (©British Museum)
4.8   Taharqa's *ushabtis*, from his pyramid at Nuri (©British Museum)
4.9   Esarhaddon towering over two captives, including Taharqa's kneeling son (Staatliche Museen zu Berlin—Preussischer Kulturbesitz, Vorderasiatisches Museum)

SCRIPTURE INDEX

AUTHOR INDEX

274

Beardsley, G. H. 41 n. 31
Becking, B. 109 n. 16
Beltrami, V. 187
Belzoni, Giovanni 67
Bennett, R. A. 212 n. 42
Ben Zvi, E. 123 n. 106
Berkowitz, L. 89 n. 70
Berlinerblau, J. 219 n. 25
Bernal, John Desmond 216
Bernal, Martin 215, 216, 217, 218, 219, 220
Berossus 124
Betto, F. 20 n. 3
Bezold, C. 101
Bietak, Manfred 61
Bimson, John 82
Bion 170
Blackburn, R. 26 n. 45
Blakely, J. A. 92, 95
Blyden, Edward W. 164
Boardman, J. 189 n. 25, 202 n. 62
Boemus, Johan 27
Bonnet, Charles 44, 51 n. 78, 62 n. 112, 64
    n. 114, 68, 69, 71, 152
Bordreuil, P. 38 n. 14, 95
Borger, R. 137 n. 167
Borowski, Oded 22 n. 18, 84, 94, 95 n. 100
Bosch, D. J. 206 n. 2
Bourriau, J. 61 n. 107
Bradbury, L. 84 n. 51
Bradley, L. R. 28 n. 55
Bradley, R. J. 151 n. 10
Braund, D. 191 n. 35
Breasted, J. H. 45 n. 51, 49 n. 69, 62 n. 111, 139
    n. 175
Bregman, J. 203 n. 67
Breton, J.-F. 92 n. 87
Brier, B. 116 n. 64
Bright, John 108, 125
Bringhurst, N. G. 32 n. 67, 32 n. 69, 33 n. 72
Briquel-Chattonet, F. 81 n. 22
Brock, S. P. 37 n. 13
Browne, S. G. 35 n. 4
Browne, W. G. 194
Bruce, D. D. 208 n. 12
Bruce, F. F. 164 n. 17, 185 n. 8
Bruce, James 149
Brunner, U. 92 n. 91
Brunson, J. 213 n. 45
Brunt, P. A. 159 n. 37
Budd, P. J. 35 n. 1
Budge, E. A. W. 67, 101, 105, 125
Bullard, R. G. 184 n. 5

Bulliet, R. W. 95
Burckhardt, Lewis 67
Burkert, Walter 220
Burns, R. J. 35 n. 1
Burstein, S. M. 52 n. 83, 67 n. 125, 114, 149
    n. 2, 150 n. 6, 154, 155 n. 24, 158 n. 32, 159
    n. 35, 164 n. 19, 171, 173 n. 46, 176 n. 49,
    220 n. 33
Burton, T. 195
Buswell, J. 29 n. 56
Buxton, D. 101 n. 138, 163 n. 7
Byron, Lord George Gordon 124

Cailliaud, F. 149
Caminos, R. A. 143 n. 189, 145
Canova, G. 99 n. 130, 100 n. 134
Cansdale, G. 83 n. 42
Caputo, G. 196
Carroll, S. T. 46 n. 55, 86 n. 59, 206 n. 5
Carruthers, J. 218 n. 21
Cary, M. 86
Chadwick, J. 41 n. 30
Chamberlain, Richard 87 n. 63
Chamoux, F. 190 n. 28
Chastel, A. 88 n. 66
Chavalas, M. W. 215 n. 2
Chevannes, B. 105 n. 153
Childs, B. S. 123 n. 103
Chittick, Neville 173
Christensen, D. L. 110
Christidès, J. 83 n. 41
Clancy, F. 188 n. 22
Clapp, Nicholas 93 n. 96, 96
Clarke, John Henrik 212
Cleague, Al 209
Clements, R. E. 123 n. 105
Cline, Eric H. 219, 220 n. 29
Clouse, R. G. 180 n. 57
Coats, G. W. 35 n. 1
Cogan, M. 83 n. 38, 92 n. 85, 123 n. 108
Cohen, H. Hirsch 20, 21, 22
Coleman, J. E. 216 n. 7
Columbus, Christopher 89, 90
Copher, C. B. 37 n. 10, 105 n. 155, 210 n. 30
Cornell, T. 184 n. 6
Cozzolino, C. 85 n. 53
Crocker, P. T. 164 n. 18
Cross, F. M. 35 n. 3, 37 n. 9, 81, 95 n. 107

Dalley, S. 115
Daum, W. 95 n. 104
Davey, C. 79 n. 17

SUBJECT INDEX